**BASIC
ELECTRONIC
TEST
EQUIPMENT:**
A PROGRAMMED
INTRODUCTION

BASIC
ELECTRONIC
TEST
EQUIPMENT:
A
PROGRAMMED
INTRODUCTION

McGraw-Hill
Book Company
New York
St. Louis
San Francisco
Toronto
London
Sydney

DONALD H. SCHUSTER
Associate Professor of Psychology
Iowa State University

BASIC ELECTRONIC
TEST EQUIPMENT:
A PROGRAMMED
INTRODUCTION

PREFACE

This book is more than the usual textbook. It presents information but, in addition, immediately tests you on that information. At the end of a page of text, you will find a question with several answers listed. Each answer has a different letter. Choose an answer and note its letter. Then check yourself on the next page. In turning to an answer, the important thing is the letter. To clarify an answer, you may wish to reread the previous page. A bookmark will be very useful.

This book is an introduction to the theory of three types of common electronic test equipment: meters, signal generators, and oscilloscopes. Chapters are arranged by pairs, with the first chapter concerning the general theory of operation and the second of the pair covering one or more pieces of actual test equipment. The last chapter covers an advanced oscilloscope. Details of operating and troubleshooting are not discussed; for these you will have to refer to the test equipment manuals.

It is assumed that the reader is already familiar with basic electronic theory; that is, you should know elementary ac-dc circuit theory, along with simple amplifier and oscillator circuits in both vacuum-tube and transistor versions. Complex circuits are explained as they are used. If you are unsure of your background knowledge, turn to the appendix and take the basic electronics test. Score your answers against the key on the following page, and interpret your score.

A review quiz is given at the end of each chapter. If upon reading the book for the first time, you feel that you already know the material in a given chapter, turn to the quiz for that chapter. Answer the quiz questions. If you score 90 percent or more correct, go on to the next chapter. If you miss more than 10 percent of the questions, review as necessary or go through the whole chapter. For review of specific topics, refer to the index which is extensively cross-referenced.

It is a pleasure to acknowledge the contributions

of others to this present volume. The author's interest in programmed instruction for electronic test equipment was stimulated some years ago in research work with J. W. Rigney and G. L. Bryan of the Electronics Personnel Research Group, University of Southern California. Selection of material to be included in this book was made in collaboration with these test equipment specialists at Collins Radio Co.: L. Petska, B. Ostler, G. Bishop, N. C. Gronert, J. W. Heath, C. L. Bohs, and D. L. McManis. These people also checked appropriate sections of the manuscript for technical accuracy. C. J. Draker of Collins Radio Co. was helpful in many ways; planning, preparing drawings, training and testing of technicians, and providing encouragement on this project. Ken Thompson of the Naval Training Device Center was helpful in getting books printed for evaluation by electronic technicians.

Numerous companies supplied technical manuals and drawings for their respective test equipment. Their names are listed on the figures appropriately, but their contributions are gratefully acknowledged here also: Thanks are due to the Triplett Electrical Instrument Co., the Heath Co., the Hewlett-Packard Co., the Allen B. Du Mont Laboratories, Inc., Division of Fairchild Camera and Instrument Corp., and Tektronix, Inc.

DONALD H. SCHUSTER

CONTENTS

BASIC ELECTRONIC TEST EQUIPMENT:
A PROGRAMMED INTRODUCTION

CHAPTER ONE   **METERS** 14 QUESTIONS

ITEM 101

INTRODUCTION

Meters are the basic yardstick for electrical and electronic measurements. Meters are used to measure current, voltage, resistance, power, phase angle, and frequency, to name some of their more common uses. Basically, the common meters all measure current flow. They measure the other quantities by an appropriate transforming or proportional means. For instance, a voltmeter basically measures current, but by virtue of Ohm's law and a proportional resistor, a meter also measures voltage. The voltage is proportional to the resistance times the indicated current.

There are three common types of meters: the D'Arsonval, electrodynamic, and moving-vane. Two less common types are the hot-wire, or thermocouple, and electrostatic, or capacitor, meters. Later we will discuss these basic types of meters individually.

If you haven't yet read the preface of this book, please do so now before trying the following question.

Q101 How does the meter mechanism in a voltmeter measure voltage? Select an answer, and turn to the corresponding item number.

ITEM 101a   It measures resistance, and by virtue of Ohm's law, voltage is proportional to the inverse of the resistance.

ITEM 101b   It measures current directly, and voltage is proportional to the current through a standard resistor.

ITEM 101c   It measures voltage directly.

ITEM 101a

You answered: **A voltmeter measures resistance directly and transforms this to voltage via Ohm's law.**

It is true that, according to Ohm's law, voltage is directly proportional to resistance. However, the meters that we are going to be talking about measure something else basically. An ohmmeter measures resistance, but even an ohmmeter measures current first. Then via Ohm's law and a calibrated scale, it converts current to resistance in a direct fashion. This is beside the point in this question, however, since the meters we are going to be talking about do not measure resistance directly. Turn back to the preceding page, reread the material, and try another answer.

ITEM 101b

You answered: **A meter mechanism, to measure voltage, first measures current but then transforms the current reading to voltage.**

The current through the meter produces a magnetic field that is proportional to the current. If a suitable precision resistor is employed to limit the current, the current is proportional to the applied voltage, and the meter can be calibrated to read volts directly.

Turn to next page.

ITEM 101c

You answered: **A voltmeter measures the voltage directly.**

Certain types of voltmeters do measure voltage directly. The electrostatic, or capacitor-type, voltmeter does measure voltage directly, and the voltage is read immediately on the scale. However, these electrostatic voltmeters are laboratory devices and are not very common. Certainly they are not the typical meter movement. As such, the basic meter mechanism that we will be talking about measures something other than voltage directly. Turn back to Item 101, reread the material there, and try another answer to the question.

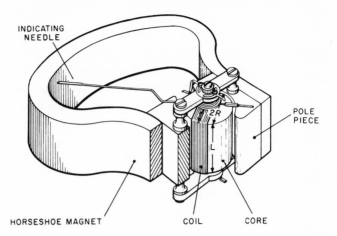

FIGURE 1-1

D'Arsonval meter
mechanism.

INDICATING
NEEDLE

POLE
PIECE

HORSESHOE MAGNET

COIL

CORE

2R

L

ITEM 102

**D'ARSONVAL
METER
MECHANISM**

Referring to Fig. 1-1, you see that the basic parts of the meter mechanism or movement are a horseshoe, or curved permanent magnet; a movable coil inserted in the gap of the magnet; and a fixed iron centerpiece, or cup, between the poles of the magnet around which the movable coil rotates. At rest, the coil is not lined up with the magnetic field from the magnet. When current flows through the movable coil, however, the current establishes a second magnetic field which tries to align itself with the magnetic field of the permanent magnet. The resulting push-pull torque is proportional to the current flowing through the movable coil. The coil then moves to a position where the torque from the current flowing through the coil is exactly balanced by the restoring force of the helical spring or taut band.

If an alternating current (ac) is used, a rectifier is used to convert this to pulsating direct current (dc). The average value of this rectified current produces an average torque on the movable coil, and the meter reading thus is proportional to the average of the pulsating current.

Q102 How will a dc meter respond to this waveform? Assume that the pulse repetition rate is well above the highest frequency to which the needle can respond.

ITEM 102a 5 ma.

ITEM 102b 10.0 ma.

ITEM 102c 6.3 ma.

ITEM 102d 7.1 ma.

10 MA

0 MA

50% ON, 50% OFF DUTY CYCLE

ITEM 102a

You answered: **5 ma.**

A square wave with 10-ma peaks half of the time will indeed have an average value of 50 percent of the peak value; the peaks and valleys are averaged to produce just half of the peak value. So you were correct; nice going. Turn to Item 103.

ITEM 102b

You answered: **10.0 ma.**

The peak value of the square wave in this case is 10 ma. Now if you rectify (in a bridge circuit) a square wave where the peak value of the current is 10 ma, you will obtain a square wave where the peaks are still 10 ma. What is the average of the peaks and the valleys in this case? It certainly isn't 10 ma, is it? Think about this a little more, and try another answer to the question back on Item 102.

ITEM 102c

You answered: **6.3 ma.**

The average value of half of a sine wave is indeed 63 percent of its peak value. The average value (both halves added together) of a sine wave with a peak of 10 ma would indeed be 6.3 ma. Most ac-dc meters in their ac positions are calibrated to read the average value of the commonly encountered sine-wave current. However, the question specifically stated that we had a square wave instead of a sine wave. Read the question a little more carefully in Item 102, and try again.

ITEM 102d

You answered: **7.1 ma.**

The effective, or rms,[1] value of a sine wave is 70.7 percent of its peak value. The effective value of current is simply defined as its equivalent heating effect, but the effective values of sine waves and square waves are considerably different. Most ac-dc meters in their ac positions are calibrated to read the average value of the commonly encountered sine-wave current. Is this waveform sinusoid?

It is suggested that you reread the question.

---

[1] Rms: Root mean square is the dc equivalent heating value of a sine wave.

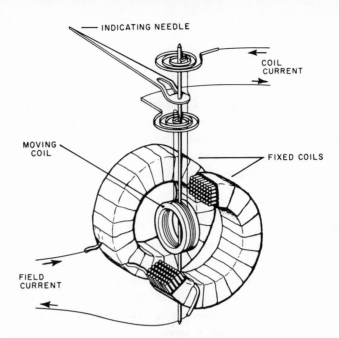

INDICATING NEEDLE

COIL CURRENT

MOVING COIL

FIXED COILS

FIELD CURRENT

FIGURE 1-2
Electrodynamic
meter mechanism.

ITEM 103

ELECTRODYNAMIC
(DUAL-COIL)
METER

Refer to Fig. 1-2. As in the D'Arsonval meter, we have a movable coil that has a helical spring attached to it. Current through this movable coil establishes a magnetic field that produces a coil and meter needle deflection proportional to the current. The permanent magnet, however, is replaced by an electromagnet. The magnetic field through the gap of the pole pieces now is not a constant, but it is proportional to the current through this second coil. The torque is proportional to the product of the two currents.

We can put a resistor in series with the fixed coils to measure the applied voltage. Now if we let the current in the movable coil measure the amperage going to a device, we can measure the product of the voltage and current, or power.

The waveform of the applied current can be of any shape, and the meter will measure both alternating and direct currents. The meter can be made to measure current, voltage, or power and responds to the rms, or effective, value. Reactance limits the current, however, when the applied frequency is too high.

Q103 What is the effective torque when equal currents applied to the coils are 90° out of phase?

ITEM 103a   Torque is proportional to I_1.

ITEM 103b   Torque is 0.

ITEM 103c   Torque is proportional to I_1^2.

ITEM 103a

You answered: **Torque is proportional to the absolute value of** I_1. In a D'Arsonval meter this is quite true. In this case it is only a half-truth since the algebraic or vector product of the two quantities is required. What you need to apply is this formula: Torque = constant $\times I_1 \times I_2 \times$ cos of the phase angle. Turn back to Item 103; apply this formula and pick another answer.

ITEM 103b

You answered: **The torque is zero.** In this particular case, the torque is proportional to the product of the two currents, $I_1 \times I_2$, but in addition, the phase angle[1] must be taken into account. When the currents in the two coils have a phase relationship of 90°, the effective product is 0. Therefore, the torque is zero. You were correct. Nice going. This relationship is also the basic one employed by phasemeters used to measure the phase angle between two electrical quantities. Turn to Item 104.

ITEM 103c

You answered: **The torque is proportional to** $I_1{}^2$. In this problem, it was stated that I_2 is equal to I_1 but at a phase angle of 90°. Your answer would be true if it were not for a phase angle. If you take the cosine of 90°, your product relationship is still true, but the multiplier turns out to be 0. Physically this means that the magnetic fields set the effective torque product. You were basically right but not completely so.

What is the average algebraic product of the two currents and their magnetic fields? Go to Item 103 and see if you can pick a better answer.

---

[1] A phase angle of 90° means that when one waveform reaches a peak, the other is going through zero amplitude. Phase angle, in general, refers to the angular difference, if any, between the same point on two similar waveforms with the same frequency of repetition.

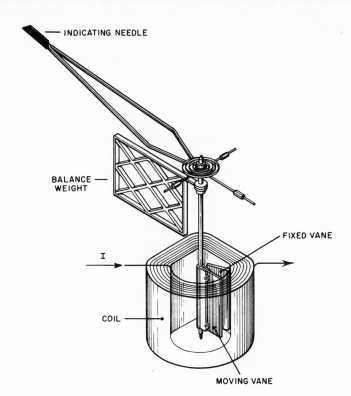

— INDICATING NEEDLE

BALANCE — WEIGHT

FIXED VANE

I

COIL

MOVING VANE

FIGURE 1-3
Moving-vane
meter mechanism.

ITEM 104

MOVING-
VANE
METER

Refer to Fig. 1-3. Two pieces of iron are in the magnetic field established by the current through the coil. One piece of iron is fixed. The other piece is movable and attached to the meter needle, or pointer. Since both pieces of iron are in the same magnetic field, they are magnetized similarly by the alternating current. The north poles will be adjacent in the two pieces and so will the two south poles. Accordingly, the two north poles and the two south poles of each magnetized piece of iron repel each other. When the alternating current reverses, the pole positions reverse, but the net effect is still one of repulsion. The strength of repulsion is proportional to the magnetic field, which in turn is proportional to the effective, or rms, value of the current. This is true for any waveshape of current. Accordingly, the torque is proportional to the effective value of the current.

Q104 What happens if dc current is applied?

ITEM 104a   The meter responds less than normal (reads 50 percent low).

ITEM 104**b**   The meter doesn't respond (reads zero).

ITEM 104**c**   The meter responds normally.

ITEM 104a

You answered: **The meter responds less than normal (reads 50 percent low).** Well, you are partially correct on this one but not entirely so. You correctly realized that when a direct current is applied to the coil, the two iron pieces will be magnetized similarly. The two north poles will repel each other on one end, and the two south poles on the other end of the vane will repel each other with a constant repelling force. However, what is the effective (rms) value for an alternating current? It is quite true that there may be slight differences between operating a meter on 60 cps ac and on 60 cps dc, but let's use the definition of "effective" in this instance. Think about this question for a minute, and try another answer back in Item 104.

ITEM 104b

You answered: **The meter doesn't respond (reads zero).**

With direct current applied to the coil, there will be no change in the current and you will have a constant magnetic field. The two pieces of iron will be magnetized similarly; there will be two north poles together at one end and two south poles together at the other end. Thus, both ends of the magnetized pieces will tend to repel each other, and you will have a constant repulsion. As such, the meter will certainly read something. See if you can puzzle this out on Item 104.

ITEM 104c

You answered: **The meter responds normally.**

The dc current through the coil will induce a magnetic field in the two iron pieces, and the effect will be to set up a repelling force and produce meter-needle torque as a result. The rms value of a dc current is its average value. There is no change involved in the dc current, but the meter will still work! Its calibration may be affected slightly because of reactance effects, but it will read close to 100 percent of what it's supposed to. Even though this answer is correct, a general recommendation is to use dc meters on direct current and ac meters, such as the moving-vane, on alternating current. Turn to Item 105.

ITEM 105

ACCURACY

Let's consider the matter of calibration of accuracy of the reading a little bit further. The accuracy of a meter usually is stated as a certain percentage of the full-scale, or maximum, reading of a meter. Typical values run from 5 percent for the commonplace bench meters to 0.1 percent accuracy for laboratory standards. The laboratory standards are sometimes referred to as "secondary standards" since the "primary standards" for voltage and resistance are set at the National Bureau of Standards in Washington, D.C., or Boulder, Colorado.

Since accuracy decreases as you go from full scale toward zero, use a range in which the meter needle reads as high as possible. However, beware of pin bending when you switch to a lower range to make the needle read higher. Check the present value to determine whether the needle will read off-scale when you switch to the next lower range. Many meters are put out of calibration this way each year. In some cases, the meters are damaged beyond being simply put out of calibration by this pin-bending process of banging the needle against the full-scale stop.

A meter's absolute accuracy stays the same regardless of the actual position of the meter needle. For a typical meter, this is 5 percent of the full-scale reading. Thus, on a 100-volt scale, the accuracy of a reading at full scale would be plus or minus 5 volts, but if the needle were reading 50 volts, then the accuracy would still be 5 percent of full scale, or plus or minus 5 volts. Now, however, the relative accuracy of reading is only half of what it was before: 5 volts out of 50 volts equals 10 percent accuracy.

To improve the accuracy of more precise meters, such as those used as secondary standards, longer scales are used and mirrors are used to reduce parallax. To make a reading on a mirrored scale, place your eye directly over the meter needle and center it over the image of the needle in the mirror under the scale. When this is done, there is no parallax and you can read the value exactly without a parallax error. In addition, the electrical components are considerably more precise than in the usual meters.

Q105 Suppose we have a typical laboratory meter with an accuracy of 5 percent of full scale. The ranges for this meter are 3, 10, 30, 100, 300, and 1000 volts. We have made a reading with the meter on the 100-volt range, and the needle reads 12 volts. How can we make this reading more accurate?

ITEM 105a Leave the meter on the 100-volt range since it is not possible to get 5 percent accuracy at 12 volts.

ITEM 105b Switch to the 30-volt range since this is a safe check.

ITEM 105c Change to the 10-volt range since the accuracy is considerably worse than 5 percent at 12 volts.

You answered: **Leave the range switch on the 100-volt scale since it is not possible to get 5 percent accuracy at 12 volts.**

Well now, on a 100-volt scale did you stop to figure out what your accuracy was? Five percent of 100 volts would be 5 volts, and 12 volts plus or minus 5 volts is quite a lot of error, isn't it? Wouldn't you like to be able to improve this somewhat? It is true in this case that you will not be able to get 5 percent accuracy on this reading of 12 volts, since the 12-volt reading does not fall near any maximum range. However, you can read the voltage applied to the meter considerably better than the approximate 40 percent error that you would get on this scale. Turn back.

ITEM 105b

You answered: **Switch to the 30-volt scale.**

Previously your meter read about 12 volts on the 100-volt scale, and you wanted to switch to a scale where the needle would read higher. Now if you switched to the 30-volt scale, the meter then would read a little bit less than half, about 40 percent of full scale; but if you switched it down to the 10-volt scale, 12 volts would bang the pin. Then this is the best answer, even though the needle still reads somewhat less than half scale. Very good; you were right. Turn to Item 106.

ITEM 105c

You answered: **Change to the 10-volt range.**

You recognized in this case that you certainly do want to change ranges, and probably you realized that 5 percent of 100 volts for the initial scale used produced 12 volts plus or minus 5 volts error, or approximately 40 percent error. This is considerable, isn't it? Thus, you may have figured that 12 volts minus 5 volts would be 7 volts and this could be measured very nicely on the 10-volt range. This is quite true, but if you happen to switch to the 10-volt range directly, you might bang a pin, because the measurement actually might have been 12 volts plus 5 volts, or 17 volts. It is not recommended, then, to switch to the 10-volt scale. Pick another answer.

Let's look at the accuracy involved here. The meter was given as having an accuracy of 5 percent of full scale. But is that the case here? Five percent of the full-scale 30 volts would be 1.5 volts. If you were measuring 30 volts, you would have an accuracy of ±1.5 volts. With 12 volts, however, you have measured 12 volts plus or minus the full-scale accuracy, or 12 volts ±1.5 volts. This is far worse than 5 percent accuracy: 1.5 volts/12 volts gives ±12.5 percent accuracy.

Not only will the accuracy of a meter vary with the care and precision used by the manufacturer, but it also will vary with the type of meter. For instance, the D'Arsonval meter measures the average current. On alternating current, this meter is used with a rectifier and calibrated for a particular type of ac waveform, usually that of the common sine wave. Because of the rectifier, the meter is less accurate on alternating current than direct current. Where the waveform is other than that of a sine wave, you would have to calibrate the meter or use a fudge factor to take the different waveshape into account. The electrodynamic and moving-vane meters, on the other hand, measure the rms, or effective, value of a waveform of any shape, but their dc accuracy is typically less than that of the D'Arsonval movement.

METER LIMITATIONS

The frequency response of meters also affects their accuracy. For instance, the D'Arsonval meter is basically a dc meter and is adapted to measuring alternating currents by the use of a rectifier. The rectifier introduces a limitation on the frequency response in that capacitive effects at high frequencies limit its response. Using a D'Arsonval meter on alternating current means that one standard conversion factor (usually for sine waves) is used to convert from alternating current to direct current.

The rectifier also produces a nonlinearity in another way. At low voltages, the rectifier's resistance affects the current flowing in the circuit. Accordingly, most voltmeters that use a rectifier will have lower scales that are slightly differently calibrated than the higher-voltage scales. The electrodynamic and moving-vane meters, on the other hand, have primarily just the frequency-response characteristics to limit their accuracy.

At high frequencies, the inductance of the coils sets a limit at which the meters no longer read accurately. At the low-frequency end there is insufficient inductance to limit the current flowing. The wires may heat up and change resistance, affecting the calibration; but before this happens, you may be in danger of injuring the meter coil winding.

Q106 What happens when you use meters above their cutoff frequency?

ITEM 106a The meters won't indicate and correspondingly aren't useful.

ITEM 106b The meters may read low or high, but they may be used with caution.

ITEM 106a

You answered: **The meters won't indicate and correspondingly aren't useful.** In the discussion about frequency response of meters, it was pointed out that the calibration accuracy would be affected at the high-frequency end. Typically, what happens is that the meter's inductive reactance limits the current flowing. Eventually a point is reached where the current starts falling off abruptly at the rate determined by the LR circuit constants. In cases with an appreciable capacitive reactance, the meter response actually may increase slightly as you approach a cutoff frequency. Above the resonant frequency, however, the meter reading drops off quite sharply with an increase in frequency. Thus, as you approach the cutoff frequency of a meter, the calibration accuracy is impaired at first and the meter reading may be higher or lower than the correct value at that frequency. The meter can be used with caution, however, particularly at one given frequency. It may even be recalibrated for that particular frequency. Try the other answer in Item 106.

ITEM 106b

You answered: **The meters may read high or low, but they may be used with caution.**

Above a cutoff frequency dependent upon the resistance and reactance of the meter, the response or indication of the meter drops off. The meter will respond, however, to frequencies somewhat above this cutoff frequency. The meter, in such cases, should be used only as a relative indicator unless it is recalibrated for each such frequency. You were correct in your thinking; now continue.

ITEM 107

VOLTMETERS

A typical and common basic meter movement will indicate 1 ma full scale. So you will find the meter movement characterized as "0–1 ma full scale." This simply means that the meter reads 0 to 1 mil and that 1 ma current is the full-scale value. Correspondingly, the meter movement will have a typical resistance value of 50 ohms. According to Ohm's law, if 1 ma produces a full-scale needle deflection across a 50-ohmmeter coil, a 50-mv IR[1] drop across the coil is produced. This usually is insignificant but in precision meters will be taken into account.

Q107 Suppose that we want our 0- to 1-ma meter to read 1 volt full scale. What resistor would we place in series with the 50-ohm coil to convert the meter?

ITEM 107a Use a resistor of 1000 ohms.

ITEM 107b Use an additional resistor of 950 ohms.

ITEM 107c I don't know.

---

[1] IR drop is a technical phrase for the voltage produced by a current I flowing through a resistance R.

You answered: **An additional resistor of 1000 ohms.**

The total resistance in this case is indeed 1000 ohms, and you have shown that you know Ohm's law quite well. One volt divided by 1 ma does give a total resistance of 1000 ohms. But what about the 50 ohms of the meter movement itself? Wouldn't this have to be subtracted from the total resistance? Return to Item 107 and make the right choice.

ITEM 107b

You answered: **An additional resistance of 950 ohms.**

Applying Ohm's law, you realized that 1 volt divided by 1 mil full-scale current gives a total circuit resistance of 1000 ohms. But since you already had 50 ohms for the meter-coil resistance, the additional resistance to add was 1000 ohms minus 50 ohms, or 950 ohms. Correct. Turn to Item 108.

ITEM 107c

You answered: **I don't know.**

Let's take a look at what's happening here. Basically, this is another application of Ohm's law. We want a full-scale deflection of 1 volt. We know that the meter, when the needle is reading full scale, is passing a current of 1 ma. Applying Ohm's law, we then have the total circuit resistance given as 1 volt divided by 1 ma equaling 1000 ohms. This is the total circuit resistance, and from this total we must subtract the resistance of the meter coil itself. Turn back to Item 107 and pick the right answer.

A meter with this characteristic of 1 ma current for full-scale needle deflection is known as a "1000 ohms/volt meter." As you can see, once you want to measure voltages greater than 1 volt, the 50 ohms resistance of the coil is insignificant. If you want to measure 100 volts, you would insert a series-multiplier resistor of 100,000 ohms. Compared with this, the 50 ohms of the meter coil is insignificant and is disregarded.

As a common practice in a multiscale, or many-range, voltmeter, a series of multiplier resistors is tapped so that the total resistance at a particular point is the necessary resistance for that voltage scale. This essentially is a long string of resistors with a switch tap between each member. In using a multiscale voltmeter, it is often quite useful to be able to take the basic meter movement sensitivity, such as 20,000 ohms/volt, and the voltage scale in use, and figure the total resistance applied to the circuit. This meter resistance will permit you to determine whether your voltmeter will load down the circuit being tested.

Q108 We have a 20,000 ohms/volt meter set on the 300-volt scale. Figure out the total meter resistance applied to the circuit. The meter reads 150 volts when applied to this particular circuit. The total meter resistance applied to the circuit is:

ITEM 108a   3 megohms.

ITEM 108b   6 megohms.

ITEM 108c   20,000 ohms.

ITEM 108a

You answered: **The total meter resistance applied to the circuit is 3 megohms.**

Perhaps the meter reading of 150 volts fooled you in this case. The meter resistance applied to the circuit is independent of the voltage that the meter is actually reading. (This assumes, of course, that you haven't burned out the meter with an applied voltage that was too high.)

In this problem you have to multiply the basic meter resistance of 20,000 ohms/volt by the maximum voltage that you intend to read on that meter switch position. Return to Item 108 and see if you can figure this one out.

ITEM 108b

You answered: **The total meter resistance applied to the circuit is 6 megohms.**

Part of this problem is to ignore the 150 volts. The meter resistance applied to the circuit is independent of the actual voltage being read. You correctly realized that the total resistance applied to the circuit is the basic meter sensitivity multiplied by the full-scale voltage desired. Turn to Item 109.

ITEM 108c

You answered: **The total meter resistance is 20,000 ohms.**

This is the basic meter sensitivity when you are trying to measure 1 volt full scale but not 300 volts full scale. Go back to Item 108 and figure out how to multiply the basic meter sensitivity by the full-scale range, in this case, to obtain the meter resistance on this range.

VOLTMETER
CIRCUIT
LOADING

The ohms-per-volt figure for the meter also gives the full-scale current. With the meter set to the 300-volt scale and a total resistance of 6 megohms, 300 volts would give what full-scale current? Algebraically, 300 volts divided by 6 million ohms equals 50 μa. Knowing this current also can be quite useful in determining circuit loading.

Q109 In this circuit, we want to measure the plate voltage. What is the error in the meter reading? This is a 5 percent meter set on the 100-volt range, and the meter sensitivity is 20,000 ohms/volt. The plate resistance of the tube is 1 megohm.

ITEM 109a   The error is approximately 5 percent.

ITEM 109b   The error is appreciably larger than 5 percent.

ITEM 109c   The error is much less than 5 percent.

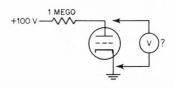

ITEM 109a

You answered: **The error in reading the plate voltage is approximately 5 percent.**

What is the total meter resistance? This is found by multiplying the meter sensitivity of 20,000 ohms/volt times the meter scale used, 100 volts. This produces a total meter resistance of 2 megohms on the 100-volt scale. In reading the plate voltage, you see that this meter resistance shunts the plate resistance of 1 megohm, which reduces the total plate resistance from 1 megohm to two-thirds of that. This is a reduction in the resistance of more than 5 percent. Try again.

ITEM 109b

You answered: **The error in reading the plate voltage is much more than 5 percent.**

Following Ohm's law, you realized that the meter resistance applied to the circuit was 20,000 ohms/volt times an even 100 volts, or 2 megohms. This was quite appreciable when shunting the 1 megohm to 0.67 megohm. This 33 percent change in load resistance was in series with the 1-megohm plate-load resistance and produced a change much more than 5 percent. You were correct. The change in the plate part of the resistance was one-third, but this was merely one-half the total circuit resistance so the total current and voltage reading will be reduced by about one-sixth. Therefore the loading error was 16 percent. Go to Item 110.

ITEM 109c

You answered: **The error is much less than 5 percent in reading the plate voltage.**

One approach to this problem is to figure out the total meter resistance. The meter resistance is found by multiplying 20,000 ohms/volt times the 100-volt scale, which gives 2 megohms total meter resistance. Two megohms in parallel with the one-megohm plate resistance produces an appreciable reduction, namely, about a one-third reduction in the total parallel resistance. Therefore, the plate resistance will be decreased by a third which would increase the error beyond the 5 percent value. Try again.

There are two words, accuracy and precision, commonly used in describing the merits of meters. The two words technically have different meanings. Accuracy is defined as a conformity to the true value. The average usually yields the best estimate of the true value being measured by a meter. Precision refers to how sharply or clearly a measurement is made. Precision is inversely related to the spread of the measurements around the average. In this respect, it is similar to the standard deviation in statistics.

Meter errors may be split into nonrepeatable or variable errors and repeatable or constant errors. Parallax is one common nonrepeatable error. That is, if you look at a meter needle from an angle rather than from straight above the needle, you will read an erroneous value. To reduce parallax, the more accurate meters use a mirror scale so that when you read the value, you see the knife-edge needle and its image superimposed.

Repeatable or constant errors usually are due to the calibration, or lack thereof, in the resistors used to change the scale ranges on a meter. That is, the resistors themselves need to be considerably better than the overall accuracy of the meter. If you want a meter with a full-scale accuracy of 1 percent, the scale or range resistors need an accuracy better than 1 percent. Since the resistances are fixed, though, the meter reading is going to be off by the same amount when the same value on the same scale is measured. However, there may be differences in the amount of calibration error from scale to scale.

Another type of constant error is that due to the springs' providing the restoring torque on the needle. The springs themselves with their bearings may have some nonlinearities so that the measurements are not quite the theoretically desired values throughout the meter range. Irregularities in the shape of the pole pieces may cause the nonlinearities in the magnetic field to introduce nonlinear but repeatable errors at different scale values.

Q110 The use of 0.1 percent precision resistors is sufficient to ensure a full-scale meter accuracy of 0.1 percent.

ITEM 110a False.

ITEM 110b True.

ITEM 110a

You answered: **False. The use of 0.1 percent resistors is insufficient to ensure 0.1 percent full-scale meter accuracy.**

The use of 0.1 percent resistors is a basic step in the direction to ensure 0.1 percent full-scale accuracy. Actually, however, since there are several errors and they add up to an rss (root-sum-of-squares) fashion, you would like to use something like 0.05 percent resistors to enable you to wind up with 0.1 percent full-scale meter accuracy. In addition to these precision resistors, you also would need a long meter-needle scale, a mirror backing to eliminate parallax, and a knife-edge meter needle. So you are quite correct: It takes a number of things to ensure a high order of accuracy. Another variable error is that due to friction. Even though the meters are quite freely suspended, the bearings do have some minimal amount of friction. And this may change slightly from measurement to measurement even when the process is repeated with the same value being measured. Still another apparent variable error is that due to temperature. When the temperature changes, the resistances in the meter change slightly and thus give a different reading on the meter. Most modern instruments, however, use calibrated resistors that are temperature-compensated. Errors due to temperature are minimized and, for most purposes, can be ignored.

Go to Item 111.

ITEM 110b

You answered: **True. The use of 0.1 percent resistors is sufficient to ensure 0.1 percent accuracy full scale in a meter.**

To answer this question you really need to go back and consider: How many sources of error are there? What happens if you have a meter movement that does not have a long scale or a knife-edge with a mirror to eliminate parallax? Or what happens if the meter movement has certain nonlinearities in it? As such, 0.1 percent (or better) resistors are one of the basic ingredients necessary to ensure 0.1 percent full-scale accuracy. More than just this is needed, however.

Turn back to Item 110 and try again.

Let's discuss how to make an ammeter or a milliammeter measure currents other than those within its basic range. If we start with a sensitive 0- to 1-ma meter movement, it's impossible, without a current amplifier or increased magnetic field, to make it measure currents less than 1 ma full scale. Let's take a look. According to the illustration, the meter resistance is 50 ohms. This corresponds to 0.02 mho.[1] Applying Ohm's law in the conductance G version, we have the following: $I = VG$. Since we must yet have 50 mv across the meter at 10 mils total current, the total conductance G_t equals 0.2 mho. We already have 0.02 mho from the meter, so that the additional conductance can be provided by a shunt resistor $G_{sh} = 0.18$, or $R_{sh} = 5.55$ ohms. Obviously, a resistance such as this would require a precise resistor, such as 1 or 0.1 percent, and might even be hand wound.

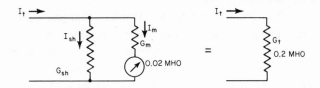

Q111 Let us define the multiplying factor K as the ratio of the new full-scale current to the existing full-scale current of the meter. That is, $K = I_t/I_m$. Using this formulation, what is I_{sh}, the shunt current?

ITEM 111a KI_m.

ITEM 111b $(1 - K)I_m$.

ITEM 111c $(K - 1)I_m$.

[1] The mho is "ohm" spelled backward and is the unit of reciprocal resistance or conductance. For example, 25 ohms = 0.04 mho. Measuring conductance in mhos is particularly helpful, as shown above, in dealing with parallel circuits.

ITEM 111a

You answered: $I_{sh} = KI_m$.

Well, this is close and is a good approximation if K is much larger than 1. However, approximations usually are not accurate enough in measuring instruments. For instance, if we wish to change the scale factor by 10 so that we read 10 mils full scale instead of 1 mil, then K would be 10. If we used your formula, we would have a 10 percent error. See if you can figure out which is the more exact formula on Item 111.

ITEM 111b

You answered: $I_{sh} = (1 - K)I_m$.

Well, isn't K as a multiplying factor much larger than 1? It appears that you may have assumed something like this in your algebraic manipulation, but you probably forgot a minus sign. The quantity in this expression $(1 - K)$ would be negative since K is much larger than 1. And since we do not wish to deal with negative multiplying factors, return to Item 111 and take another crack at the question.

ITEM 111c

You answered: $I_{sh} = (K - 1)I_m$.

The simplest way to look at this is that you want to have the normal full-scale current going through the meter and the remainder going through the shunt part of the circuit. If we have unity current going through the meter, we would like to have the multiplying-factor current minus this unity current going through the shunt branch. You were quite correct. Turn to Item 112.

ITEM 112

AMMETER
SHUNT
PROBLEM

Let's take another case where we want 50 times the normal current through the meter to make it read full scale. The shunt current is now equal to 49 times 1 ma. As before, the voltage across the meter required to produce full-scale current is the constant 50 mv. The following algebra applies to find the shunt resistor:

$$R_{\text{sh}} = \frac{V_m}{I_{\text{sh}}} = \frac{V_m}{(K-1)I_m} = \frac{R_m}{K-1}$$

Q112 In this case, where we wish to have 50 times the normal full-scale current produce the maximum current reading on the meter, what is the value of the shunt resistor R_{sh}?

ITEM 112a   2451 ohms.

ITEM 112b   1.020 ohms.

ITEM 112c   1 ohm.

ITEM 112a

You answered: **2451 ohms.**

It appears that you were thinking of the voltmeter case where you want to add a resistance in series to increase the voltage at which the meter reads the maximum. You have the correct answer for the voltmeter case, but that isn't what was asked here. Check the question more carefully, and see if you can figure out the correct answer on Item 112.

ITEM 112b

You answered: **1.020 ohms.**

The total resistance presented to the circuit when you wish to have 50 times the usual maximum current obviously must be one-fiftieth of the usual resistance. Applying our formula, however, you find that the shunt resistance isn't quite one-fiftieth but is reduced by 1 less than its maximum ratio. Therefore, the shunt resistance is the meter resistance divided by 49, or 50 ohms/49 = 1.02 ohms. You were right on the ball, and used the correct algebra when you figured this one out. Turn to Item 113.

ITEM 112c

You answered: **1 ohm.**

This answer is approximately correct. If you want to make a 50-ohm meter movement that ordinarily reads 1 ma maximum read 50 mils maximum, you want to reduce the total resistance presented to the circuit to one-fiftieth. This answer is only approximately correct, however, and in meters we usually dispense with approximations and apply the exact formula. Return to Item 112 and use the exact formula, not the approximate one.

ITEM 113

OHMMETERS

Let's take a look now at how ohmmeters work. Basically, an ohmmeter is a milliammeter with a battery added as a voltage source. Then the milliammeter with battery and calibrating resistor is applied to a circuit. You could then calculate the resistance of the external circuit from knowing the battery voltage, the current through the meter, and the calibrating resistor. This can be done simply by using Ohm's law. However, you can make the job much easier by having the scales calibrated directly in ohms of resistance instead of current. The total resistance of the circuit R_t is equal to the voltage over the current. Now, if we make the unknown external resistance R_x equal to 0, we can adjust our calibrating resistor so that the meter just reads full scale. Then $R_t = R_m$. If we open the circuit so that no current flows, the external resistance R_x is equal to infinity. A more typical and interesting case occurs when the milliammeter reads half scale. In this particular case, half of the resistance is in the external circuit and half is directly in the calibrating circuit. Thus $R_x = R_m'$, where R_m' is the total internal calibrating resistance, including that of the meter.

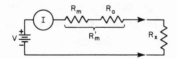

Q113 A 1-mil full-scale meter with a 1½-volt battery and an adjustable calibrating resistor R_a will have what midscale value of resistance? (What is the midscale R_x?)

ITEM 113a   1.5 kilohms.

ITEM 113b   1000 ohms.

ITEM 113c   The same as R_a, the adjustable resistor.

ITEM 113a

You answered: **The midscale value of the meter scale is 1.5 kilohms.**

Let's go back and figure out the algebra on this one. To adjust the meter to a full scale requires 1 ma of current from the applied battery voltage of 1.5 volts. Applying Ohm's law, 1.5 volts/1 ma = 1500 ohms. That is the value of the adjustable resistor plus that of the meter when the ohmmeter is calibrated at 0 ohm by shorting the test leads. Then, when the meter reads half scale, you know that a value exactly equal to the total meter circuit resistance has been placed in the external part of the circuit: $R_x = R_m'$. You were correct; the answer is 1500 ohms. Go to Item 114.

ITEM 113b

You answered: **The midscale value of the resistance is 1000 ohms.**

It appears that you may have confused the answer to this one with the meter sensitivity. A meter with a 1-ma full-scale current will have a sensitivity of 1000 ohms/volt. That is definitely true. However, that is not the same as the value of the adjustable resistor R_a in this case. Go back and reread the discussion in Item 113, and see if you can puzzle out a better answer.

ITEM 113c

You answered: **The midscale value of R_x will be the same as that of the adjustable resistor R_a.**

This is approximately true, but what is the exact value? In this particular case, the problem is to find out the value of the adjustable resistor. The problem was stated that you adjust an ohmmeter by shorting the leads and making the meter read full scale. Well, now you can calculate what that value of resistance is. Then you know that if you apply a resistor that is equal to this, the current will be cut in half because now the total circuit resistance is double that of your adjustable calibrating resistor. Turn to Item 113 and puzzle this one out.

ITEM 114   Ohmmeter ranges may be changed by changing the meter sensitivity. For instance, if a 100-μa meter movement has been used on the high-resistance range, the meter could be shunted to make it effectively a 1-ma full-scale movement, and you would be able to read resistances 10 times lower in value than before. A second way of changing the ohmmeter range is to change the battery voltage. For example, two batteries may be used, a 1.5-volt battery for low-resistance measurement and a 15-volt battery (hearing-aid size) for high-resistance measurements. A third method is to switch the meter from a series position to measuring the shunt current; this method requires two differently calibrated resistance scales on the meter face. In practice, all these methods may be used together to change ohmmeter resistance ranges.

AC VOLTMETERS   Let's consider how ac voltmeters are made from dc voltmeters. The usual approach is to use a rectifier to change alternating current to direct current. Rectifier circuits such as half-wave, voltage-doubler, or bridge circuits may be used. Quite often, a filter capacitor is dispensed with, and the only filter is that of the inductance and inertia of the meter itself.

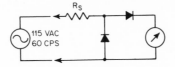

Q114 In this simple ac voltmeter circuit, what smooths the pulsating direct current presented to the meter?

ITEM 114a No smoothing is needed since a full-wave rectifier circuit is used.

ITEM 114b The inductance and inertia of the meter smooths the alternating current.

ITEM 114c I don't know.

ITEM 114a

You answered: **No smoothing is needed because of the full-wave nature of the circuit.**

First, the circuit really isn't a full-wave, or voltage-doubler, circuit. In order to keep the resistance presented to the external circuit constant, the second diode bypasses the meter on alternate half cycles. The waveform presented to the meter circuit is a series of positive half cycles. The circuit current does need some smoothing. Turn back to Item 114 and try a better answer.

ITEM 114b

You answered: **The inductance and inertia of the meter itself smooths the alternating current.**

A pulsating waveform is presented to the meter from the rectifier circuit. The pulsating dc current sets up a current through the meter. The inductance of the meter and circuit resistance provide filtering action for high frequencies to keep current flowing. Admittedly, the filtering action is not complete, but the inertia of the meter movement keeps the needle from vibrating or pulsating on all but the lowest ac frequencies. Correct and right on the ball! Go to Item 115.

ITEM 114c

You answered: **I don't know.**

Let's discuss this for a minute. The diode pointing toward the meter lets positive half cycles from the applied ac waveform pass through to the meter. The other diode shunts the alternate (negative) half cycles to ground to preserve a constant resistance to the external circuit. This also avoids high-voltage breakdown due to the blocking of the reverse ac cycle. The waveform presented to the meter is that of every other half cycle for a pulsating and positive direct current. As such, some smoothing is definitely needed, but return to Item 113 and reread the paragraph.

ITEM 115   The moving-vane meter is used much like the D'Arsonval meter in measuring current and voltage. Series resistors can be added to make the moving-vane meter perform on voltages higher than full-scale voltage for the meter movement by itself. To measure higher currents, typically, a current transformer may be used. A current transformer simply has a turns ratio so that the current being measured may be stepped up or down in direct proportion to the turns ratio. Electrodynamic meters may be used in much the same manner. If used to measure voltage or current, however, specially calibrated scales are needed because the two coils in parallel will produce a squared response characteristic. Usually, electrodynamic meters are used to measure power. Sometimes clamp-around transformers are used so that the ac current flowing in a branch does not have to be interrupted at all. Thus, ac current and power can be measured without disconnecting the circuit. The wraparound transformer is simply a transformer with the secondary winding connected to the meter, and the primary, simply the wire around which the iron core is clamped shut.

VOMS   A very common laboratory instrument is the "VOM" or the volt-ohm-milliammeter, sometimes referred to as "VOMA." These instruments usually have a basic D'Arsonval meter movement with appropriate series resistors to measure a number of voltage ranges and a rectifier so that the meter also can be used to measure ac voltages. A number of shunts are included to put in parallel with the meter coil so that many current ranges can be measured. Finally, a battery or two is included so that resistances over many ranges can be measured.

FIGURE 1-4 Triplett Model 310 VOM photograph.

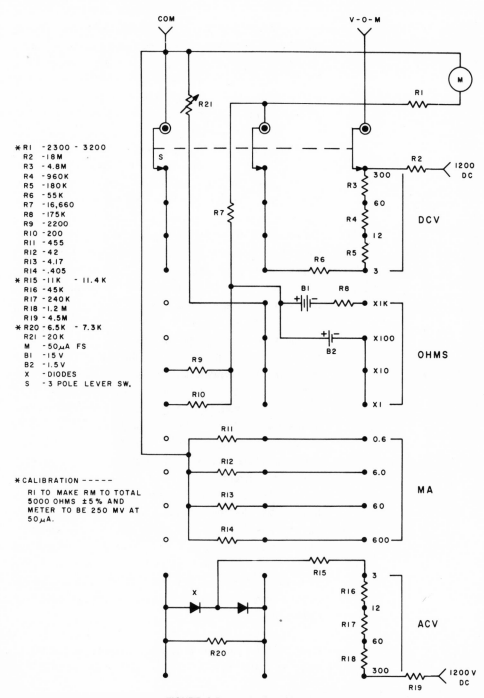

FIGURE 1-5 Triplett Model 310 VOM schematic.

Figure 1-4 shows a typical VOM, the Triplett Model 310. This VOM has these ranges: 3, 12, 60, 300, and 1200 volts dc and ac. The meter sensitivity is 20,000 ohms/volt dc and 5000 ohms/volt ac, with a special 3-volt ac scale (slightly nonlinear). The same meter also measures these currents: 600 μa, 6, 60, and 600 ma. The midscale resistances on the ohms' ranges are as follows: 200 ohms, 2, 20, and 200 kilohms. Figure 1-5 shows the wiring diagram for the meter.

Now you know about the basic types of meter movements, and when you encounter a laboratory meter of a VOM, you'll have some idea of how it works. If you are using a VOM, study the manual and find out the special precautions to take in the use of the meter. And if you scrutinize the circuit diagrams supplied with the meter, you will discover its workings to be quite similar to what we have discussed here.

There are two other types of meter movements occasionally found in the lab. The first is the "hot-wire," or thermocouple, movement in which a piece of resistance wire is thermally bonded to a thermocouple junction. A current heats the wire and thermocouple. The thermoelectric voltage is proportional to the hot-junction temperature, with the reference, or cold, junction usually at room temperature. This type of meter has a non-linear response and is used to measure high-frequency alternating currents.

The other type of movement sometimes encountered is the electrostatic, or capacitor, meter. The voltage impressed across a capacitor results in an attractive force between the plates. In a rotatable capacitor, one set of plates or a dielectric plate can be pulled into the remainder against a spring reaction. This type of meter is used to measure high-frequency ac voltages and high dc voltages.

You have now completed the first chapter in this book. Check yourself on meter concepts by turning to Item 116 and answering the questions for review in Quiz 1.

ITEM 116

QUIZ 1

Write down your answers to these questions on a separate piece of paper. The letter in parentheses after each question gives the answer paragraph on the next pages.

1 Name two types of a-c meter movements. Describe them briefly. *(E)*

2 What is the most common dc meter movement, and how is it used on alternating current? *(A)*

3 Define accuracy and precision. *(F)*

4 What is a "series-multiplying resistor," and how does it work? *(H)*

5 What is a "current shunt resistor," and how does it work? *(C)*

6 Name two ways to change the electrical ranges on an ohmmeter. *(D)*

7 In using a D'Arsonval meter on alternating current, what precautions should be kept in mind? *(B)*

8 What is "circuit loading" in using a voltmeter? *(I)*

9 What corresponds to circuit loading in ammeters? *(K)*

10 What rule(s) should be kept in mind when changing ranges on meters? *(G)*

11 What is the reason for switching ranges on a meter? *(J)*

12 What is the only true voltmeter? *(L)*

A The most common dc meter movement is the D'Arsonval meter movement. It is used on alternating current with an associated rectifier
circuit. The ac scales are calibrated in terms of a sine-wave equivalent to direct current.

B Precautions to take in using a D'Arsonval meter to measure ac voltages are to know the waveshape and if it is not a sine wave, to use
a special conversion factor in order to interpret the voltages correctly.
The frequency response of the meter must cover the basic repetition
frequency and high-frequency components if a sharply peaked waveform
is encountered. The right scale must be read as a special scale if
used on low ac voltages.

C A current shunt resistor is a resistor in parallel or shunt with a meter
so that an accurately known proportion of the circuit current will flow
through the shunting resistor and bypass the meter coil. This permits
the meter to measure currents much larger than the nominal full-scale
current for the particular meter movement.

D Two ways to change ohmmeter ranges are to use batteries of different
voltages for the voltage source and place shunt resistors across the
meter to change its current ranges.

E Two basic types of ac meters are the moving-vane and electrodynamic
types. The moving-vane meter has two magnetic vanes inserted in a
coil. When the current flows through the coil, the movable vane is
repelled by the fixed vane in proportion to the strength of the magnetic field which in turn depends upon the current. The electrodynamic
meter mechanism has two sets of coils. A fixed pair of coils has a
current passing through them with a magnetic field proportional to the
current strength. A movable coil at right angles to the other pair of
coils also has a current flowing through it, creating a magnetic field. The
two magnetic fields interact to attract or repel the movable coil with
respect to the fixed pair.

F Accuracy indicates how closely the average of repeated measurements
taken with a given meter approximates the true value. Precision refers
to the amount of spread, or standard deviation, of these repeated
measurements.

G The major rules to be followed in changing ranges are to know what
type of measurement you expect to make and to make sure your meter
is set to measure this. Secondly, start one scale higher than you think

necessary. If in doubt, start with the highest possible scale on your meter, and then keep switching to a more sensitive scale while noting the response of the meter needle. In each case, make sure that you don't pin the meter movement. Many meters are ruined by trying to measure volts with the meter set to measure current or ohms, or by trying to measure current with the meter set to measure volts or ohms, or by trying to measure 100 volts when the meter is set on the 3-volt scale!

H A series-multiplying resistor is a precision resistor inserted in series with a meter movement so that the meter will measure voltage. It does this by keeping the current through the resistor and meter in accordance with Ohm's law.

I Circuit loading refers to the current drawn by a voltmeter. Even though the voltmeter may have a very high series resistance, it will have to draw a small amount of current in order for the meter mechanism to operate. This small current can result in erroneous voltage readings in high-impedance circuits.

J The basic reason for switching ranges is to obtain as high a deflection as possible on the movement without banging the needle against the stop. This helps to get maximum reading accuracy.

K Circuit loading in a voltmeter corresponds in an ammeter to the slight voltage drop across it due to current flow through its resistance. This slight voltage drop means that the voltage applied to the circuit is less by this amount and may cause a slight error in calculating the power consumed by the circuit.

L The only true voltmeter is an electrostatic, or capacitive, meter since it responds to the effective voltage.

After you have successfully completed this quiz or reviewed the material in the chapter, take a break. Then try your hand at Chap. 2.

CHAPTER TWO

VACUUM-TUBE VOLTMETERS

ITEM 201

INTRODUCTION

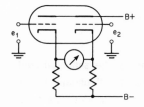

A vacuum-tube voltmeter, abbreviated VTVM, is based upon a difference amplifier circuit such as the typical one shown here. A double triode[1] commonly is used, with each half of the tube acting as a cathode follower. One voltage e_1 is connected to the grid for one tube, and a second voltage e_2 is connected to the other grid. Because of cathode-follower action, the cathode voltages are directly proportional to, and within a very good approximation of, the values of e_1 and e_2. The constant of proportionality is the same for both triodes so that the voltage difference will be measured by the meter; this difference will be the exact difference with no approximations.

A double triode with identical halves is used for this circuit; the triodes have the same amplification factor and the same plate resistance and plate currents. The temperature effect on plate current is approximately the same for both halves of the tube. This constancy of temperature in the cathode-follower circuit makes a very stable dc amplifier. If fluctuations do occur in plate current, an adjustment is provided to balance it.

When the meter resistance in a VTVM is low compared to that in the cathode resistors, the effect is similar to that of a grounded-grid amplifier where the input signal is applied to the cathode. When input voltage e_1 increases, plate current I_{p1} increases. Because of the minor cross-coupling action, second-triode plate current I_{p2} decreases slightly. When the second input voltage e_2 increases, through coupling the first plate, current I_{p1} decreases slightly.

Q201 If you consider just major effects, what is going to be the result if both input voltages e_1 and e_2 increase simultaneously?

ITEM 201a   The meter current will increase.

ITEM 201b   The plate currents will increase by the same amount with no meter change.

ITEM 201c   The plate currents will decrease by the same amount.

---

[1] Two identical triodes in one common glass or metal envelope.

ITEM 201a

You answered: **The meter current will increase.**

In this particular case when the input voltage for the left triode increases, its plate voltage is going to increase. Consequently, the cathode voltage will increase by some given amount. When the grid voltage applied to the second triode increases by the same voltage, you will have the same increase in plate current and consequently the same resulting cathode voltage as in the first tube. Now then, if we have equal voltages applied to both sides of the meter, what is going to happen to the meter current? It isn't going to increase, is it? Go to Item 201.

ITEM 201b

You answered: **The plate currents in both triodes will increase by the same amount.**

The plate voltage for both triodes will decrease in this case. An increased grid voltage permits more electrons from the cathode to reach the plate. Consequently, the cathode voltages are going to increase by the same amount; thus there will be no current through the meter. You were right on the ball with this one. Turn to Item 202.

ITEM 201c

You answered: **The plate currents for the triodes will decrease by the same amount.**

Let's take a look at this one. When grid voltage increases, it usually means that the grid voltage becomes more positive. Now it is true that in triodes where you have a negative bias, the meaning of an increase in voltage is somewhat questionable. In this particular case we do not have any bias battery, so that the only bias voltage comes from the cathode current. That settles the question about what an increase in grid voltage means. Here an increase can only mean going positive. If the grid voltage goes positive, more electrons are allowed to reach the plate. Consequently, the plate current is going to increase and by the same amount for both tubes.

Go to Item 201.

Refer to Fig. 2-1 on the next page. A vacuum-tube volt-meter is constructed basically of a difference amplifier and a tapped voltage divider. There are some refinements added to the basic difference amplifier, however. The input voltage is always applied to the left triode via some voltage divider. The second grid is tied directly to ground to provide a zero reference for all input voltages. Thus, the differences will always be a reflection of the input voltage times some multiplying factor. The multiplying factor in the voltage-measuring part of the circuit derives from the 11-megohm voltage divider. Trace this out. This voltage-divider string starts with a 7-megohm resistor at the top where the switch connection goes to the 1.5-volt scale. The voltage divider progresses downward through a 2-megohm resistor and finally all the way down to a 10,000-ohm resistor connected to ground. The switch tap at this position is 1500 volts full scale.

Note that there is a 1-megohm resistor at the very tip of the test probe, which makes the total resistance of the voltage-divider network 11 megohms. The full circuit voltage is always applied to the entire voltage-divider string, but note that you get a voltage-divider action by having the triode-grid voltage tapped down at some known fraction of the input voltage.

Note that there is an RC filter at each grid so that any ac voltage components on the dc voltages being measured will be bypassed to ground. Thus the meter will respond to the average or dc value instead of the ac components of the measured voltage. Also note the plus and minus power supplies: The plates have a potential of approximately 50 to 70 volts positive with respect to ground, and the low end of the cathode resistors and shunt resistor are at a potential of 60 to 80 volts negative with respect to ground.

Q202 With the switch on the 1500-volt scale (the triode grid connected to the junction of the 10- and 20-kilohm resistors in the voltage divider), what test-prod voltage would give a meter deflection equivalent to 1.0 volt on the 1.5-volt scale?

ITEM 202a I don't know.

ITEM 202b 1 volt.

ITEM 202c 1000 volts.

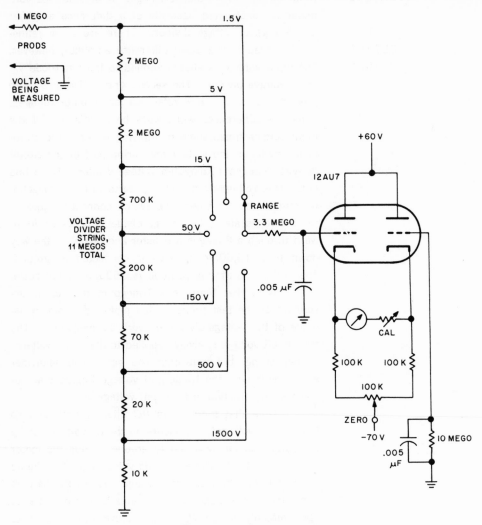

FIGURE 2-1 Basic dc VTVM circuit.

You answered: **I don't know what the maximum voltage range is.**

Let's take a look at how a voltage divider works. You have a total resistance of 11 megohms to ground in the divider string. Then there is a 1-megohm probe resistor (in the dc switch position) connected to the 7-megohm resistor at the top of the voltage divider. From the 7-megohm resistor, you progress downward until you wind up with a 10-kilohm resistor to ground.

The triode grid measures a known fraction, or percentage, of the voltage applied to the top of the string. Let's assume that we had applied 110 volts to the 11-megohm voltage divider. Where the 1-megohm probe resistor and the 7-megohm resistor meet, we would have 10/11 or 100 volts at the top of the string. Let's count down. Our 100 volts at the top of the voltage-divider string would be a mere 3 volts at the center switch position. Note that these are full-scale values. Having gone over this discussion of voltage dividers, turn to Item 202.

You answered: **One volt.**

In the circuit diagram, you have a voltage-divider string of 11 megohms total resistance to ground with a 1-megohm resistor at the probe end of the string. The voltmeter, or the triode grid, is connected between the 10- and 20-kilohm resistors at the bottom of the voltage-divider string. The multiplying factor is 10 kilohms/1100 kilohms. The applied voltage times this ratio produces an equivalent maximum voltage of 1.5 volts when the resistance is 1100 kilohms/1100 kilohms. Work this ratio backward on Item 202.

You answered: **The voltmeter indication will be 1000 volts.**

If your voltmeter-needle deflection was two-thirds of full scale, the voltage measured would be the full-scale 1500 volts times two-thirds or 1000 volts. The voltage-divider ratio of 1,000 comes from noting a resistance of 10 kilohms to ground on the 1500-volt range compared to 10 megohms total resistance to ground on the 1.5-volt range. Correct.

Turn to Item 203.

SAFETY
PRECAUTIONS

Higher voltages can be measured with caution expediently by adding even more resistance to the probe. A common high-voltage probe has a resistor of 1090 megohms, so that the total voltage divider has 1100 megohms to 11 megohms, or a reduction ratio of 100:1. The meter readings would be a mere 1 percent of the voltage applied at the high-resistance and high-voltage end of the probe. Thus, if you were to measure 100 volts full scale, you would normally be measuring 100 times that, or 10,000 volts full scale.

Safety considerations are as follows: Turn the high voltage off before attempting to measure it, and short the high-voltage terminals to ground with a heavy-duty screwdriver or shorting bar. Do not try to measure over 30,000 volts; then apply your high-voltage probe to the circuit, take your hands off, set the meter scale, and turn the high-voltage power supply on again. Read the meter, turn the high voltage off, and remove your test probe after the voltage has died to zero. In this VTVM circuit, if you want to read a negative dc voltage, you merely reverse the meter connections to the tube cathodes.

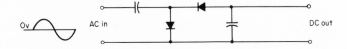

Q203 The following rectifier circuit is used in VTVMs to measure ac voltages. Assume that the capacitors are as large as those in a typical rectifier circuit, that they charge up fully each half cycle, and that they discharge only a little into the load each cycle. The question is: What type of rectifier circuit[1] is shown above?

ITEM 203a An rms circuit that measures the true value of the ac waveform.

ITEM 203b A rectifier circuit that responds to average values of the ac waveform.

ITEM 203c A circuit that measures from the negative peak to the positive peak of the ac waveform.

ITEM 203d A peak rectifier circuit that measures negative halves of sine waveforms.

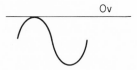

[1] Hint: The waveform to ground between the two diodes is directly above.

ITEM 203a

You answered: **The rectifier circuit will measure the true, or rms, value of the applied ac waveform.**

The rectifier circuit for conventional VOMs does measure the average value of an applied ac waveform, but even the dc average is different from the rms, or effective, value.

The circuit given will clamp the positive part of the applied ac waveform to ground so that a clamped waveform with only negative components will be supplied to the second diode. This will let the capacitor charge up to the peak voltage of the entire waveform but in a negative-going sense.

You ought to review the material dealing with average, rms, peak, and peak-to-peak voltage values in Chap. 1. Then start over with Item 203.

ITEM 203b

You answered: **The circuit will measure the average value of the applied waveform.**

The circuit, as shown, is a combination of a negative peak rectifier and a positive clamping circuit. But this has nothing to do with measuring the average value. There is no average value taking here at all. Turn to Item 203.

ITEM 203c

You answered: **The rectifier circuit measures to the plus from the minus peak.**

The circuit previously shown operates as follows: The first diode shunts the positive part of any waveform to ground so that the full peak-to-peak waveform in a negative-going fashion is applied to the second rectifier. The second rectifier thus lets the full negative voltage pass through the capacitor which charges up to the peak voltage. The peak voltage though, is that of the completely positively clamped waveform (only negative components) so that the complete peak-to-peak voltage appears across the capacitor. You were correct. The circuit also is called a half-wave voltage doubler. Turn to Item 204.

ITEM 203d

You answered: **The circuit measures the peak voltage of the negative part of the waveform.**

Nope, reread Item 203 and try again. You have it half right though.

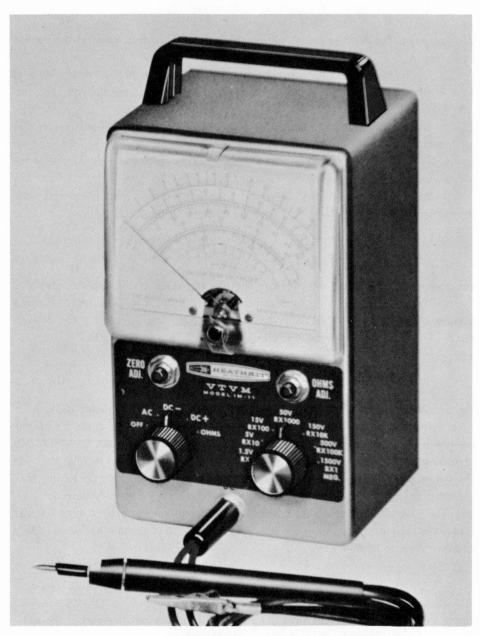

FIGURE 2-2   Heath VTVM IM-11 photograph.

Figure 2-2 on the previous page shows a picture of a VTVM. Figure 2-3 on the following page shows a circuit diagram for a typical VTVM. Let's take a look at the circuit diagram. The power supply, at the bottom right of the schematic, supplies plus 60 volts to the plates of the double triodes and a negative 70 or 80 volts with respect to ground for the bottom end of the cathode resistor and the zero-adjust potentiometer.

On ac volts, note that two voltage dividers are in the circuit. Part of the dc voltage divider is used for alternating current. In order to keep the diode rectifiers from breaking down on voltages greater than 150 volts, a separate ac voltage divider is switched into the circuit whenever the divider is switched into expected full-range voltage greater than 150 volts. This keeps the maximum rectifier voltage at a safe value.

The dc balance control is adjusted with the meter on direct current, and it simply makes the meter needle read zero. We also note that there is a dc calibrate adjustment in series with the meter on direct current, and this is adjusted to make the dc voltage scales read correctly (calibrated). Since on alternating current the meter operates in conjunction with a dc difference amplifier, it is desirable to leave the meter in dc balance when on alternating current. Not only does this separate ac zeroing, but separate calibrating controls are used. The high-resistance return from the rectifier circuit provides an ac zeroing called ac balance, and there is a separate ac calibrate control.

In measuring resistance, note that you have seven possible scales, ranging from a center, or midscale, resistance of 10 ohms to 10×10^6. Thus on the 10^6 range, the center resistance really is 10 megohms. A battery supplies 1.5 volts to calibrated resistor R_c through the probe to external resistor R_x.

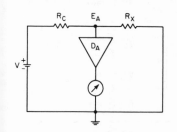

Q204 An equivalent circuit is shown above. What effect will decreasing R_x have? Consider this a voltage divider.

ITEM 204a Voltage E_a at the shunt point will increase.

ITEM 204b Voltage E_a applied to the amplifier will decrease.

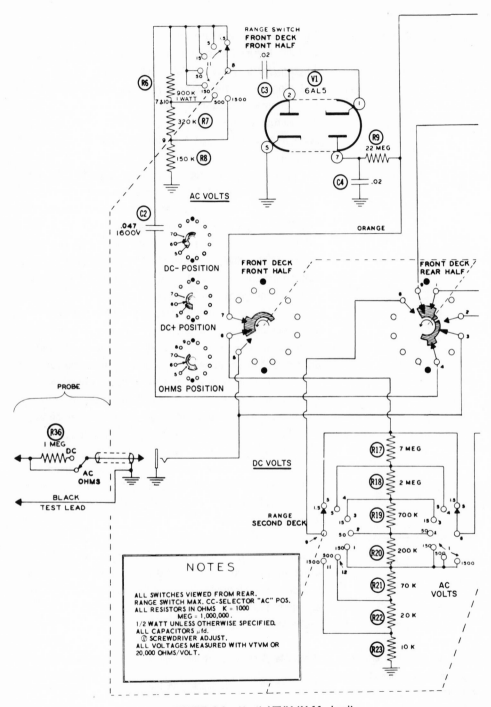

FIGURE 2-3 Heath VTVM IM-11 circuit.

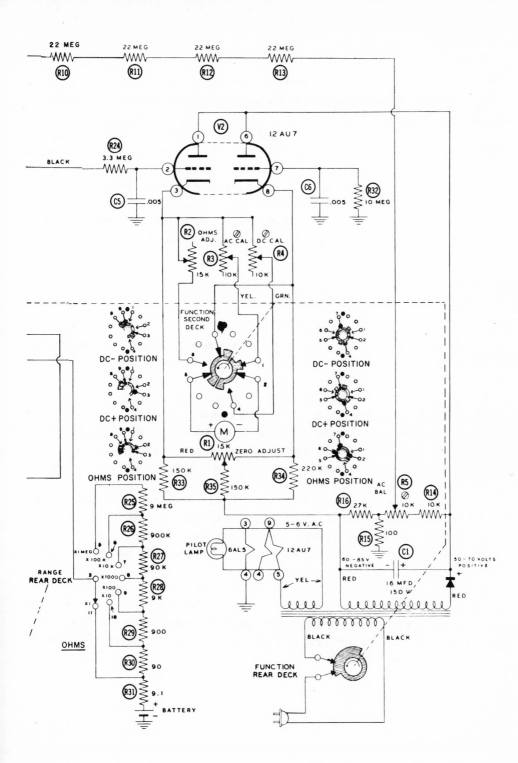

ITEM 204a

You answered: **The voltage applied to the amplifier E_a will increase when the external resistor R_x decreases.**

    The circuit is a shunt circuit, but the meter current I_a drawn by the amplifier input is negligible in comparison with the current drawn by the resistor R_x. Thus the circuit is really a series circuit, and voltage E_a reflects the approximate ratio of two resistors R_c/R_x times the supply voltage of 1.5 volts from the battery. If external resistor R_x decreases, the voltmeter or difference amplifier will be across a smaller part of the total voltage divider than it was before. Since the same voltage is applied, the current will increase, but you are now reading less (a smaller percentage) of the total voltage. Turn back to Item 204, review the circuit, and then try the other answer.

ITEM 204b

You answered: **As external resistor R_x decreases, the voltage applied to the amplifier decreases.**

    The difference amplifier supplying the meter is in shunt with external resistor R_x. In general, the difference amplifier will draw a negligible current as compared with the amount of current drawn through the external resistor R_x. Thus, the circuit is really a series-resistance voltage-divider string comprised of calibration resistor R_c and external resistor R_x. The meter simply measures the proportion $R_x/(R_c + R_x)$ times 1.5 volts. So you were quite correct: The voltage applied to the difference amplifier and meter will decrease as R_x decreases.

    The frequency response of a VTVM when measuring ac voltages is quite important. The typical response for a vacuum-tube voltmeter when measuring voltage from a 600-ohm source resistance ranges from 42 cps to 7.2 Mc ± 1 db. The meter will read the full peak-to-peak voltage, from the plus peak to the minus peak, for the entire waveform, and it would not read a different voltage if the leads were reversed. However, you may get a slightly different reading if you reverse the leads because of a different effect, namely, the shunt capacity through the power supply of the meter. But for sources where the shunt capacity is negligible, reversing the leads would show exactly the same peak-to-peak voltage. This isn't true for r-f probes (probes used at radio frequencies). Go to Item 205.

ITEM 205

R-F PROBE

To extend the frequency range of the VTVM to higher frequencies, a special r-f demodulator probe is used. This r-f probe will extend the frequency response of the VTVM typically from 1 kc to 100 Mc.

There are limitations in using this type of probe. For instance, the peak-to-peak r-f voltage must be less than the peak inverse voltage, usually 30 to 300 volts, to keep the diode from breaking down. The dc level of the circuit must be less than the voltage rating of the coupling capacitor, commonly 500 volts.

This circuit is a half-wave rectifier and will measure only the peak value for one-half the ac waveform. The positive r-f component charges the input capacitor to the positive peak voltage. For the negative waveform component, the diode is an open circuit and little current flows. The input capacitor tends to hold its peak charge, and the meter is connected to the negative side of the capacitor via the output RC filter.

In using such an r-f probe, bear in mind that you may be dealing with very high frequencies and that you must measure as closely as possible to the circuit in question. Place the low-inductance ground lead close to the circuit being monitored.

Q205 On an unsymmetrical r-f waveform, will the reading of the VTVM with this r-f probe be different with the probe leads reversed?

ITEM 205a No.

ITEM 205b Yes.

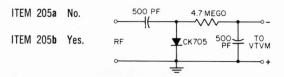

ITEM 205a

You answered: **No, the meter with this r-f probe will not read differently on unsymmetrical r-f waveforms.**

The resultant voltage for this r-f probe is the peak value of the positive half of the waveform. The peak value of an r-f waveform is the value to which the capacitor will charge, and that's the voltage presented to the meter difference amplifier. If the waveform is unsymmetrical, as is the one following, and has a big peak value for the positive half of the waveform and a small value for the negative part, then the positive half will provide a much greater value across the capacitor. Thus, you would get a much larger reading on the positive half of the waveform than you would with the probe reversed to measure the negative half of the waveform. This is a little bit different from your answer. Try the other answer on Item 205.

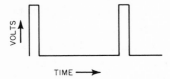

ITEM 205b

You answered: **Yes, when measuring an r-f waveform that is unsymmetrical, the typical r-f probe will measure different voltages with the leads reversed.** You were correct, since the r-f probe measures peak voltage for either the positive or negative half of the waveform but usually not for both.

In order to minimize circuit loading at high frequencies, one may use a smaller coupling capacitor so that less r-f energy is coupled into the r-f probe. Since there is less energy coupled into the probe, a more sensitive meter is required.

Turn to Item 206.

ITEM 206

VTVM ZEROING

It is interesting to note that a semiconductor diode, such as the one in the diagram on Item 205, would have no effect on the zeroing of the meter but that a hot diode (vacuum tube) would have an effect. Electrons, as they boil off the cathode of a hot diode, gain a certain amount of kinetic energy. When they reach the plate of the hot diode, their kinetic energy is transformed into potential energy, which shows up as a slight voltage, with the plate negative with respect to the cathode.

Adjusting or zeroing a vacuum-tube voltmeter is an interesting and intricate procedure. Refer to Fig. 2-3, the VTVM schematic. First, zero the meter mechanically; then set up the lowest possible dc voltage scale, and short the probe to the ground lead. Next, adjust the zero adjust so that the meter needle reads zero. Switch to a low ac voltage scale, again short the probe, and this time adjust the ac balance control for zero. Switch back to direct current and recheck.

Calibration is a process to make the meter read accurately once the meter is zeroed. This is different from the previous zero adjusting as it adjusts the range proportionality factor appropriately. Calibration typically is a factory adjustment and usually does not need to be done in the field because of stable amplifiers.

To repeat, the adjustment sequence is as follows. Let the VTVM warm up for half an hour. Then zero the meter on direct current, and check the meter against a known voltage on direct current. Switch to the lowest ac voltage scale, and adjust the balance control. Then, upon measuring resistance, each time you use the meter, you must adjust the needle deflection so that it reads full scale on each separate range.

Q206 Is it necessary to calibrate a VTVM every hour in order to stay within the 5 percent tolerance on the meter?

ITEM 206a   No.

ITEM 206b   Yes.

You answered: **No, it is not necessary to calibrate a VTVM every hour in order to keep within the 5 percent stated tolerance.**

Typically, a VTVM will drift only in the zero or dc offset portion of the circuit. This corresponds to the average value of the voltage being measured, and as such, once you readjust the zero of a VTVM, the calibration is relatively constant because of the high linearity of a cathode follower.

The adjustment procedure becomes even more involved when you are measuring resistance since the meter must be calibrated to the full-scale deflection each time. On ohms, the probe is left unshorted without a resistor connected, and the meter is adjusted so that the meter reads full scale. Recheck the zero because it may have changed slightly. On ohms, you may have to recheck the zeroing and full-scale adjustments on each scale or range because they may change slightly. On the lowest resistance range, the lead resistance may be an important part of the total circuit resistance external to the meter. The zero adjustments must be checked periodically because they change slightly with changes in temperature, as the chassis warms up from the vacuum tubes.

Turn to Item 207.

You answered: **Yes, it is necessary to calibrate a VTVM every hour in order to keep the meter tolerance within the 5 percent stated tolerance.**

The primary causes of drift in a VTVM are dc or average-level changes. The actual range of calibration of the meter, once the zero has been adjusted each hour, is yet within the 5 percent, or quite often 3 percent, stated accuracy of the full-scale deflection of the meter. Try another answer on Item 206.

BASIC AC
VTVM

A vacuum-tube voltmeter, to measure alternating current, is a little bit of a different story.   An ac vacuum-tube voltmeter, in addition to having a rectifier or meter circuit, has a stabilized high-gain ac amplifier.   The gain is stabilized by generous use of negative feedback.   The frequency response of a typical "audio" VTVM is from 20 cps to 5 Mc, with a gain variable from 0 to 80 db in 10-db increments.   Other ac vacuum-tube voltmeters cover even wider ranges of frequency and voltage.

Q207 Is it necessary to adjust the zero-adjust control frequently of an ac **VTVM?**

ITEM 207a   Yes.

ITEM 207b   No.

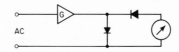

ITEM 207a

You answered: **Yes, it is necessary to readjust the zero-adjust control of an ac VTVM frequently.**

In the discussion of zeroing a dc VTVM, you found that the most frequent readjustment needed is zero adjusting for all measurements. However, most waveforms are symmetrical; thus, there is no dc zero adjustment on an ac amplifier. It is true that the gains are stabilized with large amounts of negative feedback; this is necessary to ensure that the meter stays accurately calibrated. But this is different from having to compensate for a nonexistent dc shift in a zero adjustment.

Try the other answer on Item 207.

ITEM 207b

You answered: **No, it is not necessary to readjust the zero adjustment frequently on an ac VTVM.**

In order to ensure accurate calibration of voltage readings on the meter, the ac amplifier used with an ac VTVM must have a highly stabilized gain. But this gain is entirely at some ac frequency, since the amplifier usually will not amplify dc voltages. Thus, there is no necessity of the amplifier's having a zero adjustment to compensate for slight shifts in the dc voltage level. Therefore, it is not necessary to adjust the zero adjustment frequently simply because there is no dc zero adjust. There is no frequent need for adjusting the calibration control, since large amounts of feedback are used to ensure gain stability and consequent meter calibration.

Turn to Item 208.

ITEM 208

TRANSISTORIZED
VOLTMETER

Let's consider briefly a transistorized voltmeter. This meter is a conventional voltmeter (without an amplifier) plus a transistor current amplifier plus a voltage- or current-divider string.

The input impedance changes in this transistorized voltmeter, just as it changes with different scales in a conventional VOM. A typical input resistance with this circuit, however, is approximately 100,000 ohms/volt instead of the 1000 or 20,000 ohms/volt for typical meters. Note that you could use a constant input resistance of 100,000 ohms and then use current shunts to vary the voltage ranges. But many times this would result in an input impedance so low that it would cause circuit-loading problems. The stratagem illustrated here is typically used. This circuit also has zeroing problems since transistors are somewhat more sensitive to temperature changes than are vacuum-tube triodes.

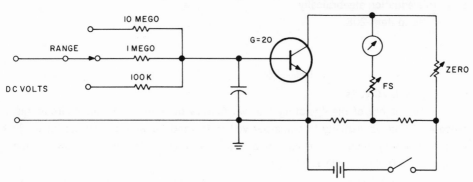

Q208 With the meter switch as shown on the center position connected to a 1-megohm input resistor, what voltage will produce full-scale deflection of the meter? The sensitivity of the meter is 100,000 ohms/volt.

ITEM 208a   1 volt.

ITEM 208b   100 volts.

ITEM 208c   10 volts.

ITEM 208a

You answered: **1 volt.**

Consider the concept of dimensionality in solving this algebraic equation. You would like to multiply ohms per volt, the sensitivity of this meter, by a factor which would eliminate ohms and leave just volts in the numerator. This could be done quite easily if we were to divide the total circuit resistance by the meter sensitivity. That is, volts = 1 megohm/(100,000 ohms/volt). As you see, the units of ohms cancel and the volts have been inverted twice, leaving this as the sole term in the expression. Solve this equation.

Go to Item 208.

ITEM 208b

You answered: **100 volts.**

Employing the concept of dimensionality, we would like to wind up with an expression including volts in the numerator. The total meter input resistance in this range is 1 megohm if we neglect the input resistance of the transistor which is much, much smaller than a 1-megohm resistor. The meter sensitivity is the second factor that you need, 100,000 ohms/volt. You would like to combine these two expressions to eliminate ohms and leave volts in the numerator of the resulting expression. One way to do this is to combine them as follows: 1 megohm/(100,000 ohms/volt) = volts. Solve this equation algebraically.

Go to Item 208.

ITEM 208c

You answered: **10 volts.**

The object of manipulating the two factors of total meter input circuit resistance and meter sensitivity in ohms per volt is to wind up with an expression for just volts, eliminating ohms. The correct and easy way to do this is as follows: 1 megohm/(100,000 ohms/volt) = 10 volts.

Go to Item 209.

ITEM 209

MULTIPURPOSE PROBES

Many types of probes are quite useful additions to the VTVM. A multipurpose probe is shown following. When the switch is in the position shown, the probe is connected directly to the meter, which allows using the VTVM as an ohmmeter. In the next position, a 1-megohm resistor is inserted in series with the probe, as it is in measuring dc voltage. Switching to the next position would provide a high-frequency-compensated probe. This switch position could be utilized for an r-f voltage-doubler circuit. A high-voltage probe using this switch circuit is unwise because it would not be able to handle 10,000 volts with safety. The last position, with a capacitor and diode, shows a typical r-f probe. This is a half-wave shunt rectifier, or positive clamping circuit. Filtering is accomplished by wiring capacity and meter inertia.

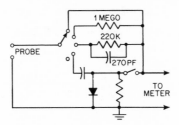

Q209 The compensated r-f position would be used on what types of frequencies?

ITEM 209a   Radio and intermediate frequencies.

ITEM 209b   Radio, intermediate, and audio frequencies.

ITEM 209c   Radio frequencies only.

ITEM 209a

You answered: **Radio frequencies and intermediate frequencies.**

It is quite possible to use the r-f position of the meter on frequencies ranging from direct current or audio frequency up through the highest radio frequency the meter will handle. Obviously, you would stop short of the ultrahigh frequencies because of the high-frequency limit of the regular ac voltmeter circuit. The capacitor in shunt with the input resistor in this lead provides a combination capacitive-resistance voltage divider that is frequency independent, since the ratio of the capacitive reactance and resistances is 1:1. However, using the r-f probe on direct current or other frequencies means that the meter would not be calibrated; therefore, measuring these voltages thus is not recommended. Accordingly, you hit the answer right on the head: a coverage not too broad, a coverage not too narrow.

Now try the quiz for Chap. 2. Go to Item 210.

ITEM 209b

You answered: **Radio frequencies, intermediate frequencies, and audio frequencies.**

The purpose of the capacitor's shunting the probe resistor in the r-f position is to compensate for the shunt capacity to ground in the ac part of the meter. This capacitor makes a capacitance voltage divider which is shunted by an identical ratio-resistive voltage divider. Thus, the voltage divider is frequency independent. This probe could be used for its wide range of frequencies, from the low limits (a-f) of the ac range of the meter up to its highest ranges (r-f). One drawback, however, is that the meter must be recalibrated. For this reason, the use of the r-f probe is not generally recommended at audio frequencies. Instead, use the meter on its ac ranges.

Turn to Item 209.

ITEM 209c

You answered: **The probe in the r-f position would be used for measuring only radio frequencies.** Nope, try 209 again.

1 Which has a higher input impedance, a vacuum-tube voltmeter or a 20,000 ohms/volt VOM set on the 1500-volt scale? *(G)*

2 Which has a higher input resistance, a typical VTVM or a 20,000 ohms/volt VOM on the 1.5-volt scale? *(D)*

3 On an ac voltmeter, a measured 30 volts equals how many volts rms? *(A)*

4 Ten volts measured with an r-f probe is how many volts rms? *(H)*

5 If we assume that a frequency response of a VTVM ranges from 42 cps to 5 Mc, can such a voltmeter provide useful information on a 30-cps signal? *(E)*

6 A VTVM at one point in a circuit measures 6.1 volts dc. Your VOM at the same point measures 6.5 volts. What is wrong? *(C)*

7 In measuring a high-power low-resistance resistor, your VTVM reads 0.1 ohm. When the measurement is rechecked, it reads 0.9 ohm. What is wrong? *(I)*

8 You are attempting to measure a symmetrical 60-cps signal. You reverse the leads, and find that your reading is somewhat different. What causes this with a VTVM? *(F)*

9 You find that your VOM and VTVM give different readings when measuring the output voltage of a constant output voltage transformer. Why is this? Note: These two meters agree when measuring the line-voltage side of the transformer. *(B)*

10 A rectifier-type VOM and an iron-vane meter are used to measure a symmetrical 60-cps square wave which has peaks of 10 volts. Which meter will read higher? *(J)*

11 What would be the full-scale voltage of a 20,000 ohms/volt meter if you used a series resistance of 11 megohms, the input resistance of a typical VTVM? *(L)*

12 In measuring a voltage with a 10 percent third harmonic on an ac VTVM, should you consider the phase of the harmonic with respect to the fundamental? *(K)*

13 Which has greater accuracy and resolution, a differential VTVM or a mirrored-scale D'Arsonval VOM? *(M)*

A   The VTVM may read peak-to-peak or rms voltages on alternating current. Thirty volts peak-to-peak is 2.8 times the rms voltage. Solving
this equation in reverse produces 10.6 volts rms which is equivalent to
30 volts peak-to-peak. No conversion is needed for voltages read on
an rms scale.

B   What happened is that you are measuring the third harmonic of the
sine wave, because of the regulating characteristics of the transformer. The peak-to-peak reading of the VTVM includes this. The
VOM responds only to the average value and ignores the third-harmonic
component in the output voltage.

C   Assume that the accuracies of the VTVM and VOM full scale are plus
or minus 5 percent. This corresponds to plus or minus 0.3 volts when
measuring approximately 6 volts; the meter readings are within 10 percent of each other. There is nothing wrong with the meters.

D   For a typical VTVM, the input resistance is 11 megohms regardless of
the scale used. The resistance of the VOM is 20,000 ohms/volt times
the 1.5-volt range which produces 30,000 ohms. This illustrates a
major advantage of VTVMs.

E   Yes, the VTVM will provide useful measurements beyond its frequency
range if the measurements are kept purely relative. The frequency
range of the VTVM was specified as 42 cps to 5 Mc plus or minus
1 db. Actually, the frequency response of the meter probably is yet
within 3 db of its maximum value. However, when we ignore absolute
measurements, the VTVM here will be quite useful to measure gain.

F   What you encounter here is capacity from the power line to the ground
side of the VTVM. The only way to circumvent this phenomenon is to
use an isolation transformer so that you may have even the ground
side of the VTVM "hot" with respect to the circuit.

G   The sensitivity of the VOM is 20,000 ohms/volt, and this times the
1500-volt scale is 30 megohms. The input resistance of a typical
VTVM is 11 megohms so that the VOM has the higher resistance.

H   An r-f probe typically measures the peak voltage for one side of the
measured waveform. If the peak voltage is 10 volts, 10 volts times
0.707 produces an rms voltage of 7.07 volts (read on the dc scale) if
the waveform is a sine wave.

I   Even without reversing the leads in measuring very low resistances, you may get slightly different resistance readings because of different contact resistance. The remedy here is to scrape the test probes on the surface of the conductor a little bit so that they wear through the oxide coating and provide a low-resistance path to the resistor.

J   The average and rms values of the full-wave rectified 60-cps square wave are the same, 10 volts. However, the meters are calibrated with 60-cps sine waves, with approximate conversion factors of 0.6 and 0.7 times peak for the VOM and iron-vane meters respectively. These factors have been applied erroneously to our square wave (effectively the same as direct current) so that the meter readings must be unconverted by the reciprocals 1/0.6 and 1/0.7. Thus the VOM reads higher.

K   For a harmonic measuring 10 percent of the peak amplitude of the fundamental, it certainly does make a difference, especially in peak voltage, whether the harmonic adds to the fundamental peak, in phase, or subtracts from it, out of phase. The root-sum-of-squares formula applies for power.

L   Apply the rational-units equation: 11 megohms/(20,000 ohms/volt) $=$ 550 volts. Note that for full-scale voltages higher than this, the VOM has a higher resistance than the typical VTVM.

M   This was purposely a poor question to make you think. The mirrored-scale D'Arsonval VOM meter at high voltages probably would be more accurate and the differential VTVM would be used to compare two high floating voltages accurately.

Put this book down for a while before tackling the next chapter on oscillators.

CHAPTER THREE

BASIC OSCILLATORS _{13 QUESTIONS}

ITEM 301

INTRODUCTION

Basically, oscillators may be viewed as energy converters; that is, they convert dc energy into ac energy with a given period or frequency. Oscillators may be used to produce sine waves, square waves, or other shapes.

There are two basic types of oscillators: those involving inductance and capacitance (LC) and those involving resistance and capacitance (RC). In both types, the purpose of the active element, such as a tube or transistor, is to provide power gain and not necessarily phase shift. The circuit and type (LC or RC) determines the amount of phase shift required of the active element. Most oscillators use regenerative or positive feedback in producing the sustained oscillations. In addition, most oscillators use some form of limiting or negative feedback to produce a constant amplitude output.

Where to draw the dividing line between an oscillator and a signal generator is a good question. Typically, the difference between an oscillator and a signal generator is that the signal generator will have one or more oscillators within it, and, in addition, will have some extra components such as attenuators, meters, and range or scale changes; however, an oscillator may have many of these also. Therefore we conclude at this point that an oscillator is a relatively simple circuit, whereas a signal generator will have a number of additional items.

Noise generators may be a special type of signal generator. Noise generators may use a gaseous, thermionic, or solid-state diode to generate thermal noise directly. A pulse generator may be used as a noise source at radio frequencies, because a narrow pulse has a certain amount of r-f energy inherent within it. These two types of noise generators usually do not involve inductance or capacitance, but they do involve a resistance, and the diode type does not use feedback in signal generation.

Q301 What type of feedback is usually found in oscillators?

ITEM 301a Positive feedback.

ITEM 301b Negative feedback only.

ITEM 301c No feedback.

ITEM 301a

You answered: **Positive feedback is usually used in oscillators.**

In a few cases, a signal generator may use no feedback, such as in a noise source using a gaseous diode. Many oscillators use both positive and negative feedback. The negative feedback or gain limiting is used to stabilize the level of the oscillations. By a process of elimination we see that in most vacuum-tube oscillators, positive feedback is used so that the signal will be applied from the plate to the grid to keep the oscillations going. Go to Item 302.

ITEM 301b

You answered: **Negative feedback only.**

Negative feedback is used quite widely in oscillators. It also is true that gain limiting in oscillators is used quite frequently to provide a constant level of oscillation. In high-fidelity amplifiers, negative feedback is commonly used to provide gain stabilization, lower distortion, and to provide a flatter frequency response. However, in this case we're not talking about hi-fi amplifiers; we're concerned about another case where we're interested in "low fidelity" because we're interested in nonlinearity. If we had negative feedback only, we would not have regeneration, the basis of most oscillators. In this case, negative feedback is not the right answer. See if you can figure out the right answer back on Item 301.

ITEM 301c

You answered: **No feedback usually is used in oscillators.**

No feedback is used in one generator to produce noise, i.e., one that employs a gas or solid-state diode for the noise source. In a pulse generator, negative feedback may not be used, but positive feedback is used to produce the pulses. Typically such pulses are produced with a multivibrator circuit, but in some cases, the pulses are produced by a fast relay, such as a mercury-wetted relay. In most oscillators, however, a combination of feedback is used. Turn again to Item 301, and figure out which is the most usual type of feedback in oscillators.

ITEM 302

OSCILLATOR USES

Oscillators are used for many purposes, and they have many different applications. Oscillators are used simply as a source of ac energy. The frequency may vary widely; for instance, audio-frequency (a-f) oscillators are used as an energy source for a-f bridges to measure inductance, capacitance, and resistance at audio frequencies. An r-f oscillator may supply energy to a bridge for measuring these same quantities at much higher frequencies. In addition to measuring inductance and capacitance, an oscillator may be used to compare the values of inductance and capacitance.

Variable-frequency oscillators are used quite widely in the design of receivers. A receiver is calibrated with one; that is, its frequency coverage and intermediate frequencies are set up or made to agree with the frequency for a standard oscillator set at the desired frequencies.

Oscillators are also used to check the response of hi-fi amplifiers. The frequency response simply means that the gain of the amplifier (with a known input signal level) is measured and calibrated by comparing the output voltage versus the input voltage for a wide range of frequencies. A linear or flat response means that the amplifier amplifies all frequencies within its given range the same amount within a given tolerance (usually ± 3 db).

One other interesting use of oscillators is that they may be used to modulate the output of other oscillators. They may vary the output signal level, the phase, the frequency, or a combination of these.

Other miscellaneous uses of oscillators are in Q meters, impedance (Z) meters or bridges, frequency meters, and timing-events counters.

Q302 How many uses does an oscillator have?

ITEM 302a It is used to measure and compare inductance, capacitance, and resistance.

ITEM 302b Oscillators have all these uses, including modifying another oscillator's output.

ITEM 302c It is used as a source of sustained oscillations.

ITEM 302a

You answered: **An oscillator is used to measure and compare inductance, capacitance, and resistance.**

Frequency bridges must have as their input an oscillator at an appropriate frequency to measure inductance and capacitance. In some cases, bridges are direct current but when inductance and capacitance must be measured, one must use an oscillator of some kind as an energy source to the bridge. However, oscillators do have other uses. Turn to Item 302 and pick the right answer.

ITEM 302b

You answered: **Oscillators are used for all the other purposes, including modifying another oscillator's output.**

This is indeed the case. Actually, oscillators have considerably more uses than those given in the previous item. You were correct; continue.

A very common type of oscillator is one termed "inductance-capacitance" (*LC*). The inductance and capacitance are used in either a series or parallel circuit to provide 180° of phase shift to couple the output back to the input. Typically, a common-cathode or common-emitter circuit is used in the amplifier itself, so that a 180° phase shift occurs in it. When an additional 180° phase shift occurs in the feedback network, the output signal is fed back in phase to the input to cause the signal to be amplified; this regenerative feedback causes oscillations to occur.

Some voltage gain is required in this oscillator, which means that a common-plate amplifier (or cathode follower) cannot be used here. The oscillations build up until the tube or transistor is driven so far into its nonlinear region that the loop gain is unity.

Turn to Item 303.

ITEM 302c

You answered: **The use of an oscillator is as a source of sustained oscillations.**

Oscillators in this capacity are used as signal generators to supply a source of constant oscillation to other measuring instruments. This is just one use of oscillators.

Return to Item 302 and pick another answer.

LC OSCILLATORS

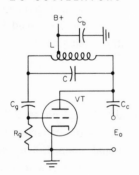

FIGURE 3-1 Hartley oscillator circuit.

Let's look at the Hartley oscillator circuit shown below. A vacuum-tube triode is used, and 180° of phase shift occurs to a signal entering the triode on the grid and leaving on the plate. A parallel LC circuit is used to couple the signal from the plate back to the grid. Across a tank circuit such as this one, the signal is reversed by 180°. If a positive sine wave exists at the plate, then a 180° phase shift means that the sine wave at the grid end of the tank circuit is negative-going. Note that the B+ or plate supply is tapped close to the grid end of the coil. A capacitor C_b bypasses any radio frequency to ground at this point. The tap functions as a voltage divider. The signal at the plate is much larger than the signal at the grid because of the gain of the vacuum tube and coil ratio: B+ provides an r-f reference point such that most of the voltage drop occurs at the plate end of the coil, and only a small amount at the grid. The tube, of course, amplifies this small voltage back up to the large voltage at the plate of the tube. The output voltage is taken from the plate via a coupling capacitor. The B+ voltage is kept from the grid by a grid-coupling capacitor C_g. A grid resistor R_g provides self-bias for the tube when grid current flows on r-f peaks.

Q303 What element provides the necessary 180° phase shift in the Hartley oscillator?

ITEM 303a The LC inductance-capacitor tank.

ITEM 303b The series tank capacitor C and the grid capacitor C_g.

ITEM 303c The grid resistor R_g and grid capacitor C_g.

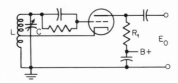

FIGURE 3-2

Hartley oscillator

circuit variation.

ITEM 303a

The 180° of phase shift for the oscillator is supplied by the LC tank circuit.

Because of the reactances in opposite directions, there is indeed a total of 180° of phase shift across a parallel LC tank circuit such as the one shown for the Hartley oscillator. The B+ tap is at ac ground and the reference point for the phase shift. The r-f voltage to ground at one end of the tank is 180° out of phase with the r-f voltage at the other end. An insignificant amount of phase shift occurs across the grid capacitor C_g and grid resistor R_g. Righto, old chap!

A variation of the Hartley oscillator is to place the cathode at the tap, place the plate at ac ground, and have one end of the LC tank grounded and the other end applied to the grid. See Fig. 3-2. This provides a circuit with several advantages. One side of the tank capacitor can be grounded. This is a definite advantage in minimizing r-f leakage and maximizing safety when the capacitor is controlled or adjusted from the front panel. Another advantage is that an output circuit can be placed in the plate which will be nearly independent of the feedback circuitry causing oscillations.

Go to Item 304.

ITEM 303b

The series tank capacitor and the grid coupling capacitor provide 180° of phase shift.

The phase shift from plate to grid is indeed reflected across the capacitor C. However, the capacitor C by itself also would provide an additional amount of phase shift. Merely putting C_g in series with this capacitor without some other element such as a resistor or inductance at the junction of the two capacitors will not give you more than 90° of phase shift. Some other element is needed along with the tank capacitor C to provide 180° of phase shift in this circuit. Return to Item 303 and determine the missing component, Mr. Holmes.

ITEM 303c

You answered that **the grid resistance R_g and the grid capacitor C_g provide the 180° of phase shift.** The 180° of phase shift is needed because a total 360° of phase shift is necessary to produce a signal at the grid fed back in phase with the signal existing at the grid. Since 180° of phase shift occurs in the grid to plate, another 180° phase shift is needed. However, not very much of the phase shift comes from the coupling grid capacitor C_g and the grid resistor R_g. The time constant of this combination is selected so that the RC product is much longer than the period of the oscillation. However, it should not be extremely longer since cutting off the tube current would cause intermittent oscillations. As such, an insignificant phase shift occurs across these two circuit components.

Turn back to Item 303 and reread the material.

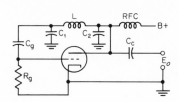

FIGURE 3-3 Colpitts
oscillator circuit.

ITEM 304

**COLPITTS
OSCILLATOR**

The Colpitts oscillator is another inductance-capacitance (LC) oscillator. There are several differences in the circuit from the Hartley oscillator. Note that the plate current is fed in shunt; B+ comes to the plate via an r-f choke (RFC). Thus, the tank coil L and the B+ feed choke RFC are in parallel, viewed from the plate. Also, there are two capacitors instead of one, C_1 and C_2. The two capacitors in series give an effective tuning capacitance C, the same as is given in the Hartley oscillator. The center connection between the two capacitors is grounded. This is quite an advantage, since it minimizes the amount of r-f energy that sneaks out the front panel via the rotor of the capacitor to the front panel. This minimizes frequency changes due to hand capacity. In this connection the feedback ratio is determined by the ratio of the reactances of the two capacitors, C_1 and C_2. Their reactances form a voltage divider to step down the voltage from the plate to the grid. Only a small amount of grid drive is needed since the tube supplies the gain necessary to make up for losses in the circuit as well as to supply an output voltage E_o via a coupling capacitor C_c. As in the Hartley oscillator, no appreciable phase shift occurs across the grid coupling capacitor C_g and the grid resistor R_g.

Q304 For proper voltage-dividing action,[1] what should the capacitance ratio C_2/C_1 be?

ITEM 304a Capacitor C_1 should be much greater than C_2.

ITEM 304b Capacitor C_1 should be much less than C_2.

ITEM 304c The two capacitors should be equal, $C_2 = C_1$.

---

[1] Hint: Voltages are proportional to the capacitive reactances which in turn are inversely proportional to capacitances.

You answered: **To provide proper voltage-divider action across the tank coil, capacitor C_1 should be much greater than C_2.**

To take advantage of the tube's gain, you want to have a considerably smaller amount of voltage across the grid-side tank capacitor C_1 than you do across the plate-side capacitor C_2. Voltages are inversely proportional to capacitances; in this case, to keep the voltage small on the grid side, we want a small reactance on the grid side as compared to that on the plate side. This means that we do indeed want capacitor C_1 much larger than capacitor C_2. This is correct, and a typical ratio is from 5 to 25.

A similar circuit to the Colpitts oscillator is the ultra-audion oscillator wherein the two tank capacitors are really the tube's internal grid-cathode and plate-cathode capacitances. Another similar oscillator is the Clapp oscillator, also called the series-tuned Colpitts oscillator. As the name implies, the series-tuned Colpitts oscillator has capacity in series with the inductance in the tank circuit, so that the tuning is done by this series capacitor. (The Clapp circuit is mentioned because of its high degree of frequency stability.) Turn to Item 305.

You answered: **The ratio of the two tank capacitors is such that C_1 should be much smaller than C_2.**

If C_1 is much smaller than C_2, then the reactances of the two capacitors are going to be in the opposite direction, that is $X_{C1} \gg X_{C2}$. This means that most of the voltage is dropped across the grid end of the tank coil instead of across the plate end. This would tend to make the grid voltage much greater than the output voltage if the tube didn't reduce its gain accordingly. A tube when it is overdriven would obligingly try to reduce its gain to meet your stipulation. That is, the tube would be driven so hard that the gain of the stage would reduce, because of plate-current limiting and grid-current clipping, to get the gain down to slightly above 1 as your answer implied. This is not a very efficient way to run an oscillator since most of the energy of the oscillator would be going back into the grid circuit to supply drive. Not much energy would be left over to be taken off as a useful output voltage E_o. Put your thinking cap on, turn to Item 304 again, and select a different answer.

You answered: **To provide proper voltage-divider action, the tank capacitors C_1 and C_2 should be equal.**

For your arrangement, you would be supplying the full output voltage as drive to the grid circuit; that is, E_g equals $-E_o$. With two equal capacitances, their reactances would be equal and you would split the total tank voltage in two parts. Thus, the grid voltage is equal in magnitude but opposite to the output voltage. What about the gain of the tube? Wouldn't this result eventually in the output's being much greater than the grid voltage? Well, the circuit would try to do this, but it would overdrive the tube, and eventually the gain of the tube would reduce from some high value to approximately 2. This would cause loss of energy, which is not a very efficient way to run an oscillator. Do you remember what we said about wanting to have the grid voltage considerably lower than the output voltage, so that the tube gain will bring the smaller grid voltage back up to the output level again? Turn back to Item 304 and put your thinking cap on.

ITEM 305

BEAT-FREQUENCY OSCILLATORS

This heterodyne type of circuit has two major uses: it can be used as a local oscillator or beat-frequency oscillator (BFO) in receivers to provide a heterodyne to bring an unknown signal down to a lower frequency so that it can be measured by a lower-frequency-measuring instrument.

As the illustration shows, oscillator 1 puts out a constant frequency and amplitude signal. Oscillator 2 also puts out a constant amplitude signal, but its frequency is varied externally. In such a BFO signal generator, the frequencies of the two oscillators are fairly close. Thus, a considerably lower frequency results from the difference of these two as the output of the mixer. In a communications receiver, however, oscillator 1 may be replaced by the i-f received signal at 465 kc. Oscillator 2, or BFO, is quite close to this in a frequency of 466 kc. The difference in the two frequencies will come out of the mixer as an audio frequency of 1000 cps, a typical difference frequency.

Used in a signal generator, the two radio frequencies would be quite close together. The output mixer would be a variable audio frequency depending on how far apart the two oscillators were in frequency. Engineers do this to achieve a range that is linearly related to capacitance change in the variable oscillator.

FIGURE 3-4

Beat-frequency oscillator diagram.

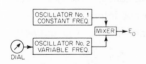

Q305 A beat-frequency oscillator is so called for one of the following reasons:

ITEM 305a One oscillator is synchronizing the other oscillator.

ITEM 305b It is in common use as a means to produce a highly repetitive musical rhythm.

ITEM 305c Two audio oscillators that have frequencies close together produce a much lower difference tone when their outputs are mixed.

ITEM 305a

You answered: **A beat-frequency oscillator is so called because one oscillator is synchronizing, or beating, the other.**

When two oscillators are close together and there is coupling between them, it is quite true that one oscillator will pull the other oscillator into its same frequency. Thus the two oscillators will be synchronized, although in most cases this is unintentional. If one oscillator is "pulled" or synchronized with the frequency of a second, then no difference or beat frequency exists. We want the difference frequency in this case, and the oscillators usually are isolated from each other to prevent "pulling" and insure the desired beat frequency.

This is not the right definition of the word "beat" either. This is a usage of two oscillators in a different way from what the term "beat-frequency oscillator" implies. Beat a path back to Item 305, and try another answer that is not so off-beat.

ITEM 305b

You answered: **A beat-frequency oscillator is so named because this device is commonly used as a metronome to establish a constant musical rhythm.**

Most metronomes either are mechanical or employ a blocking oscillator or multivibrator to set up a series of "ticks." Metronomes do not usually use two oscillators with frequencies that vary only slightly to produce the beats in the musical rhythm. One might say that this was an "off-beat" answer. As such, you had better beat a path back to Item 305, and try again.

ITEM 305c

You answered: **A beat-frequency oscillator is so called because two oscillators, with frequencies that are close together, produce a much lower difference tone that sounds like "beats" when their outputs are mixed or beat.**

This actually is the origin of the word "beats." When two musical tones are quite close together in frequency, a much lower difference frequency actually is heard and appears to pulsate, or beat. The two musical tones do not interact to pull each other closer in frequency; this actually is an acoustical phenomenon. You answered correctly on this one.

Go to Item 306.

If one tries to take an output directly from an oscillator, load variations may be coupled back into the tank circuit of the oscillator. This may change the output level or frequency of the oscillator. For this reason, some form of isolation, such as constant-impedance attenuator pads or isolation amplifiers, is used to isolate the oscillator from the output terminals of a signal generator. A change in the power-supply voltage may have the same effect as a load change. The operating point changes with a different effective source resistance.

Many times an oscillator generates signals at a low level. When more power than this is desired from the output, a power amplifier must be used to provide the desired power level at the output terminals. Quite often a voltmeter is provided to monitor the output level and an attenuator to permit adjusting the output to any desired value. The attenuators may be continuously variable or discrete (switched in steps). When a wide range in attenuation is desired, several attenuators may be switched in series. These different sections are shielded from each other to reduce undesirable leakage coupling of the signal.

In addition, when a modulated signal is desired at the output, an isolation amplifier frequently is used to isolate the oscillator from the modulation process. This ensures that the output level of the oscillator is relatively constant and reduces any incidental frequency modulation of the oscillator due to load variation during modulation.

Note that in this section we are starting to add a number of features to basic oscillators. This really introduces the discussion of signal generators. One distinction, admittedly a loose one, between signal generators and oscillators is that signal generators have an additional number of features. But we will discuss this in more detail in the next chapter.

Q306 The basic reason for using an isolation amplifier at the output of an oscillator is:

ITEM 306a To monitor the output power level and to provide attenuation with little signal leakage.

ITEM 306b To keep variations in the load from affecting the oscillator frequency and output level.

ITEM 306c To supply large amounts of power gain.

You answered: **The basic reason for using an isolation amplifier at the output of an oscillator is to provide power-level monitoring and attenuation with little leakage.**

Don't you think that if you put a voltmeter directly across the output terminals of an oscillator, it would measure the output voltage? And if you shielded the entire oscillator (which is usually done anyhow), you could also use a shielded attenuator so that you could reduce the output signal level considerably below the output level of the oscillator.

This is a very good feature unquestionably, but this is not really the basic reason for providing an isolation amplifier at the output of an oscillator. Guess again on Item 306.

ITEM 306b

You answered: **The basic reason for using an isolation amplifier at the output of an oscillator is to prevent load variations from affecting the oscillator frequency and output level.**

Changes in the load reactance, if no isolation is provided, can indeed shift the oscillator frequency undesirably. A similar thing can happen with load resistance changes. Consequently, you are very much on the ball with this answer. Continue with Item 307.

ITEM 306c

You answered: **An amplifier is used at the output of an oscillator basically to provide a large amount of power.**

Actually, you could build an oscillator to supply a kilowatt or more output power if you wanted. This is done in certain commercial applications. For instance, a radar transmitter may use a klystron or magnetron which are modulated oscillators. R-f heaters or ovens, putting out kilowatt power, typically are oscillators at a high power level. So you see, the power gain is only one reason to use an isolation amplifier. There are other reasons for using isolation amplifiers at the output of oscillators. Reread the material on Item 306, and try again.

An oscillator, or its output amplifier as a signal generator, has a definite generator, or source, impedance. An oscillator will supply its rated output power only at the rated value of load impedance. Typically, this load impedance is specified at 600 ohms for a-f generators and 50 (or 72) ohms for r-f generators. This is stated, or load, impedance. A typical a-f oscillator may have a source impedance of 10 ohms or less and yet have a rated output load impedance of 600 ohms. R-f generators are another story: In order to improve the standing-wave ratio, the generator impedance is usually matched to the load impedance. Thus, an r-f generator with a stipulated load impedance of 50 ohms also has a generator, or source, impedance of 50 ohms.

When a load impedance other than the rated impedance is used with an oscillator, the output voltage may be considerably different from that specified with the rated load impedance. This is particularly true of high-frequency generators, designed to be used with equal source and load impedances. An output-level meter may be used so that the output voltage level can be adjusted as desired; the power then has to be calculated by Ohm's law.

Variations in the generator, or source, impedance of a signal generator are undesirable. To minimize the variations in generator impedance with frequency, wide-band (high-fidelity) amplifiers with a wide frequency range are typically used; usually cathode or emitter followers are used in the output stage. Grounded-grid, or base, amplifiers give even more isolation. To minimize the effect of load changes in shunt with the generator impedance, a constant-impedance attenuator pad may be used. Such an L or T pad preserves a constant output impedance.

Q307 The source impedance of a signal generator cannot be kept constant with changes in output frequency or load impedance:

ITEM 307a False.

ITEM 307b True.

You answered: **The source, or generator, impedance cannot be kept constant with changes in frequency or load impedance. False.** I hope the double-negative aspect of this statement didn't fool you. Apparently it didn't, because this was the correct answer. Variations in the frequency and amplitude of oscillation can be minimized by the use of isolation amplifiers and constant-impedance attenuation pads.

Load and source impedances may be equal or different. The source imped-ance may or may not be affected by the load impedance; there is no interaction if a suitable attenuator pad is used between the two.

When the source impedance is lower than the load impedance, the load imped-ance can "reflect" some change on the source impedance. The low source impedance is usually obtained by negative feedback, and the applied load can thus affect the amplifier's gain.

Turn to Item 308.

You answered: **The generator output impedance cannot be kept constant with changes in load and frequency. True.**

The use of a wide-frequency-range amplifier for isolation can minimize the load's effect on frequency or generator impedance of an oscillator. For all practical purposes, compensation over the range of an oscillator is good enough so that there are no changes in the output impedance. The use of constant-impedance attenuator pads, such as T or L pads, also keeps the output impedance constant in spite of load or impedance changes due to frequency.

Don't feel bad about having picked this answer since the answer to this ques-tion depends on the interpretation of "for all practical purposes." Over the usable range of the signal generator, the changes in source impedance can be kept insignifi-cantly small for all practical purposes. Try the other answer on Item 307.

AMPLITUDE MODULATION

The simplest way to look at amplitude modulation (AM) is shown in the accompanying illustration. The modulation signal adds algebraically to the B+ voltage to produce variations in the output level in the r-f energy from the amplifier. The output level of the r-f voltage is directly proportional to changes in level of the modulating signal. The frequency, or rate of change, in the output signal is related directly to the frequency, or rate of change of the modulation signal. When there is no modulation signal, the B+ voltage is unaffected and produces the unmodulated carrier level.

When modulation is in progress, the output power level actually increases as the amplitude of the modulating signal increases. For example, when the modulation signal has raised the peak voltage of the r-f output to a level exactly twice what it was before (the modulating signal is equal to the resting or carrier level), the power output has increased by 22 percent over the unmodulated or resting carrier level. Since the modulated amplifier is essentially a nonlinear device, care must be taken to reduce the distortion in the signal. For instance, the modulated r-f signal should not increase to more than twice the resting carrier level. Exceeding twice the carrier level results in clipping and splatter during the time that the modulation voltage has reduced the B+ voltage to zero or less.

In addition to the resting carrier frequency during amplitude modulation, there are two sideband frequencies spaced by the modulation frequency up and down from the resting or carrier frequency.

FIGURE 3-5

Amplitude-modulation diagram.

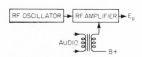

Q308 In amplitude modulation, what aspect of the modulated radio frequency stays constant:

ITEM 308a   The output power level.

ITEM 308b   The output carrier frequency.

ITEM 308c   The output bandwidth.

ITEM 308a

You answered: **In amplitude modulation, the output level stays constant.** Actually the r-f output under 100 percent modulation may change from its resting or unmodulated value all the way down to zero and up to twice the resting peak level. When this happens, the energy put out by the amplifier increases slightly. Thus the output level under modulation does not stay constant. The concept of amplitude modulation is that it is the level or output voltage for the amplifier that is changing directly. Turn back to Item 308 and pick a different answer.

ITEM 308b

You answered: **In amplitude modulation, the carrier frequency stays constant.**

In amplitude modulation, the sidebands are spaced a distance away from the carrier frequency by the modulation frequency. Although the sidebands' frequency may vary, the carrier frequency stays constant and represents the contribution of the unmodulated, or carrier, frequency as a reference. Any change in carrier frequency during modulation is termed frequency modulation (FM) and is undesirable in AM transmitters.

Your answer was entirely correct. Go to Item 309.

ITEM 308c

You answered: **In amplitude modulation, the output bandwidth stays constant.** Actually, output bandwidth was not discussed directly. However, the bandwidth is directly related to the separation of the upper and lower sidebands, which are spaced above and below the carrier frequency by the modulation frequency. Thus, the bandwidth is proportional to twice the modulation frequency. As you can see then, if you vary the modulation frequency, you are going to be varying the bandwidth needed to propagate this signal. Thus, the output bandwidth is not going to be constant when you transmit a varying modulating-signal frequency. Try another answer on Item 308.

ITEM 309

FREQUENCY MODULATION

As the name implies, in frequency modulation, the frequency of the r-f output varies around some resting, or unmodulated carrier, frequency. The power output is constant. Looking at the illustration, you see that we have added a modification to make the tank capacitor vary with a modulation signal. The rest of the Hartley oscillator circuit is the same as shown previously. The modification is that the tank capacitor has one set of plates mechanically connected to a modulating device. The modulating device is much like a loudspeaker except that the capacitor plates are attached to the voice coil. When the voice coil moves in response to the modulating signal, the rotor of the tank capacitor C is moved. The stator of the capacitor C remains fixed. Thus for small signal changes, the tank capacitor C changes linearly, and the output changes in frequency linearly. This is frequency modulation. At the same time that the frequency is changing, the output voltage level stays the same.

Instead of using an electromechanical transducer, one may use other devices to vary the frequency. This method was shown for illustration only; other methods are more practical. Frequently used these days is a solid-state device called a "varicap," or voltage-variable diode. This is a back-biased diode, and its capacity varies inversely with the applied voltage. To achieve an electronically controlled capacity another way, you can control the input capacity of a tube by varying the gain with the input bias. Still another way to control the tank resonant frequency is to use a reactance tube modulator. This is a circuit arranged to produce a plus or minus 90° phase shift in the output signal with respect to the input signal. Yet other devices, such as saturable reactors, may be used to produce frequency modulation.

FIGURE 3-6

Frequency-modulation diagram.

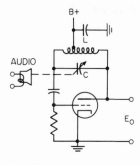

Q309 Only the capacitance of a tank circuit can be varied to produce frequency modulation:

ITEM 309a   True.

ITEM 309b   False.

You answered: **True, only a changing capacitance is used to provide frequency modulation.**

This is generally true but not always so. We mentioned two cases where this would not be true. A reactance tube can be used to provide a phase shift of plus or minus 90°. A negative phase shift corresponds to the effect of a capacitor. A plus 90° phase shift corresponds to the action of an inductor. Thus a reactance tube modulator that produces a phase shift of plus 90° is in effect a controllable inductance. In addition, we also mentioned saturable reactors that are controllable to produce frequency modulation. Finally, instead of having the voice coil control the tank capacitor C, we might have made it control a slug in the tank inductance L. When the voice coil moved in response to an input modulating signal, the slug would move and change the inductance of tank coil L. This would change the tank frequency. Thus, you can see that if you pick the other answer on Item 309, you are going to be correct. Please do so.

You answered: **False, varying the capacity of the tank circuit is not the only way to produce frequency modulation.**

Although varying the capacity of the tank circuit is the usual way to produce frequency modulation, it is by no means the only way. Your answer was correct. Good.

A reactance modulator that produces 90° phase shift is equivalent to varying the inductance. In addition, saturable reactors or an electromechanical transducer that varies the inductance of the tank circuit are other ways to vary the frequency of the tank circuit by utilizing a controllable inductance.

Turn to Item 310.

RC OSCILLATORS

Resistance-capacitance (RC) coupled oscillators are practical in frequency ranges where RC coupling is practical in amplifiers. This oscillator covers a range which extends from a few cycles per second to a few megacycles per second. Since the Wien-bridge oscillator is by far the most common audio oscillator, we shall consider it first.

Shown below is an abbreviated circuit for a Wien (pronounced "ween" or "veen") bridge oscillator. There are two types of feedback: positive and negative. The positive feedback is through the series-parallel RC network consisting of R_1C_1 in series and R_2C_2 in parallel. The amplifiers must provide sufficient gain to make up for the voltage-divider losses through R_1C_1 and R_2C_2. Note that the grid input E_i to the amplifier is taken at the junction of the series-parallel network. This series-parallel network provides an in-phase feedback (360° phase shift). The other arm of the bridge consists of R_3 and the nonlinear resistance lamp NL. The cathode input to amplifier 1 comes from the junction of R_3 and NL. This provides negative feedback for amplitude stabilization. The output of the bridge thus is the input for the first amplifier and is $E_i - E_{NL}$.

FIGURE 3-7
Simplified circuit for
Wien-bridge oscillator.

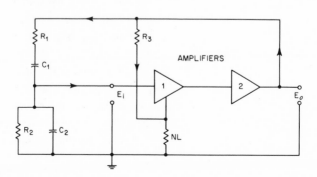

ITEM 310A   The input voltage for amplifier 1 is the difference between its grid and cathode voltages, the bridge output. These voltages are in phase at the operating frequency. The phase shift caused by R_1C_1 is cancelled by that of R_2C_2, and R_3NL causes zero phase shift. Each amplifier contributes exactly 180° phase shift, with an overall loop phase shift of 360 or 0°. The frequency selectivity of this oscillator is due mainly to its phase-shift characteristics and only somewhat to its attenuation characteristics. Typically the values of R_1 and R_2 are set equal, as are C_1 and C_2. Thus at the operating frequency, the reactances equal the resistances: $X_{C1} = X_{C2} = R_1 = R_2$. Below the operating frequency, the impedance of R_1C_1 predominates to produce a net capacitive phase shift. Above the operating frequency, an opposite phase shift is produced by R_2C_2. The operating frequency is changed by varying C_1 and C_2 the same amount. Even so, the phase shift stays the same at the operating frequency, and the reactance ratio remains constant.

Let's consider in detail just the left side of the bridge, R_1 and C_1 in series and R_2 and C_2 in parallel, at the operating frequency with equal resistances and reactances. The upper-leg impedance $Z_U = R_1 - X_{C1} = 1.414R_1 \angle -45°$. Similarly for the lower leg, $Z_L = (1/R_2 - 1/X_{C2})^{-1} = R_2(1 + X_{C2}R_2)/(1 + X_{C2}R_2)^2 = 0.717R_2 \angle +45°$. Note that the phase shifts are equal and opposite and that the magnitude of the upper impedance U is twice that of the lower impedance L. To oscillate, the overall loop phase shift has to be 360°. The series-parallel RC network behaves as a phase discriminator for frequency components near the frequency of oscillation, and only that frequency component with a phase shift of 0° through the RC network regenerates.

The amplifiers operate over their linear region, so that some method of amplitude stabilization is needed to ensure purity of output waveform. A nonlinear element is included to provide feedback for this purpose, typically a lamp such as the NL symbol on the diagram. As the amplitude of signal increases, more current flows through the nonlinear lamp element; its resistance increases nonlinearly according to some power function, thus providing negative feedback to stabilize the signal amplitude. Under these circumstances, the oscillator provides an output sine-wave signal of low distortion (high purity) at a very constant amplitude.

It is easy to change capacitors C_1 and C_2 either by using variable capacitors or by switching in different capacitors. Accordingly, this oscillator is used to cover a wide range of frequencies in the "audio" range, extending from 0.01 cps to 1 Mc (actually "r-f").

Q310 E_i is the output voltage from the series-parallel RC network that goes to the amplifier grid input; E_o is the oscillator output voltage that is fed back as input to this same network. The ratio E_o/E_i or output/grid voltage:[1]

ITEM 310a Varies with the oscillator output frequency because of the series and shunt capacitors.

ITEM 310b Is equal to 3 only at the frequency of oscillation.

ITEM 310c Is constant at all frequencies, whether measured at the oscillating frequency or not.

[1] Hint: Review the impedance magnitude relationships.

You answered: **The loop gain of the oscillator varies directly with the oscillator frequency because of the series-shunt capacitors.**

You apparently have this one slightly out of cause-and-effect order. It is quite true that the capacitors C_1 and C_2 are deliberately varied, but they are varied to change the frequency of oscillation. This is the cause-and-effect sequence: Varying the two capacitors changes the frequency at which the reactances are equal to the resistances, and this makes the voltage-divider action, loop gain, and phase shift constant for just one frequency. The voltage-divider action and loop gain for frequencies other than this frequency of oscillation (or resonant frequency) does indeed vary for frequencies both above and below the operating frequency where the resistances and reactances are equal. As a matter of fact, the loop gain decreases on both sides of the resonant frequency because of first, the action of one capacitor and second, the action of the other capacitor. Turn back to Item 310, and see if you can select the correct answer now.

ITEM 310b

The loop gain of the oscillator is a constant 3 only at the frequency of oscillation.

The voltage-divider action at the oscillating frequency is a constant 3 in the circuit used. You are correct, and right on the ball with this one! At a frequency lower than the resonant frequency, the effect of C_2 is such that it is an open circuit compared to resistor R_2. The reactance of C_1 also is increasing as frequency decreases below resonance, and accordingly the voltage-dividing ratio approaches X_{C1}/R_2. Obviously this ratio gets much larger than 3 as frequency decreases. Thus, the gain of the amplifiers is indeed 3 only at the resonant frequency.

However, remember that it is the 0 or 360° phase shift through the series and parallel RC networks which determines the operating frequency. Keep your thinking cap on, and proceed to Item 311.

ITEM 310c

You answered: **The loop gain for the oscillator is constant for all frequencies, resonant and nonresonant, because of the nonlinear negative feedback.**

At the resonant frequency the two capacitive reactances are equal to the two resistances, and the voltage-divider action is then constant. The gain of the two amplifiers provides a constant amplitude output and must just equal the loss in the RC voltage divider. The nonlinear resistance compensates for slight changes in gain so that the gain at the resonant frequency does indeed stay constant. The R_1C_1 and R_2C_2 voltage divider changes phase shift also. The capacitor C_1 above the resonant frequency becomes a virtual short, as does capacitor C_2. The voltage-dividing action at frequencies much above the oscillating frequency is the ratio of R_1/X_2. A similar situation occurs at frequencies lower than the resonant frequency. Turn to Item 310.

**PHASE-SHIFT
OSCILLATOR**

The phase-shift oscillator, as the name implies, adds another 180° of phase shift to an existing 180° of phase shift through an amplifier, to provide a total of 360° of phase shift for in-phase, or positive, feedback. A minimum of three RC sections in series will provide a total of 180° of phase shift. Refer to the diagram below. Approximately 60° of phase shift occurs in each of the three RC sections, if we assume that the ratios of the capacitors and resistors are equal in each of the three sections. There are slight differences in the amount of phase shift per section due to the loading of the following RC network upon the preceding one. The reactance of the capacitor and the resistance in each section form a reactance voltage-divider network. (See Fig. 3-8.) The ratio of output to input signal of the network is represented by the cosine of the phase shift, 60°; this is 0.50. Multiplying this factor by itself three times produces a total attenuation of ⅛. To produce sustained oscillations at a constant amplitude, the amplifier, in addition to providing 180° of phase shift, must provide a constant gain of 8 to make up for the voltage-divider action and loss in signal.

Q311 The amount of phase shift which is required of the amplifier in the RC phase-shift oscillator is:

ITEM 311a   225°.

ITEM 311b   360°.

ITEM 311c   180°.

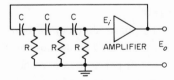

FIGURE 3-8

RC phase-shift oscillator.

You answered: **The necessary phase shift to be supplied by the amplifier in the phase-shift oscillator circuit is 225°.**

If you assumed 45° phase shift per section, there would be a total of 135° for the three RC sections. This phase shift is produced by the frequently used example of having equal resistive and reactive elements in each network section. Subtracting 135° from 360° leaves 225° for the amplifier. However, it is an unusual amplifier that will produce 225° of phase shift at all frequencies, which is the requirement of the amplifier in this case. A phase shift of 45° per section can happen, but it turns out that 180° total is required for oscillation in this case. Turn to Item 311 and pick the right answer without hesitation.

You answered: **The necessary phase shift to be supplied by the amplifier in the phase-shift oscillator is 360°, as in the Wien-bridge oscillator.**

In the RC phase-shift oscillator, there is no comparing the phase shifts above and below the resonant frequency. The voltage gain or voltage-divider action of the three-section RC network actually varies with frequency. As you can readily see, if a frequency much higher than the frequency of oscillation were to be fed through the network, the effect of the three series-capacitive reactances would become negligible so that the overall attenuation or gain factor would be due only to the three resistors R in parallel. At frequencies much lower than the frequency of oscillation, the capacitive reactance of the three series capacitors would become the predominant factor, and the gain in the voltage divider (attenuation) would approach infinity at very low frequencies, leaving no output signal to be fed back to the amplifier. The frequency of oscillation for this oscillator is determined primarily by requiring that the oscillator frequency be sensitive to 0° phase shift, which is the same as 360° for sine waves. We have a total of 180° of phase shift across the three RC networks. The required difference is simple enough to figure out. Return to Item 311.

You answered: **The phase shift required of the amplifier in the RC phase-shift oscillator is 180°.**

The phase shift per section is set at 60°, in order to produce the total of a 180° phase shift. Two sections of 90° each are not practical. With three sections, the phase shift per section does not have to be 60°, but the total must be 180°. This is true because a total of 0 or 360° phase shift is required to produce in-phase or positive feedback. Since the given three RC sections are added in series with a typical amplifier and since we had stated that the three RC sections produce a 180° phase shift, the usual amplifier is left producing a 180° phase shift. But you used your head, my dear Watson, and selected the correct answer. Proceed to Item 312.

There are a number of types of multivibrators. However, we are going to discuss one of the simplest types, the RC-coupled multivibrator. In the diagram, note that there are two transistors, each supplying 180° of phase shift. The RC coupling networks from collector to the other base provide coupling and time delay but do not contribute to the required 360° of phase shift. Assume that transistor Q_1 is conducting (just turned on). Capacitor C_1 had just been charged to full-supply voltage; consequently when the collector voltage Q_1 falls, this voltage across C_1 reduces the base voltage of transistor Q_2, cutting it off. Transistor Q_2 had just been conducting and now is turned off. Capacitor C_2 had been discharged to approximately zero voltage since both the collector of transistor Q_2 and the base of transistor Q_1 were at approximately the same potential. When transistor Q_2 cuts off, the collector of Q_2 rises to the supply voltage. Since capacitor C_2 has no voltage across it initially, this full-supply voltage is coupled to the base of Q_1 turning it on even harder. Thus, positive feedback around the loop ensues until capacitor C_1 discharges, permitting Q_2 to turn on again. As soon as transistor Q_2 goes on, the state of affairs reverses and transistor Q_2 is on with transistor Q_1 off.

Note that the time at which transistor Q_2 turns on is determined at some point in the RC timing cycle, not necessarily the RC time constant. It will be the same point in the cycle each time, whether it is exactly the RC time or, as is typical, somewhat longer.

FIGURE 3-9 Simple multivibrator circuit.

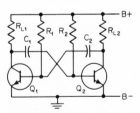

Q312 The output point for signals, so that the load has little effect on the period of the timing in this multivibrator, should be as follows:

ITEM 312a Between the base and the collector of transistor Q_2.

ITEM 312b The base of transistor Q_2 to ground.

ITEM 312c From the collector of transistor Q_2 to ground.

ITEM 312a

You answered: **To minimize the effect of load variations upon the period, the output point in the multivibrator circuit should be taken between the base and collector of transistor Q_2.**

The load resistor at this point would have an interesting effect, namely, providing negative feedback in the circuit. This would stabilize the gain of the transistor, with the transistor swinging between saturation and cutoff. How much gain stabilization is needed? One side of the load resistor typically is grounded, and neither point (collector or base) can be grounded in this circuit without seriously degrading the performance of the circuit. (This is true only when a common power supply is used.) With this additional information, try a second thought about the selection of a suitable output point on Item 312.

ITEM 312b

You answered: **To reduce the effect of load variation on the period, the output point from the multivibrator should be taken at the base of the second transistor Q_2 to ground.**

The base resistor R_2 is such that it is usually much higher than the collector resistor R_{L2}. If you place a load resistor in parallel with a high-valued resistor such as R_2, you would lower the RC discharge time for capacitor C_2. Thus, you would have placed your load resistor in a spot where it would markedly affect the RC discharge time. This is not the effect that you had intended. Try another answer on Item 312.

ITEM 312c

You answered: **To minimize the effect of load variations upon the period of the multivibrator, the output should be taken from the collector of Q_2 to ground.**

The load resistor typically has a value comparable to that of the collector resistance R_{C2}. The base resistances usually are considerably higher than the collector load resistances. Since placing a resistor at the base either to collector or to ground would affect the circuit's time constant, it would be undesirable. Consequently, you selected the right answer. Nice going.

Similar multivibrator circuits may have different coupling arrangements between the transistors. A typical arrangement is that they may have coupling between the two emitters, with a common load resistor. Go to Item 313.

ITEM 313

OTHER
OSCILLATORS

When a constant frequency of oscillation is desired, a crystal oscillator is often used. The active element is a piece of quartz ground and polished to a particular thickness. The crystal vibrates physically, and the vibration is picked off electrically and coupled to the oscillator circuit. The crystal effectively is an extremely high Q circuit (LC tank) with very low resistive losses. One type of crystal oscillator is quite similar to a Colpitts oscillator. When a stable variable frequency is desired, a variable-frequency oscillator (VFO) is used, such as the Clapp, or series-tuned Colpitts, circuit.

Another interesting type of oscillator circuit is the negative-resistance oscillator. This device, effectively or actually, has only two terminals, and the phase shift at the frequency of oscillation must be 0°. Certain devices, such as neon tubes, tunnel diodes, some tetrodes, pentodes, and certain amplifiers, exhibit a negative-resistance characteristic. That is, as voltage is increased, the current in such a device actually decreases either abruptly or linearly. If a device that has a periodic function, such as an LC tank, is connected to a negative resistance, oscillations at the frequency determined by the LC tank will ensue. A negative resistance is like a resistor, but instead of absorbing power, a negative resistor supplies power. For sustained oscillations, the negative resistance must equal or exceed the lossy (positive) resistance.

Multivibrators by themselves produce square- or rectangular-shaped output waveforms. By proceeding to integrate a rectangular waveshape with an RC filter, triangular waveforms can be produced. By coupling these triangular waveforms into a tank circuit, sine waves may be produced. Alternatively sine waves may be produced directly in multivibrators by replacing one of the RC coupling elements with a series LC tank. Pulses may be produced by differentiating the multivibrator output. Unsymmetrical waveforms may be produced, with a pulse-to-period ratio considerably different from 1:2. Such spikes produce narrowband high-frequency noise.

Q313 In a crystal oscillator, how much phase shift is required of the amplifier portion of the circuit?

ITEM 313a   360°,

ITEM 313b   180°.

ITEM 313c   Either 180 or 360°.

ITEM 313a

You answered: **In a crystal oscillator, the amplifier portion of the circuit provides 360° of phase shift.**

In a negative-resistance oscillator, 0° of phase shift is supplied by the negative resistance which operates as an amplifier to supply power to the circuit. Power to the circuit is supplied at a rate determined by the LC combination. Since the power must be delivered in phase with the tank circuit, obviously 0 or 360° of phase shift results. But how about the typical LC oscillator? Isn't something other than 360° required in this case? Try another answer in Item 313.

ITEM 313b

You answered: **In a crystal oscillator, the amplifier portion supplies 180° of phase shift.**

In a typical Colpitts oscillator, which is the equivalent circuit for one type of crystal oscillator, it is true that 180° of phase shift is supplied by the amplifier portion. But do you remember that we stated that a crystal is a high-Q LC tank circuit and that LC tank circuits may be used with negative-resistance oscillators? Well, your answer is correct for one type of circuit, but is this the only possibility? Try another answer in Item 313.

ITEM 313c

You answered: **In a crystal oscillator, the amplifier portion of the circuit can supply either 180 or 360° of phase shift.**

In an LC oscillator such as the Colpitts, the tapped tank supplies 180° of phase shift and the amplifier, an additional 180°, to supply a total phase shift of 360°. In a negative-resistance oscillator, the negative resistance supplies power in phase to the shunt tank circuit, so that the total phase shift supplied by the amplifier is 0° phase shift, which in terms of a sine wave is equivalent to 360°. Thus, crystal oscillators may be used with amplifiers that supply either 360 or 180° of phase shift. Your answer is entirely correct.

Turn to Item 314.

ITEM 314

**OSCILLATOR
STABILITY**

Oscillator circuits are rated by their accuracy, or how closely they adhere to a given frequency. The initial tolerance on this frequency may be specified in so many parts per million that the oscillator frequency will be off from its specified frequency. A second consideration is stability of oscillation. Many factors cause the oscillator to drift or even change abruptly in its frequency of oscillation. In general, these drifts in frequency are undesirable. Drift may be caused by a number of factors, such as heat or vibration, which results in small changes in the tank circuitry or in the amplifier circuitry to produce changes in gain or reactance. The input capacity to a vacuum tube may change as the grid bias or plate voltage (and gain of the tube) is changed. The input capacitance of a triode is determined by the grid-to-cathode capacity plus the plate-to-cathode capacity multiplied approximately by the gain of the stage. Thus, you can see that if the grid bias or the plate voltage changes, the operating characteristic of the tube is changed so that the gain will cause a change in input capacity, which may cause a change in oscillator frequency because of a capacitance variation. Although this effect is used in certain types of frequency modulation, it is generally undesirable in an oscillator used as a standard or with amplitude modulation.

Oscillator tank circuits generally use a low ratio of inductance to capacitance (L/C) which produces a low tank impedance and a high tank current. When this is true, the tube circuits load down the tank circuit to a small extent, so that tube variations do not affect tank oscillations so much. The Clapp (series-tuned Colpitts) oscillator in particular employs low loading of the tank circuit to minimize the effect of tube variations upon the frequency of oscillations. In addition, screen-grid tubes are employed in Hartley oscillators, where the basic oscillator is composed of the cathode, grid, and screen grid acting as plate. With the screen grid effectively grounded at radio frequency, the plate circuit may be used as the output circuit since it is effectively shielded from the grid-cathode oscillating circuit. Needless to say, oscillators usually are supplied with voltages that are regulated carefully. To further ensure stability of oscillation, the entire oscillator is placed in a temperature-controlled environment and protected from excessive humidity.

That is enough of this chapter on oscillators. Let's see how much you remember. Turn to Quiz 3, Item 315.

ITEM 315

QUIZ 3

Write down your answer to each question on a separate sheet of paper. The letter at the end of each question gives the answer on the next pages.

1 Name two basic types of oscillator circuits. List their essential features, and compare them. *(G)*

2 What features typically distinguish a signal generator from an oscillator? *(C)*

3 A high-fidelity amplifier (constant gain over a wide frequency band) is required in a Wien-bridge oscillator. (True/False) *(H)*

4 What two factors provide gain stabilization in *LC* oscillators? *(B)*

5 All vacuum-tube oscillators require 180° phase shift of the tube. (True/False) *(F)*

6 All amplifiers for *RC* oscillators are required to produce 180° of phase shift. (True/False) *(I)*

7 Amplitude modulation (AM) usually is done at an amplifier stage following the oscillator. (True/False) *(D)*

8 Frequency modulation (FM) usually is done at an amplifier stage following the oscillator. (True/False) *(A)*

9 Differentiate between a Hartley and a Colpitts oscillator. *(E)*

10 What features help to produce oscillator frequency stability. *(K)*

11 What is the major purpose of a transistor or tube in an oscillator? *(J)*

12 A multivibrator produces this waveform. Which letter refers to the period of the pulse? *(L)*

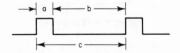

A False. You have to affect the frequency in the generating stage.

B When the grid swings positive, the grid draws current and absorbs power. When sufficient power is absorbed from the tank circuit, less power is available for the output. As the grid goes more and more positive, an increasing amount of grid power is absorbed in nonlinear fashion. As the plate voltage swings higher and higher, the tube gain reaches the nonlinear region. The transfer characteristic thus provides less gain in the tube (the mu or gain factor of the tube decreases).

C Both devices basically include an oscillator. The additional features are those, in general, that differentiate a signal generator from an oscillator. Additional features are various types of modulation, load isolation, amplitude monitoring, and control.

D True. This is done to prevent incidental frequency changes during modulation.

E The major difference is in what performs the voltage-dividing action. In a Hartley oscillator, the voltage divider is the tapped coil, and in a Colpitts oscillator, the voltage-dividing action is performed by two capacitors in series.

F False. The Wien-bridge oscillator has an associated amplifier that produces 360°. Most *LC* oscillators, on the other hand, do have an associated amplifier that produces 180° of phase shift.

G Two basic types of oscillator circuits are those where frequency-controlling and phase-shifting networks are composed of inductance and capacitance *(LC)* and those employing a combination of resistance and capacitance *(RC)*. *RC* oscillators are limited to intermediate radio frequencies and audio frequencies. *LC* oscillator circuits generally operate over a wider range of frequencies than their *RC* counterparts. The *LC* oscillators have two components, each of which provides an energy-storing function. *RC* oscillators have just one energy-storage device, a capacitor.

H True. This device typically covers a wide range of frequencies, three to five or more decades usually, which makes this requirement necessary. There are single-frequency oscillators of this type, however, that need not have wide-range amplifiers.

I False. The Wien-bridge oscillator is an exception, as is the twin-*T*—feedback oscillator. This statement is true in general, however.

J Power gain to overcome losses and sustain oscillations is the major reason.

K Rigid mechanical mounting of all parts, use of temperature-compensated circuits, a low L/C tank circuit ratio, use of load or output separation from the frequency-generation circuits (such as a Clapp oscillator or frequency doubler), and use of voltage-supply regulation.

L The pulse period is letter c; the reciprocal of the pulse repetition frequency, prf. Letter *a* refers to the pulse width PW.

You have now finished another chapter. Nice going! When you feel up to tackling the next chapter, please do so.

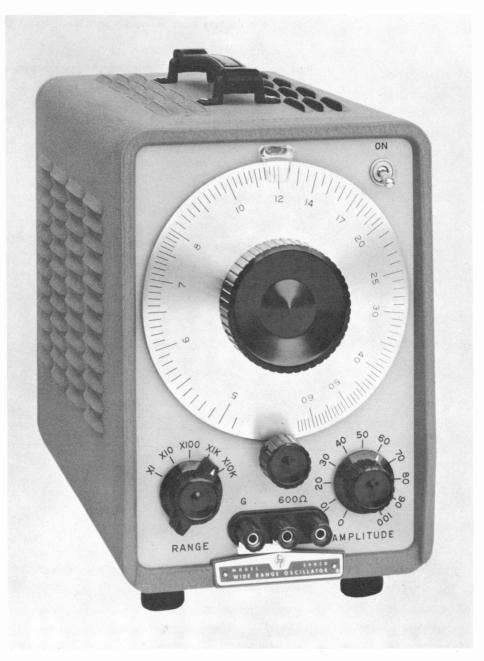

FIGURE 4-1 Photograph of the HP Model 200CD wide-range oscillator.

CHAPTER FOUR   SIGNAL GENERATORS 14 QUESTIONS

ITEM 401

The major difference between oscillators and signal generators is that typically a signal generator has many extras compared to an oscillator. In this chapter we are going to study three different types of signal generators so that you may become familiar with them. The first signal generator that we are going to consider is called an oscillator, although you will note that the term is somewhat misleading since the oscillator to be discussed has many additional features besides its wide frequency range.

THE HP 200CD WIDE-RANGE OSCILLATOR

Refer to Fig. 4-1 for a picture of the HP 200CD wide-range oscillator.

The Hewlett-Packard Model 200CD wide-range oscillator covers frequencies from 5 cps to 600 kc. This frequency range is accomplished by using five overlapping decade bands. The 200CD oscillator may be operated with either a balanced output or an unbalanced output into a 600-ohm load. This device will furnish up to 10 volts of signal into a 600-ohm load (equivalent to 160 mw) for any frequency within its range. Some of the applications of this test set are checking audio amplifiers, audio-range transducers, telephone carrier systems, and low r-f devices.

Q401 The Hewlett-Packard Model 200CD is:

ITEM 401a An audio oscillator.

ITEM 401b An r-f signal generator.

ITEM 401c A combination audio oscillator and low r-f oscillator.

ITEM 401a

You answered that the Model 200CD is an **audio oscillator.** Although this is true, the Model 200CD is more than just an audio oscillator. When you reread Item 401, you will notice that the frequency range is from 5 cps to 600 kc. Since 600 kc is well above the audio range, the Model 200CD may also be used for the low radio frequencies. Try again; don't let this discourage you.

ITEM 401b

Your answer was that the Model 200CD oscillator is an **r-f signal generator.**

This is not entirely correct. The audio frequencies are also included in its 5 cps to 600 kc range. Reread Item 401; then choose the right option.

ITEM 401c

Right! With a range of 5 cps to 600 kc, **the Hewlett-Packard Model 200CD may be used for both the audio frequencies and the lower radio frequencies.** Now continue with Item 402.

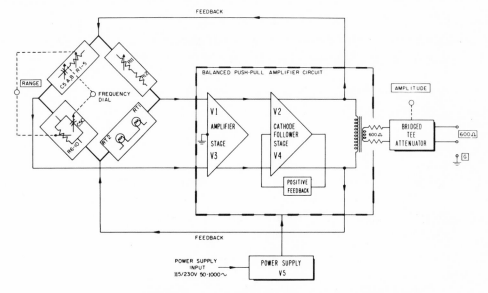

FIGURE 4-2   HP 200CD wide-range oscillator (block diagram).

ITEM 402

HP 200CD
BASIC THEORY

Figure 4-2 is a block diagram for the Hewlett-Packard Model 200CD oscillator. Notice (left) the frequency-controlling bridge network, an RC bridge circuit controlled by the range switch and frequency dial. The range switch [$\times 10$, $\times 100$, etc. (dial multiplier)] selects the resistors in the two left-hand legs of the bridge, that is, R_1 through R_5 and R_6 through R_{10}. There will be one resistor in each leg on any range. R_1 will be in the circuit at the same time as R_6, R_2 with R_7, and so on to R_5 with R_{10}.

To vary the frequency within a range, C_5 with its sections A, B, and C is varied. This capacitor is coupled mechanically to the calibrated frequency dial.

In the right leg of the bridge, R_{T1} and R_{T2} are temperature-sensitive resistors. They are in the circuit to ensure amplitude stability via negative feedback. The variable resistor R_{11} is a factory adjustment to ensure the proper amount of output at the terminals of this oscillator. The only time this control should need adjustment is if R_{T1} or R_{T2} is replaced.

Q402   The resistors R_1 through R_5 and R_6 through R_{10}:

ITEM 402a   Vary the frequency of the bridge circuitry.

ITEM 402**b**   Set the range of the oscillator.

ITEM 402**c**   Are dc blocking resistors.

ITEM 402a

Although the resistors R_1 through R_5 and R_6 through R_{10} do cause a wide variation in the frequency of the bridge circuit, it is more nearly correct to say that they set the range (decade multiplying factor) for the oscillator. The capacitor C_5 varies the frequency within the ranges set by these 10 resistors. Continue to Item 402b.

ITEM 402b

You are correct. Remember that capacitor C_5 varies the frequency within the range set by the 10 resistors. The sections A, B, and C of capacitor C_5 are always in the circuit to vary the frequency. Just one pair of the range-setting resistors is in the circuit at a given time. These R-C elements provide the frequency-controlling positive feedback. Continue with Item 403.

ITEM 402c

You are way off base. These resistors do **not** block direct current. Capacitors will block direct current, but resistors will conduct current, both ac and dc currents. Reread Item 402 and try another answer.

In Fig. 4-2 there are two push-pull amplifier stages in the balanced-amplifier circuit. Tubes V1 and V3 make up one pair and are used as a voltage amplifier in a balanced push-pull configuration. Tubes V2 and V4 make up a special push-pull cathode-follower stage, used to compensate for load variations. The function of this second stage is to provide a constant output regardless of the load-impedance changes. Included in this cathode-follower stage is a positive feedback path which effectively provides a gain of 1 for this stage. This stage also has 600-ohm resistors in the output leads to present a 600-ohm source to the output.

Another major function of this cathode-follower stage is to provide a signal feedback to the bridge circuit to sustain the oscillations.

Q403 The balanced-amplifier circuit consists of:

ITEM 403a A push-pull voltage amplifier and a push-pull cathode-follower stage for load isolation and regenerative feedback.

ITEM 403**b** Two parallel amplifier stages with 600-ohm output circuit.

ITEM 403**c** A range-multiplier circuit plus a voltage amplifier for compensation.

Very good! You chose the right answer. **The balanced push-pull amplifier section is made up of a balanced push-pull voltage amplifier and a push-pull cathode-follower stage for impedance matching and regenerative feedback to the bridge circuit.** Proceed to Item 404.

Your answer of **two parallel amplifier stages with a 600-ohm load** is wrong. The balanced push-pull amplifier consists of (1) a balanced push-pull voltage amplifier and (2) a push-pull cathode-follower stage to match load impedance and provide a regenerative feedback path for the oscillator circuit. Now go back to Item 403 and reread it; then choose the right answer and continue.

Nope. Read and reread Item 403; then take the service handbook for the Hewlett-Packard Model 200CD oscillator and read pages 3-1 and 3-2. When you have finished this, return to Item 403 and choose another answer.

ITEM 404

THE 608D VHF SIGNAL GENERATOR

Figure 4-3 shows a picture of the Hewlett-Packard Model 608D vhf signal generator. Examine the front panel and controls. This signal generator furnishes r-f signals from 10 to 420 Mc. The signals may be amplitude modulated by externally applied sine waves or pulses, or by internally generated sine waves, or left unmodulated (CW).[1] The output voltage level of the signal may be adjusted by an output attenuator which can be calibrated to read in decibels or volts by an output voltmeter. The attenuator is calibrated to read directly into a 50-ohm resistive load and has an accuracy of plus or minus 1 db over the entire frequency range. This signal generator is also supplied with a crystal calibrator so that at 1 and 5 Mc points throughout the frequency range of the instrument, a calibration signal may be obtained to check the accuracy of the frequency dials.

This test instrument can be used for calibrating, testing, and trouble shooting of vhf radios and of vhf circuits; for measuring antenna and transmission-line characteristics; for measuring standing-wave ratios and receiver sensitivity, to name its common uses.

Q404 The 608D vhf signal generator provides what modulation capability?

ITEM 404a   Frequency modulation.

ITEM 404b   No modulation (pure CW).

ITEM 404c   Amplitude modulation.

[1] CW: Continuous wave, or constant-height waves.

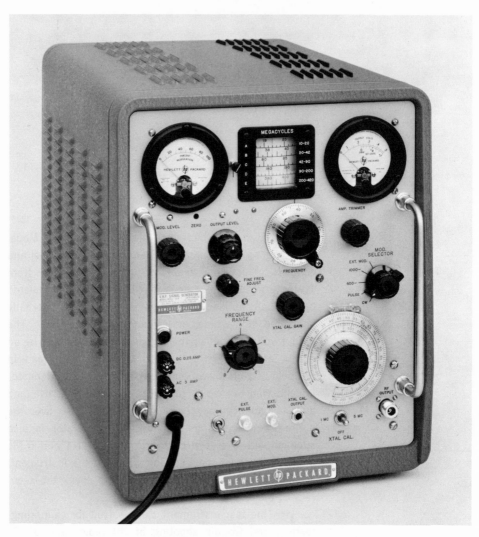

FIGURE 4-3 Photograph of the HP Model 608D vhf signal generator.

ITEM 404a

You answered that the 608D vhf signal generator provides **frequency modulation** of the output signal. There is some minute frequency modulation in the signal generator, but it is purely unintentional and held to an extremely low level. The frequency modulation of the frequency generator is so low that this type of modulation is useless for any practical purposes. It is held to less than 1000 cps throughout the entire frequency range. Thus you can see that for a typical frequency-modulation signal where you might want plus or minus 10 percent frequency change, this 1000 cps out of 100 Mc is useless. Reread the material on Item 404, and try another answer.

ITEM 404b

You answered that the Model 608D vhf signal generator provides **no modulation** capability at all.

It is quite possible that you looked at the photograph of this signal generator in Fig. 4-3 entirely too closely. On the modulation selector switch on the front panel, there is one position of the switch on which the oscillator is unmodulated; that is, it puts out a continuous wave. However, this is not the best use of the device, since for testing receivers and trouble-shooting purposes the signal generator is more useful if it produces amplitude modulation. However you are partially correct; proceed to Item 404c.

ITEM 404c

You answered that the 608D vhf signal generator provides **amplitude modulation** of the output signal.

Either from reading the descriptive material or from looking at the picture of the front panel of the signal generator, you gathered quite correctly that this signal generator does indeed provide amplitude modulation of the output signal. This modulation signal may be turned off (CW), or in the amplitude-modulation positions, either 400 or 1000 cps may be applied as modulation, or external sine waves or pulses may be applied for modulation.

Go to Item 405.

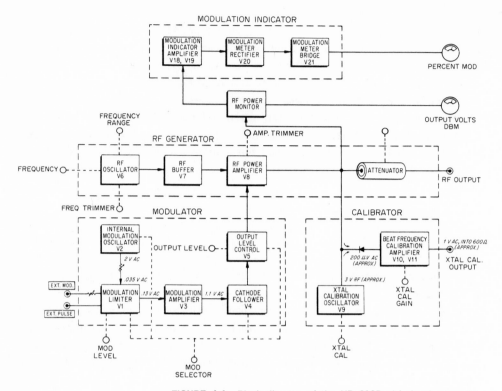

FIGURE 4-4 Block diagram of the HP 608D vhf signal generator.

Refer to Fig. 4-4 which shows a block diagram for the 608D vhf signal generator. A Colpitts oscillator generates sine-wave signals and supplies these signals to a buffer amplifier and then through a power amplifier to the output. The buffer amplifier primarily isolates the oscillator stage from the output stage and also provides some power gain. The output of the power amplifier may be connected straight through to the output connector, or various levels of attenuation may be used.

A sine-wave oscillator is used as a modulator to provide amplitude modulation at either 400 or 1000 cps. Note that high-level cathode modulation is used as the modulation signal is applied to the cathode of the power-output stage. An output voltmeter is used to monitor the r-f output signal level. A rectifier samples the r-f output voltage applied to the attenuator and serves to energize the meter. Thus any output r-f level that is desired may be set, and the calibrated attenuator then attenuates this reference level to any desired value. Another meter reads percentage of amplitude modulation directly. This percentage-of-modulation indication is independent of the attenuator setting.

A calibrator stage provides 1 and 5 Mc harmonics throughout the range of the signal generator. By connecting an earphone to the Xtal Cal Output connector (crystal calibrator output), the harmonics of the two calibration oscillators may be heard beating with the output frequency from the power amplifier. The frequency dial can be set exactly to some megacycle multiple by tuning for zero beat between the harmonic and power-amplifier output.

Q405 A crystal calibrator is used to:

ITEM 405a Check the signal-generator frequency at certain points.

ITEM 405b Adjust the oscillator frequency dial.

ITEM 405c Adjust the oscillator-output amplitude.

You answered that the calibrator in the signal generator is used to **check the signal-generator frequency at certain points.**

The calibrator provides harmonics of two basic frequencies, 1 and 5 Mc. These harmonics are spread throughout the range of the vhf signal generator. Whenever the signal generator produces an output frequency that is close to one of the harmonics of the calibrator, a difference tone is generated. This r-f difference tone is detected and supplied to the output jack. You may listen with a pair of earphones to this difference signal. When the difference signal goes to zero as you vary the oscillator frequency dial, you know that the oscillator frequency and the calibrator harmonic are extremely close together in frequency. This is the way the oscillator frequency dial is calibrated. Your answer was completely correct. Proceed to Item 406.

You answered that the calibrator in the signal generator is used to **adjust the oscillator frequency dial.** If by adjusting, you meant calibrating the frequency dial, this is close but not quite right. The oscillator frequency dial is certainly turned, but there is no provision for reading the frequency to a high accuracy directly on the frequency dial. This is a procedure that could be done but isn't. The calibrator is used with another type of output indication. Turn back to Item 405 and reread the material.

You answered that the calibrator is used to **adjust the amplitude of the output signal from the oscillator.**

The output of the power amplifier can indeed be adjusted by an output control, either by the output level control or by the output attenuator. However, the calibration for output level is done by observing the output meter for signal level or amplitude instead of the crystal calibrator. The crystal calibrator has to do with frequency instead of amplitude. Determine the exact use of the calibrator by rereading the material on Item 405.

The oscillator generates sine-wave signals in five frequency bands to cover the range from 10 to 420 Mc. A "pencil" triode tube is used in a Colpitts circuit which is tuned by a precision capacitor and five separate coils. The tuning capacitor is especially constructed for high stability and resetability. The five inductors (one for each band) are mounted on a revolving turret which is actuated by the frequency-range-selector knob. Refer to Figs. 4-4 and 3-3.

Stable heater voltage for the oscillator tube is obtained from the regulated dc supply. The oscillator tube has special filters on all supply buses to provide high attenuation at r-f energies to prevent r-f energy from leaking outside the instrument.

The tuning transformers or the oscillator coils have a loosely coupled secondary winding. The secondary winding couples some energy from the oscillator through a coaxial cable to the buffer stage. The buffer stage is a miniature triode connected as an untuned grounded-grid[1] amplifier which isolates the oscillator circuit from the effects of modulation in the power amplifier. The buffer also helps to reduce incidental frequency modulation to a very low value.

The third stage, the r-f power amplifier, amplifies the r-f energy from the buffer or intermediate stage. The power amplifier is another "pencil" triode, connected as a grounded-grid cathode-modulated amplifier. The plate circuit is tuned in the same manner as the oscillator, that is, with a split-stator capacitor and five coils on a revolving turret. The tuning capacitor for the oscillator and the amplifier are ganged mechanically for frequency tracking.

Q406 The oscillator has which triode connection (see Fig. 3-3)?

ITEM 406a A grounded plate.

ITEM 406b A grounded grid.

ITEM 406c A grounded cathode.

[1] "Grounded" here refers only to the signal and not necessarily power or bias. A typical oscillator has its cathode grounded both for the signal and power. A cathode follower, on the other hand, has its plate at signal ground but not power ground.

ITEM 406a

You answered that the oscillator has **a grounded-plate triode connection.**

This indeed would be possible and is sometimes done, but it is not the case here. A grounded plate, incidentally, means only that the plate is at r-f ground and obviously is not at dc ground for the B+ supply. What about a typical Colpitts oscillator? Read again the oscillator description on Item 406.

ITEM 406b

You answered that the oscillator has a triode in **a grounded-grid connection.**

You read the material all right, but you connected things wrong. The power amplifier does indeed utilize a triode in a grounded-grid connection, but what about the Colpitts oscillator? Reread the description of the oscillator section back on Item 406.

ITEM 406c

You answered that the triode oscillator has **a grounded-cathode connection.**

The grounded-grid connection is usually used for r-f amplifiers, and the grounded-cathode amplifier may be used for oscillators, such as the Hartley or Colpitts oscillator. The grounded-plate amplifier may be used with oscillators too, but in this particular circuit, the Colpitts oscillator is indeed a grounded-cathode amplifier. Go to Item 407.

ITEM 407

R-F OUTPUT

Refer to Fig. 4-4. An unusual attenuator is used to couple power from the r-f power amplifier to the output connector. This is a piston attenuator: At one end of the attenuator a one-turn loop picks up energy from the plate circuit of the r-f amplifier. The r-f power supplied to the attenuator then goes through a shielded connection to the attenuator, so that only the desired energy feeds through it. The one-turn-loop's distance from the output turret coil is varied to control the amount of energy transferred. The power supplied to the attenuator is monitored continuously by a small detector assembly. A capacitive lead picks off some energy from the r-f inductor loop which is detected and operates the "output volts" meter, calibrated in rms values.

Q407 The output level of the power amplifier is varied by:

ITEM 407**a** Shielded potentiometers arranged in series.

ITEM 407**b** A doubly shielded lossy coax.

ITEM 407**c** Varying the distance of a pickoff loop from the output tank circuit.

ITEM 407**a**

You answered that the r-f output level in the power amplifier is varied by **shielded potentiometers in series.**

The output level of signal generators can be controlled by the use of output potentiometers, one feeding into the input of a second potentiometer in tandem. Although this procedure works, it is somewhat difficult to get an accurate attenuation ratio, particularly at radio frequencies, because of capacity and inductive coupling through the various sections of the attenuator. Even though this sounds like a plausible answer, it certainly isn't the right one. See if you can find the correct answer back on Item 407.

ITEM 407**b**

You answered: **The r-f output level from the power amplifier is varied by a doubly shielded lossy coax.**

You certainly didn't see anything like this; you must have been imagining things. A lossy coax, as the term implies, would certainly attenuate an r-f output signal, but you would have the problem of controlling or adjusting the degree of attenuation. Putting a tap on the center connector of the coax is difficult when you try to make it continuously adjustable. I suggest you take a look at the material back on Item 407, and try again.

ITEM 407**c**

The output level of the power amplifier is varied by **changing the distance of the output pickup loop from a power-amplifier tank circuit.** This one was somewhat tricky; this is indeed the case. The output of the attenuator is simply a function of how close the pickup coil is to the output tank circuit. This utilizes the well-known inverse-square law; that is, field strength falls off as the square of the distance. You are correct and perceived the truth. Please proceed to Item 408.

The crystal calibrator consists of a 5-Mc oscillator, a 1-Mc oscillator, a detector, and a high-gain RC amplifier. Refer to Fig. 4-4. The 5-Mc section of the calibrator is a crystal-controlled electron-coupled oscillator. Both the plate and screen circuits are tuned to this frequency. The 1-Mc triode section of the oscillator is adjusted so that its fifth harmonic locks in with the 5-Mc signal from the crystal-controlled oscillator. This arrangement produces a source of accurate 1- and 5-Mc signals for calibration of the variable oscillator in the signal generator.

The output of the calibrator is coupled to a mixing diode. Some signal from the r-f power amplifier is inductively coupled to the same mixing diode. Harmonics from one of the two calibration oscillators are mixed with the r-f signal to produce beat-frequency signals at the output of the mixer diode. Only the harmonic that is closest to the r-f output signal will produce a beat, or frequency difference, that is within an a-f distance.

Beat-frequency audio signals from the mixing diode are filtered and then given several stages of gain. The output from the amplifier is coupled to a front panel connector, the crystal calibrator output jack. Headphones are plugged in at this connector to listen to the audio beat frequency. In use, the r-f control is turned until the beat frequency goes to zero. This means that at that particular point on the frequency dial, the r-f output frequency is exactly in agreement with one of the harmonics from the crystal oscillator. This ensures accurate dial calibration and an extremely accurate knowledge of output frequency.

Q408 The calibrator mixer diode is similar to what stage in a superheterodyne receiver when you are listening to a steady unmodulated signal with the BFO (beat-frequency oscillator) energized?

ITEM 408a   The second detector.

ITEM 408b   The mixer, or converter, stage.

ITEM 408c   The a-f amplifier.

ITEM 408a

You answered that the calibrator mixer diode is similar to **the second detector** in the receiver.

You had to put your thinking cap on for this one, but this is indeed the case. To receive continuous-wave signals at the second detector of a receiver, you must supply a beat-frequency signal. The combination of an intermediate frequency and a local-oscillator frequency is mixed or detected in the second detector; the output is an a-f signal. This is exactly the same case as the calibrator mixer diode. Your answer is correct. Carry on, maestro, with Item 409.

ITEM 408b

You answered: **The calibrator mixer diode is similar to the mixer, or converter, stage in a receiver.**

A local oscillator and r-f energy from the antenna are the input signals to the mixer, or converter, stage in the receiver. The output signal is, however, at the intermediate frequency and not at the audio frequency. Although the concept is similar, the output frequencies for the calibrator mixer and the mixer in a receiver are considerably different. Try again on Item 408.

ITEM 408c

You answered: **The calibrator mixer diode is similar to an a-f amplifier stage in a receiver.**

Part of the calibrator circuit does involve a high-gain a-f amplifier. However the amplifier does no changing or converting of types of signals; it accepts a weak a-f signal for presentation to the headphones. Thus the calibrator mixer diode and an a-f amplifier are quite dissimilar. See if you can do better than this on Item 408.

The modulator section serves several purposes: the generation of a-f signals at 400 and 1000 cps for internal sine-wave modulation of the r-f generator, the amplification of the signals externally applied to modulate the power amplifier, and the control of the level of power of the r-f power amplifier by varying its bias.

Refer to Fig. 4-4. The modulator oscillator is a Wien-bridge oscillator which generates the 400- and 1000-cps sine waves. This circuit consists of two RC-coupled amplifier stages with positive feedback, or regeneration, coming through a frequency-selective network and negative feedback to stabilize the level of oscillation.

When pulse modulation is desired from externally supplied pulses, the peak amplitude of the modulating pulses must be limited; the input modulating pulses are fed directly to the grid of the limiting amplifier. The limiting action is such that somewhat more than 100 percent modulation of the output signal can be achieved. Signals corresponding to less than 100 percent modulation pass through the filter unchanged.

The level of sine-wave modulation applied to the power amplifier is measured with a rather interesting circuit. The circuit consists of a bridge diode-triode rectifier. With no modulation signal applied to the power amplifier, the steady-state potential is coupled to the grid of both triode tubes in the modulation-monitoring circuit. Under this condition, equal signals are applied to the two triode grids, the bridge is balanced, and the meter reads zero. When a modulation signal is rectified, the peak value of the rectified r-f voltage is applied to a one-triode leg in the bridge, unbalancing the bridge and causing the meter to read upscale. The triode in the other leg of the bridge is unaffected by the modulation signal because of its time constant. Thus the modulation-measuring circuit indicates any modulation of the r-f output signal between 0 and 100 percent within 10 percent accuracy.

Q409 Which types of modulation are available in this signal generator?

ITEM 409a Internal sine-wave modulation, 400 and 1000 cps.

ITEM 409b No modulation, or continuous wave.

ITEM 409c All the other answers.

ITEM 409d External modulation, including pulse and sine-wave.

ITEM 409a

You answered that **internal sine-wave modulation is available in this vhf signal generator.** You are quite correct, but the capability of the signal generator goes farther than this.   In addition to internally generated 400- and 1000-cps sine-wave modulation, the generator is capable of being modulated by external signals.   Turn back to Item 409 and select the correct answer.

ITEM 409b

You answered that **the vhf signal generator has the capability of producing a continuous wave, or unmodulated r-f signal.**

This is indeed the case, even though it wasn't clearly stated.   In the picture for this vhf signal generator, you may have noted that the modulation switch showed an OFF position in which case the output would be a continuous wave.   However, since you noted the modulation switch, you should have noted the other positions.   The signal generator also is capable of producing various modulated outputs.   Reread the material on Item 409 and pick the right answer.

ITEM 409c

You answered: **The vhf signal generator has all these types of modulation: internal sine-wave modulation, external sine- or square-wave or pulse modulation, and no modulation at all (CW).**

Correct and right on the ball.   Please proceed to Item 410.

ITEM 409d

You answered that **the vhf signal generator has the modulation capability for external sine-wave and pulse modulation.**

This is quite the case, but there is more to it than this.   The signal generator can be modulated by external signals, but it also can be modulated by internal signals or not at all.   As such, try a different answer on Item 409.

FIGURE 4-5 Photograph of the DuMont 404B standard-pulse generator.

ITEM 410

**THE DUMONT
404B PULSE
GENERATOR**

Refer to Fig. 4-5, which shows a picture of the DuMont 404B pulse generator. Study the picture and examine the front panel controls.

The 404B is a general-purpose pulse generator which provides high-quality pulses at a useful power level for most purposes. This instrument generates pulses ranging in widths from 0.05 to 100 μsec at a repetition rate that varies from 10 to 250,000 pps (pulses per second). Pulse width is accurately calibrated, and the circuitry is stabilized to minimize pulse jitter.

An automatic overload circuit limits the danger of damaging the instrument regardless of the pulse width and repetition rate setting. The product of the pulse width and repetition rate is automatically limited to a duty-cycle limit of 10 percent.

There is an output trigger available to trigger external equipment either before or after the pulse from the 404B starts. There is a precision ladder attenuator which accurately controls the output pulse amplitude in $\frac{1}{2}$-db increments, ranging from 0- to 59.5-db total attenuation. The output pulse may be turned off optionally and yet have the trigger output pulse operative so that external equipment may be triggered.

Q410 Referring to the diagram shown right, let's check on your background knowledge of pulse terminology. What directly indicates the repetition rate in pulses per second?

ITEM 410a B.

ITEM 410b $1/B$.

ITEM 410c $1/A$.

ITEM 410d A.

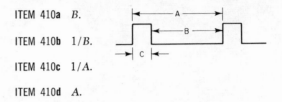

ITEM 410a

You answered that **letter B directly indicates the pulse repetition rate.**

Letter B measures from the trailing edge of one pulse to the leading edge of the next pulse and measures the interpulse spacing, or the pulse OFF time. This is not at all directly related to the repetition rate. Return to Item 410 and try again.

ITEM 410b

You answered that **letter B inversely, or $1/B$, measures the pulse repetition rate.**

Letter B measures from the trailing edge of one pulse to the leading edge of the next pulse. This gives you the total OFF time, or interpulse interval. This has nothing to do at all with the pulse repetition rate. You can find a better answer than this on Item 410.

ITEM 410c

You answered that **letter A inversely, or $1/A$, measures the pulse repetition in pulses per second.**

You were quite correct. None of the other answers do directly measure repetition rate or frequency. The closest was letter A, which gave the period T, or time between pulses. The reciprocal, or inverse, of the period T will give the pulse repetition rate. Go on to Item 411.

ITEM 410d

You answered: **Letter A indicates pulse repetition rate.**

This time interval is measured from the leading edge of the first pulse to the leading edge of the second pulse and gives the time interval, or period T, between successive pulses. This is inversely related to the frequency of the pulses. That is, $1/T$ equals the repetition frequency. Since you are so close to being correct, proceed to Item 410c.

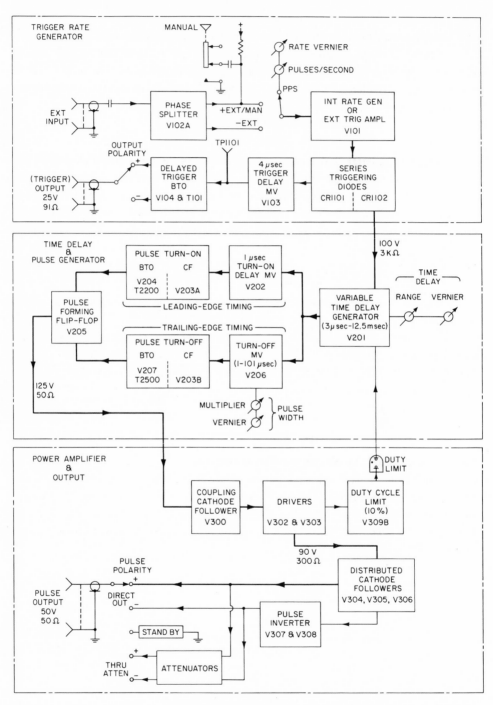

FIGURE 4-6 Block diagram of the DuMont 404B standard-pulse generator.

Refer to Fig. 4-6, the simplified block diagram for the pulse generator. The pulse generator can be divided into four basic sections or blocks: the trigger rate generator, time-delay and pulse generator, pulse power amplifier and output, and power supplies. The circuit description that follows will relate directly to the functional block diagram. For further details, refer to the circuit diagrams at the back of the equipment manual for the 404B pulse generator.

For trigger operation, refer to Fig. 4-7, the timing diagram for the delayed trigger output. The purpose of the trigger circuit is to produce a reference, or starting trigger, at time T_0' for subsequent starting of external equipment. This trigger has a delay of approximately 4 μsec with respect to the initial time T_0.

The internal rate generator, tube V101, is a free-running multivibrator. The waveform developed at the plate is differentiated, resulting in waveform $1B$.

The leading edge of waveform $1B$ is coupled through a series-triggering diode CR1101 to the delayed-trigger multivibrator V103 which generates waveforms $1C$ and $1D$. Waveform $1D$ has a fixed duration of approximately 4 μsec and is available at test point TP1101. The delayed output from V103 is used to initiate the delayed-trigger blocking oscillator V104. The output waveform $1E$ is available at the trigger output, and either the positive or negative waveform may be selected by the output polarity switch. When the pulses-per-second switch is set to external or to external manual, the multivibrator tube functions as a two-stage amplifier. Thus external triggers are amplified and shaped before they trigger the pulse generator in the next stage.

The pulse generator can be pulsed manually at a repetition rate determined by how fast the operator punches the manual trigger button. Depressing this push button provides a trigger signal for V101. From this point on, the pulse generator proceeds through the normal pulse-generating cycle.

Q411 The trigger output from the rate generator is:

ITEM 411a   Square waves.

ITEM 411b   Sine waves.

ITEM 411c   A series of spikes.

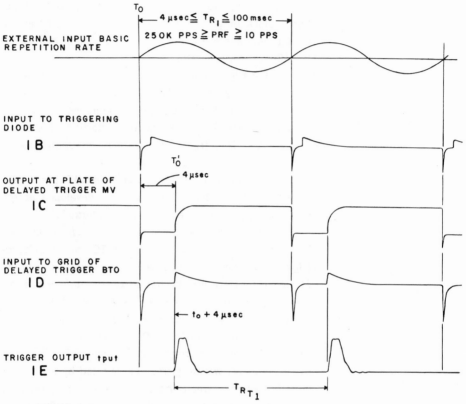

T_0
$4\,\mu sec \leqq T_{R_I} \leqq 100\,msec$
$250K\ PPS \geqq PRF \geqq 10\ PPS$

EXTERNAL INPUT BASIC
REPETITION RATE

INPUT TO TRIGGERING
DIODE
I B

T_0'

$4\,\mu sec$

OUTPUT AT PLATE OF
DELAYED TRIGGER MV
I C

INPUT TO GRID OF
DELAYED TRIGGER BTO
I D

$t_0 + 4\,\mu sec$

TRIGGER OUTPUT tput
I E

$T_{R_{T_1}}$

LEGEND:

t_0 = Initiation of Internal Rate Generator or External Trigger Amplifier

T_{R1} = Period of Internal Rate Generator:
100 milliseconds $\geqq T_{R1} \geqq 4$ microseconds
or the repetition rate is from
10 pps to 250 K pps

T_{RT1} = Period of Delayed Trigger Generator:
100 milliseconds $\geqq T_{RT1} > 3$ microseconds:
when $4\ \mu sec > T_{RT1}$, then $T_{RT2} = 2T_{RT1}$

T_W = Period of Pulse Width

T_D = Period of Time Delay
Waveforms are keyed to the over-all schematics.

FIGURE 4-7 Delayed-trigger output-timing diagram.

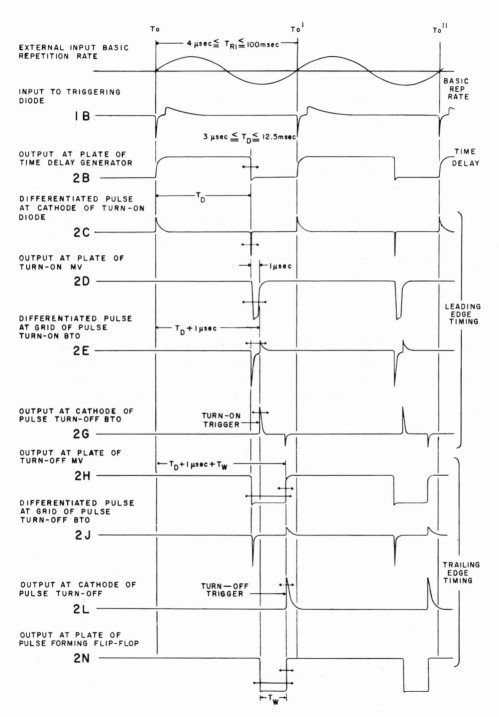

FIGURE 4-8 Basic pulse-timing diagram.

ITEM 411a

You answered: **The output from the trigger generator is a series of square waves.**

A multivibrator producing a rectangular waveform is in the signal flow path leading to the trigger output. However the multivibrator output is differentiated and triggers a blocking oscillator which produces something other than square waves at the trigger output. Return to Item 411 and select a different answer.

ITEM 411b

You answered: **The output from the trigger generator is a series of sine waves.**

Sine waves by themselves do not make very good triggers, because the time at which the voltage reaches a maximum or a minimum is so uncertain. Usually a sine wave has to be shaped and differentiated before it is useful for triggering circuits. The manufacturer had this disadvantage of sine waves in mind; thus the trigger output definitely is not a series of sine waves. Return to Item 411 and pick a different answer.

ITEM 411c

You answered: **The trigger output from the rate generator is a series of spikes.**

Sine waves may be fed into the trigger generator, but they are certainly not part of the output. Even square waves or rectangular waves have to be differentiated to produce a series of spikes which will produce accurate trigger waveforms. Thus you were correct and right on the ball in selecting this answer. Proceed please, maestro, to Item 412.

Refer to the block diagram Fig. 4-6 and to Fig. 4-8, the basic timing diagram.

The purpose of the time-delay circuit is to produce a trigger which occurs 2 μsec to more than 12 msec after time T_0. This permits the start of the input pulse to be advanced a maximum of 2 μsec or delayed a maximum of 12.5 msec with respect to the delayed output trigger. This is done in three overlapping ranges.

The waveform $1B$ from the triggering diodes is coupled through a series diode CR1102 to the variable-time-delay generator V201 which generates waveform line $2B$. The time delay is adjustable by the front panel controls, the time-delay vernier and range controls. The output waveform $2B$ is differentiated to produce waveform $2C$, which is used to trigger both the turn-on multivibrator V202 and a turn-off multivibrator V206. These outputs, as the names suggest, turn on and off the pulse-forming flip-flop to control output pulse width.

The waveform $2C$ is applied through a diode to the turn-on multivibrator V202. This stage is triggered and produces waveform $2D$, which is differentiated and results in waveform $2E$. The waveform from the pulse turn-on blocking oscillator yields waveform line $2G$. The sharp leading edge of waveform $2G$ is applied to turn on the normally nonconducting section of the pulse-forming flip-flop V205. Simultaneously, the turn-off multivibrator V206 has also been triggered. The duration of the waveform $2H$ from this multivibrator is controlled from the front panel controls, the pulse-width multiplier, and the microsecond vernier controls. Thus the timing of the turn-off signal is determined by the trailing edge of the waveform $2H$. This is differentiated to produce waveform $2J$ which is in turn applied to the grid of the pulse turn-off blocking oscillator yielding waveforms $2K$ and $2L$. Waveform $2L$ is applied to the flip-flop to turn off the main pulse. At this time, the action of the timing and initial pulse-generation phases is complete, with the net result consisting of a negative pulse waveform $2N$ with fast transitions and controlled duration and position.

Q412 The pulse width is determined by:

ITEM 412a The ON time of the pulse-forming flip-flop.

ITEM 412b The turn-on multivibrator.

ITEM 412c The turn-off multivibrator.

ITEM 412d The variable-time-delay generator.

You answered: **The pulse width is determined by the ᴏɴ time of the pulse-forming flip-flop.**

You were quite correct. The variable-time-delay generator initiated both the turn-on and the turn-off multivibrators. Clipped pulses from these two multivibrators determine the start and stop times for the pulse-forming flip-flop. Continue with Item 413.

ITEM 412b

You answered: **The pulse width is determined by the turn-on multivibrator.**

The turn-on multivibrator with its leading edge determines the time at which the output pulse does indeed turn on. However there is more to a pulse than just the time at which it turns on. You are missing half the story. Turn again to Item 412 and discover the other half of the story.

ITEM 412c

You answered: **The pulse width is determined by the turn-off multivibrator.**

The turn-off multivibrator determines the times at which the output pulse is stopped. Thus the turn-off multivibrator partially determines pulse width, but you are missing half the story. Return to Item 412 and discover the rest of the story.

ITEM 412d

You answered that the **variable-time-delay generator determines the pulse width.**

The variable-time-delay generator merely determines the delay before the turn-on and turn-off multivibrators start. Thus the variable-time-delay generator has nothing to do with determining the pulse width of the output pulse; it merely determines the start-time delay. Having gained this much more knowledge about how the circuit works, return to Item 412 and pick the right answer.

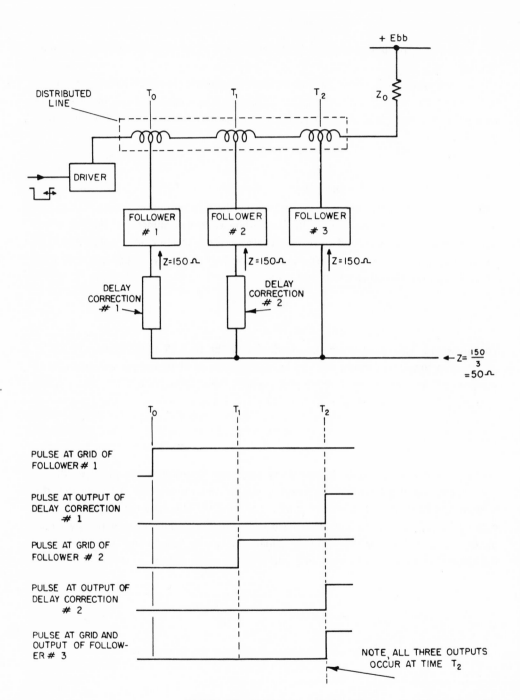

FIGURE 4-9 Distributed cathode followers, simplified schematic.

Refer to Fig. 4-9. The coupling cathode follower receives waveform $3A$ from the main pulse generator. A neon bulb E3001 is shunted across this network and permits the dc level of the waveform to vary with the setting of the bias adjustment without attenuation. The proper dc level of the waveform $3A$ is picked off the arm of the bias-adjusting potentiometer and is applied to the grid of the cathode follower V300. This output waveform is applied to the drivers V302 and V303.

The driver stage consists of a pair of pentodes with the control grids clamped to approximately zero bias through the cathode-follower driver. When the input waveform appears at the control grids, the plate current is abruptly cut off, resulting in a large positive waveform at the plates. The driver plate load consists of the input end of a lumped constant transmission line terminated in its characteristic impedance of 300 ohms. This line serves to separate the input capacitance from the drive plates, keeping rise time short and making possible the use of three parallel stages.

Each of the grids of the distributed output cathode followers is connected to a different point on the delay line in sequence. The grid tapping is spaced along the line so that the signal at each grid arrives at a time slightly later than that of the preceding grid. Correction for this time delay is made by short lengths of coax. The first tube V304 on the delay line receives its signal first since it has the longest delay correction in its cathode. The second tube V305 has only one-half of the input delay correction of V304 and has half of the output delay correction in its cathode. Thus when all three output signals meet at a common point, all three signals have been delayed the same amount and are additive.

Q413 If the rise time T_R† is 15 nsec maximum in the output followers, what is the effective circuit capacitance:

ITEM 413a   750 pf.

ITEM 413b   140 pf.

ITEM 413c   300 pf.

† Hint: Use the rise-time equation $T_R = 2.2RC$ where $R =$ resistance in ohms, $C =$ capacity in farads, and $T_R =$ time in seconds. Pf is the abbreviation for picofarad, which is a "micromicrofarad" and equals 10^{-12} fd.

ITEM 413a

You answered: **If the rise time T_R is 15 nsec maximum, then the effective circuit capacitance is 750 pf.**

Let's take a look at this one. To solve this equation you have to draw on your general circuit knowledge that the rise time T_R is the product of the effective circuit resistance and capacitance, or $T_R = 2.2RC$. When you solved this equation for capacitance, it appears that you forgot to divide appropriately. Recheck your algebra and arithmetic on this, and pick a different answer back on Item 413.

ITEM 413b

You answered: **With a rise time of 15 nsec maximum, the effective circuit capacitance is 140 pf.**

You figured quite correctly. You had to rely on your background knowledge to know that the rise time is the product of 2.2 × the effective circuit capacitance and resistance. When three cathode followers are in parallel, their output impedance of 150 ohms is effectively in parallel, resulting in the nominal output of 50 ohms. Solving the rise-time equation for the capacitance does indeed produce this answer. You are correct. Proceed to Item 414.

ITEM 413c

You answered: **If the rise time T_R is 15 nsec maximum, the effective circuit capacitance is 300 pf.**

First, let's see what the output impedance is. The output impedance of each cathode follower is 150 ohms. When the three of them are in parallel, the effective output impedance is only 50 ohms. Thus you have to plug 50 ohms into the rise-time equation which is $T_R = C_{eff} \times R_{eff} \times 2.2$. Solving this equation for the capacitance produces a result that is different from the numerical answer that you got. You slipped a factor somewhere, didn't you? Figure your arithmetic again, and try another answer on Item 413.

ITEM 414

PULSE OUTPUT

Either positive- or negative-polarity output pulses may be selected at the output. The pulse inverter is used to change polarity.

Some circuits in a pulse generator operate with very high peak currents, approaching 2 amp. Therefore it becomes necessary to limit the duty cycle[1] to a point where the average power dissipation does not exceed safe component ratings. A positive safety feature has been incorporated to prevent operating beyond these ratings. When the duty cycle reaches approximately 10 percent, relay K3001 operates. This applies a negative voltage to the duty limit indicator which then operates the duty limit lamp on the front panel. This light flashes, indicating that the duty limit has been exceeded. When the pulses are reduced, the relay releases allowing normal operating to resume. If the lamp keeps flashing, the average power input to the output stage is automatically reduced to a safe value.

A series of five 10-db attenuator steps are arranged in ladder configuration so that any attenuation up to 50 db may be used. Six additional push buttons provide attenuation in smaller steps, 0.5 to 9.5 db. The maximum possible attenuation is 59.5 db. An advantage of this step system is that a true impedance match exists under any possible combination of attenuator settings, thereby minimizing output pulse waveform distortion. The output impedance remains 50 ohms.

Q414 Assume that the output stage can produce peak currents to 2 amp and that the duty cycle (pulse ON time per period) is limited to a maximum of 10 percent. What is the maximum peak pulse[2] power?

ITEM 414a   2 watts peak power.

ITEM 414b   You don't know, or have no idea.

ITEM 414c   200 watts peak power.

ITEM 414d   20 watts peak power.

---

[1] Duty cycle is the percentage of time the pulse is on, pulse width PW per period P.

[2] Peak, or pulse, power is computed by using Ohm's law with peak current and the output resistance load.

ITEM 414a

You answered that the **peak power was 2 watts.**

The peak current was given as 2 amp, and the duty cycle (pulse ON time per period) as 10 percent. You had to dig for information that the load, or output, resistance was 50 ohms. What you have computed, however, is the average power, not the peak power. You computed average power using an average current figure of 10 percent of the peak current, or 0.2 amp. You went too far in your eagerness, and bit on the irrelevant information of duty cycle. Many times in a real engineering situation, you will have more information than needed. Return to Item 414.

ITEM 414b

You answered that **you didn't know, or had no idea,** what the pulse, or peak, power was. You are to be congratulated for being honest. The maximum, or peak, current was given at 2 amp. The duty cycle was assumed to be 10 percent, but this is irrelevant information in computing the peak power. (It is needed in computing average pulse power.) Power, whether peak or average, is determined from the product of current squared and resistance. That is, $P_{\text{peak}} = I_{\text{peak}}^2 R_{\text{output}}$.

Apply this equation now in the questions in Item 414.

ITEM 414c

You answered that the **peak power in the pulse was 200 watts.**

Peak current has been given as 2 amp. To compute average power, you would indeed take the duty cycle (pulse ON time per period) into account. To figure the peak power, all you needed, in addition to peak current, was to remember that the load impedance was 50 ohms. You applied Ohm's law correctly in coming up with this answer. Go to Item 415.

ITEM 414d

You answered that the **peak power was 20 watts.**

The peak current was given as 2 amp, and the duty cycle (pulse ON time per period) was 10 percent. You had to read back for the information that the load, or output, resistance was 50 ohms. What you have computed, however, is the average power, not the peak power. You computed average power by using the dc power as if the pulse of 2 amp were flowing continuously into a 50-ohm load and then taking a 10 percent fraction of this. You went too far in your eagerness, and bit on the unnecessary information of duty cycle. Many times in real situations, you will find that you have more information than needed to solve the problem. Turn back to Item 414.

Noise generators are useful for the reason that they can produce a signal with a known amplitude and a known but relatively wide bandwidth. Any portion or slice out of this band has the same amount of energy as any other segment; the voltages for any two portions will be equal. This type of signal is called "random," or "white," noise and has a "normal," or gaussian, distribution. Note that the noise energy is directly related to the total bandwidth and that the noise voltage accordingly is proportional to the square root of the bandwidth.

Noise in an electron tube, such as a diode or pentode, usually is undesirable. This inherent noisy property of electron tubes is used to an advantage in two types of diode noise generators, vacuum and gaseous. In a vacuum diode with a hot cathode emitting electrons, the electron flow is limited by the cathode temperature, not by space charge. Since electrons leaving the cathode actually represent tiny current impulses at random, there is a certain amount of variation, or noise, in the diode current. This noise is a predictable quantity depending upon the total current and controlled by the cathode temperature.

In a gas diode used as a noise generator, the noise comes from the ionization process as electrons are stripped away from the gas molecules colliding in a potential field. The applied voltage determines the molecules' velocity and number of collisions. The noise output is a function of the particular gas used.

Impulse generators are also used to produce noise. A single, narrow pulse (a "spike") generates frequency components in a wide band. By using only frequencies far above the basic pulse repetition rate, noise is obtained which is close to that of white noise in frequency and randomness. Such a noise source is a mercury-wetted relay operating at a 60-cps rate. With suitable high-pass filters, this generates usable noise from the high audio frequencies well into the gigacycle range.

But that's enough of this chapter on signal generators. Let's see how you do on the Quiz #4, Item 416.

1 With an output meter and calibrated attenuator on a signal generator, the voltage or power indication will be accurate for any output power level or resistance. (True/False) *(H)*

2 An audio generator designed for a 600-ohm load has a 600-ohm source impedance. (True/False) *(J)*

3 The output impedance of a pulse generator typically is the same as its rated load impedance. (True/False) *(G)*

4 Referring to Fig. 4-2 for the HP 200CD oscillator, how often should resistor R_{11} be adjusted: (a) when R_{T1} or R_{T2} is replaced, (b) upon arrival of the set from the factory, (c) each time the range is changed. *(B)*

5 The amplifiers in the HP 200CD wide-range oscillator achieve their wide frequency coverage through: (a) a series of coils switched one at a time appropriately, (b) being high-fidelity, wide-bandwidth audio amplifiers, (c) a series of RC networks switched in appropriately. *(I)*

6 The output frequency of the HP 608D vhf signal generator can be set only to within ±0.5 percent, which is the accuracy of setting the frequency dial. (True/False) *(D)*

7 What is the frequency coverage of the HP 608D vhf signal generator: (a) 10–420 Mc, (b) 30–300 Mc, (c) 300–3000 Mc, (d) 30–450 Mc. *(F)*

8 The DuMont 404B pulse generator can be triggered: (a) internally, (b) externally, (c) manually. *(A)*

9 How does the DuMont 404B pulse generator achieve its high-power output pulses: (a) use of series and shunt peaking coils, (b) push-pull high-power triodes with a common load, (c) three distributed cathode followers in parallel, (d) all of these. *(C)*

10 Which of the following may be used as a noise generator: (a) hot vacuum diode, (b) gas diode, (c) sine-wave oscillator, (d) mercury switch. *(E)*

A All these.

B a. This is a screwdriver setting.

C c.

D False. Also use the calibrator.

E a, b, and d. c is not usually used this way.

F a.

G True, to avoid reflected or spurious signals.

H False, this depends on the terminating or load resistance.

I b. It's really this simple.

J False, in general; true for pulse generators.

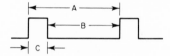

Feel like tackling the next chapter? Better take a break first. But good luck when you do!

CHAPTER FIVE   BASIC OSCILLOSCOPES 11 QUESTIONS

ITEM 501

INTRODUCTION

We are going to approach the subject of the oscilloscope by considering an electromechanical device that is very similar, the oscillograph. See Fig. 5-1 on the next page. A moving piece of paper records the time history of a variable that is being monitored by a meter; the variations in the meter reading are recorded on the paper as the paper strip flows uniformly under the pen. Essentially this device operates in two dimensions: First, the paper is moving along uniformly under the pen and second, a very lightweight pen attached to the meter needle moves across the paper.

Although the paper runs at a constant speed, it is usually very convenient to be able to change speeds. A number of paper speeds, typically 5 to 10, are available through a gearbox to change the reduction ratio from the output shaft of a constant-speed motor. To change ranges on the recording meter, one merely has to change the range resistor. The pen on the meter may actually "write" with electricity, heat, or light on especially prepared papers.

There are obvious speed limitations in this mechanical oscillograph. The paper can move only so fast and then it is subject to tearing and slipping. Likewise, although the meter needle can move much faster than the paper, it too has a frequency limitation above which it will be unable to respond.

Q501 What does an oscillograph plot?

ITEM 501a It plots the time history of one variable or quantity as a function of time.

ITEM 501b It plots the time course of two variables or quantities that vary with time.

ITEM 501c It plots two variables or quantities versus each other that are independent of time.

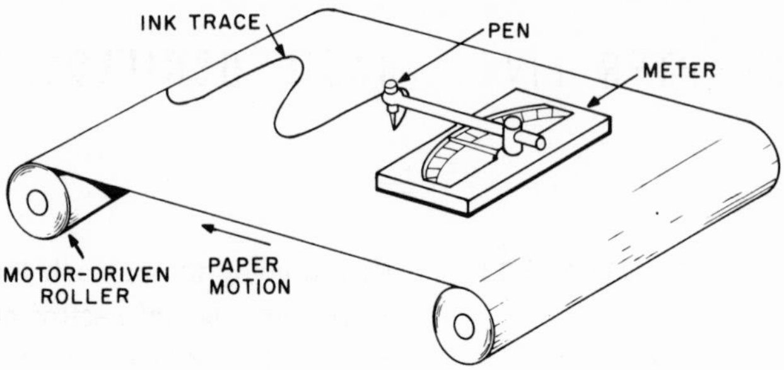

FIGURE 5-1 Basic oscillograph mechanism.

INK TRACE

PEN

METER

MOTOR-DRIVEN ROLLER

PAPER MOTION

ITEM 501a

You answered that the **oscillograph typically plots the history of one variable or quantity as a function of time.**

The dimension or direction in which the paper is moving uniformly corresponds to a linearly changing time variable. When another variable, such as that recorded by a moving pen, writes on the moving paper, what the pen writes is indeed the time history, the time course or history of the dependent variable. "The moving finger writes and having writ moves on." Shades of Omar Khayyám. But since you have written the correct answer in this case, move on to Item 502.

ITEM 501b

You answered that an **oscillograph typically plots the time course of two variables or quantities that vary with time.**

Time itself is usually considered to be the independent variable, and the other variable is the dependent variable which is plotted against time so that its variations may be observed. This is true only because the paper usually moves at a constant uniform rate, although this rate may be changed in steps. Thus with one pen, only one dependent variable can be plotted against time, and the time course or variation of just one variable versus time can be obtained. To plot two dependent variables against time would take a three-dimensional pen, or two pens, to plot the time history. Turn to Item 501.

ITEM 501c

You answered that an **oscillograph typically plots two variables or quantities versus each other that are independent of time.**

This is partially true. An oscillograph typically plots two independent variables against each other; one of the variables is almost always time, and it is linearly varying or changing at a constant rate. Thus a better paraphrase would be that although indeed two variables are plotted against one another, one typically is a dependent variable plotted against the independent variable, time. You certainly had close to the right idea. Turn to Item 501a.

ITEM 502

**CATHODE-RAY-
TUBE (CRT)
FUNDAMENTALS**

A CRT basically is an electronic version of the oscillo-graph that we have just discussed. Instead of using a paper moving at a uniform speed and a pen to write on the paper, we use an electron beam to perform both functions. The electron beam is caused to move in one direction linearly and is moved as a dependent variable in a direction at right angles (vertically usually). The beam writes the result of these two variables so that it effectively traces the time course, or the history, of the variable or quantity plotted against time. Obviously the electron beam can only go so far, and then it hits the side of the cathode-ray tube. When this happens, the beam is rapidly deflected to the start of the trace and proceeds to sweep repetitively. The electron beam has negligible inertia and has no appreciable lag until the beam is forced to move at an appreciable fraction of the speed of light itself.

CRTs are used in many places to inspect or display waveforms; this is another way of stating that the oscilloscope presents the history of signals. Typical uses are in test oscilloscopes (inspect waveforms), TV, and radar.

Refer to Fig. 5-2 which shows a sectional view of a CRT. The left-hand section comprises what is called the "electron gun." An electron gun, as the name implies, generates a pencil-thin electron beam. A heated tungsten wire heats the cathode to a high temperature. The rare earth oxide "cathode" becomes sufficiently hot and emits electrons. The electrons are repelled, or repulsed, by the negative intensity grid, with the result that only a few electrons are able to leave the cathode and whiz through the hole in the solid intensity grid. The diverging beam of electrons coming through the intensity grid is focused electrostatically by a similarly structured electrode. The focusing electrode is positive with respect to the cathode, so that the electrons are attracted and thereby focused into a fine beam after they leave the focusing electrode.

ITEM 502A

The thin beam of electrons then enters the deflection system. The deflection system may be magnetic, such

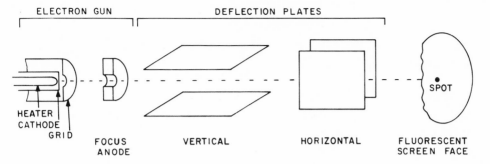

ELECTRON GUN   DEFLECTION PLATES

HEATER
CATHODE
GRID

FOCUS
ANODE

VERTICAL

HORIZONTAL

SPOT

FLUORESCENT
SCREEN FACE

FIGURE 5-2   Cross-sectional view of a cathode-ray tube.

as a pair of coils placed at right angles to this section of the tube. Here we have shown an electrostatic deflection system: two pairs of plates that straddle the beam. These pairs of plates are at right angles to each other, so that the effective motion of the electron beam is in two different dimensions. The pair of electrodes, or set of flat plates, above and below the electron beam produces vertical deflection. When the top plate is positive with respect to the bottom plate, the electrons are attracted to it and, consequently, strike the screen at a higher spot than they otherwise would. When the back electrode on the right side is positive, it pulls electrodes to the right; consequently, the electron beam is deflected in that direction.

Finally, the electrons strike the phosphorescent screen with energy sufficient enough to create visible light. The screen usually has a very thin and transparent metallic coating on it to minimize reflections and spot halos. The yoke of the tube may have an internal graphite coating, Aquadag, charged to a high positive potential with respect to the cathode of the tube, so that the electrons are accelerated to a high velocity before they strike the screen. The phosphorescent material used in the screen may have different colors, varying from blue to green typically. The spot light persistence also varies.

Q502 Which of the following are parts of a CRT?

ITEM 502a   The electron gun, the phosphorescent screen, and the power supply.

ITEM 502**b**   The electron gun, deflection plates, and sweep amplifier.

ITEM 502**c**   The electron gun, deflection system, and phosphorescent screen.

ITEM 502a

You answered that the parts of a CRT are **the electron gun, the phosphorescent screen and the power supply.**

Obviously, the electron gun and phosphorescent screen are essential parts of a cathode-ray tube. But when you included the power supply, you went one step too far. The power supply is a section of an oscilloscope that is outside the tube envelope of the CRT. In addition you are yet missing one essential part of the CRT. Try another answer on Item 502A.

ITEM 502b

You answered: **The parts of a CRT are the electron gun, deflection plates, and the sweep amplifier.**

Essential parts of a cathode-ray tube are indeed the electron gun and the deflection plates. But when you included the sweep amplifier, you included part of a typical oscilloscope that is outside the glass envelope of the cathode-ray tube. In addition you omitted one essential part of a CRT. Turn back to Item 502A.

ITEM 502c

You answered that the parts of a cathode-ray tube are **the electron gun, deflection system, and phosphorescent screen.**

The essential parts of a cathode-ray tube are indeed the electron gun, deflection system, and phosphorescent screen. Above and beyond this, it takes a power supply, a sweep amplifier, and usually vertical and horizontal amplifiers to round out the complement of an oscilloscope. But you picked the correct answer as we asked for only the essential parts of a CRT, not a complete oscilloscope. Proceed to Item 503.

**ELECTRON-BEAM
DEFLECTION**

Let's consider now in detail how the electron beam is deflected and modulated. There are two sets of deflection plates, vertical (VDP) and horizontal (HDP). There are three axes in the CRT, as shown in the diagram, Fig. 5-3, below. An X axis involves moving the beam to the right; the beam is deflected in this direction when a positive voltage is supplied to the plate on the edge farthest from the reader. The Y axis is usually considered to be the vertical direction; the electron beam is deflected in this direction when a positive voltage is applied to the top plate. The Z axis is in line with the motion of the electrons in the beam; a signal applied in this direction affects the speed with which the electrons strike the phosphorescent screen. Consequently the modulation signal in the Z axis affects the intensity of the spot of light.

Typically a repetitive sawtooth or linearly varying waveform is applied to the X axis to sweep the spot smoothly from left to right across the tube. An independent signal is applied to the Y axis, so that as the beam moves uniformly to the right, the beam moves up and down vertically to trace the history of the electric signal. The Z axis typically is left at a constant intensity level while the beam is moving uniformly to the right, but when the beam snaps to the left, a negative blanking voltage is applied to the Z axis to keep the electrons from hitting the screen. Thus the oscilloscope really is an electrical analog of the oscillograph.

FIGURE 5-3
Deflection of the
CRT beam.

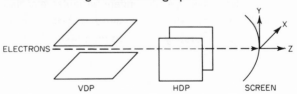

ELECTRONS

VDP   HDP   SCREEN

Q503 How many signals can be applied to an oscilloscope?

ITEM 503a   Three.

ITEM 503b   Two.

ITEM 503c   One.

ITEM 503a

You answered: **The number of signals that may be applied independently to an oscilloscope is three.**

As we have discussed, there are three mutually perpendicular axes in a CRT. Any signal may indeed be applied independently of the other signals to each axis. Thus you may have a sweep voltage applied to the horizontal plates, an unknown signal applied to the vertical deflection plates, and a modulation signal applied (possibly time markers) to the Z axis to modulate the intensity of the spot as it writes. You are correct and very much on the ball.   Proceed, please, to Item 504.

ITEM 503b

You answered that **two** signals might be applied independently to an oscilloscope.

As discussed, an oscilloscope might be thought of as consisting of three independent axes of which the Z axis typically is left constant.   Then two independent signals may be applied, such as a sweep to the horizontal deflection plates and an unknown signal to the vertical deflection plates.   Moreover, there is that third axis, the Z axis, which may be intensity modulated.   A third signal could be applied to it, don't you think?   Try another answer on Item 503.

ITEM 503c

You answered that **one** independent signal could be applied to an oscilloscope.

One signal by itself can be applied to an oscilloscope—this is done upon occasion when it is desired to use the oscilloscope as a voltmeter.   Simply measure the deflection of the spot on the screen, compare this with a calibrated base, and measure the voltage of the applied signal.   Typically, however, an oscilloscope is operated with more than one independently applied signal to it.   Perhaps the discussion about independent and dependent variables may have misled you.   The variables are applied independently in the sense that they may be applied to the deflection plates and Z axis separately.   Turn to Item 503.

PATTERN
GENERATION

Let's consider briefly how different patterns are generated on a CRT. Refer to the diagram below which shows a view facing the screen, looking at the writing end of the electron beam. Let's take a sawtooth signal and apply it to the horizontal deflection plates, shown as lines on the sides of the screen. The sawtooth is a voltage waveform in which the voltage is changing at a linear, or uniform, rate. This voltage, as it grows more positive, will pull the spot from the left side of the CRT face at a uniform rate to the right side of the tube. When the voltage abruptly returns to negative minimum, the spot will snap back instantly and later resume its slow uniform rise. We would see a horizontal line (shown at left).

If we applied the same voltage to the vertical deflection plates (represented by short lines at the top and bottom of the screen), we would find a spot moving up and down in the center of the screen at a uniform rate. The spot would move slowly and uniformly from the bottom to the top of the tube and then would snap back almost instantly to the bottom of the tube to resume its slow upward journey. A vertical line results.

The Z-axis voltage, in this case, is left constant except for the period when the spot is snapping from its positive peak to its negative peak. During this period of time, a large blanking pulse may be applied to the intensity grid of the electron gun to stop the electrons from leaving the hole in the intensity grid. The intensity modulation of the Z axis may or may not be necessary since when the spot moves very fast, it does not have time to excite a large number of phosphor molecules in the screen; consequently, the retrace is barely visible even without intensity blanking.

Q504 Which of the following waveforms represents the pattern that appears when a sine wave is applied on the horizontal deflection plates? No signal is applied to the vertical deflection plates.

ITEM 504a ITEM 504b ITEM 504c

You answered: **The pattern, when a complete cycle of a sine wave is applied to the horizontal deflection plates, is as follows:**

It takes at least two signals applied to an oscilloscope to generate the composite waveform, such as displaying a sine wave applied as a vertical deflection signal. When a signal is applied to move the spot in only one dimension, the spot is going to move along only one axis, and that is exactly the case here. The other two axes of the CRT are assumed to have no signals applied in this case; a constant intensity beam of electrons was assumed to be hitting the screen. Thus, applying a signal, even though a sine wave, will make the spot move more slowly at the ends since the slope of the sine wave is changing slowly at these points. Therefore you will indeed get a signal traced on the scope with slight differences of intensity between the center and the ends of the line. If you had the deflection system calibrated, this question would be an excellent application of the scope as a voltmeter. When a square grid is placed over the screen, the deflection amplification factors can be calibrated, so that voltages may be read directly by the total amplitude or the excursion of the signal.

Just to refresh your memory, when you change the intensity of electrons hitting the screen, perhaps by varying the voltage applied to the intensity grid, the intensity of the spot will actually vary: this variation can be used to provide further information. Also, if the sine wave had been applied simultaneously to the vertical deflection plates, a line with a slope of 45° would have been seen on the scope face if you assume equal deflection sensitivities.

You were correct and right on the ball with your answer. You recognized that an oscilloscope can be used as a one-dimensional voltmeter. Proceed to Item 505.

You answered: **The pattern, when one complete sine wave is applied to the horizontal deflection plates, is as follows:**

If we had a sawtooth voltage applied to sweep the spot uniformly from top to bottom (applied to the vertical deflection plates) and if, at the same time, we applied your sine wave to the horizontal deflection plates, we would indeed get this waveform. In this problem, however, we are dealing with just a one-dimensional signal and so do not have a linear sawtooth applied to the vertical deflection plates. Thus we would get only a collapsed version of this waveform. Figure out which way it would collapse, and try again on Item 504.

You answered that **if a signal sine wave were applied to the horizontal deflection plates, the following pattern would be seen on the CRT screen:**

Do you remember what we said about the electron beam's requiring two signals to provide a deflection in two dimensions? An oscilloscope typically has a linearly changing waveform, such as a sawtooth, applied to the horizontal deflection plates as a sweep, and the unknown signal would be applied to the vertical plates. If that were true, you would be able to see the time course of the sine wave, as you do in the pattern you picked.

In this case, you have just one signal applied to the horizontal deflection plate. Try again on Item 504.

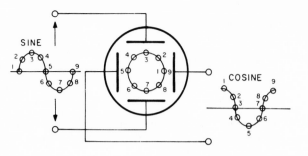

FIGURE 5-4   Lissajous patterns.

ITEM 505

**LISSAJOUS
PATTERNS**

Let's consider what happens when sine waves are applied to a cathode-ray tube with a 90° phase angle between the two sine waves. The electron beam is constant; that is, no signal is applied to the Z axis. Look at the left-hand part of Fig. 5-4. This type of figure is called a Lissajous ("Liss'-ah-jew") figure. The numbered dots trace the curve of the electron beam as a function of the history of the two sine waves. Simply stated, when one sine wave is zero, the other sine wave is at an extremum (that is, maximum or a minimum). Thus the spot will go to all four of the extreme positions in turn. Halfway in the 45° points, each of the two sine waves will be at a value down to 0.707 of its peak value. Thus the spot will be deflected at an angle of 45° since the two voltages are equal. This frequency ratio is 1:1 between the two deflection signals. Lissajous figures are quite often used when different frequencies are applied to the deflection plates. The pattern then made, when stationary, may be used to compare the frequency ratio between signals merely by counting the number of times that the electron beam touches the pairs of sides. To repeat, if the phase angle between the two sine waves is zero, the circle collapses to a straight line of 45°.

To make this sort of phase measurement and to display Lissajous figures, the voltages must be equal when applied to each deflection system, and only the phase or frequency can vary. If you use an oscilloscope to measure phase angle, you must take care that the amplitudes of the two signals are equal, or you may get misleading information about your estimated phase angle.

Q505 Referring to the right-hand figure in Fig. 5.4, what is the phase angle between the two sine waves to create this pattern?

ITEM 505a   25°.

ITEM 505b   45°.

ITEM 505c   90°.

ITEM 505a

You answered: **The phase angle in the Lissajous pattern is 25°.**

When you set out to measure the phase angle between two sine waves utilizing a Lissajous pattern, you must first make sure that the peak signal amplitudes in both the vertical and horizontal dimensions on the scope waveform are equal. That wasn't the case here. Take a second look at the ratio of signal amplitudes for the vertical and horizontal components of the signal. Then choose a different answer on Item 505.

ITEM 505b

You answered that the phase angle is **45°.**

Before you can measure phase angle even roughly by a Lissajous pattern, you must equalize the gain for the signals applied to the horizontal and vertical deflection plates so that the amplitudes of the signal in both the vertical and the horizontal dimensions are equal. You see that the peak signal amplitudes were not equal; take a second look at the figure. Try another answer back on Item 505.

ITEM 505c

You answered: **The phase angle for the Lissajous pattern is 90°.**

To get a rough estimate of the phase angle between two sine waves applied to a cathode-ray tube, you must first make sure that the peak signal amplitudes applied to the deflection plates are equal. This was not the case with our pattern; you correctly observed that the vertical deflection was approximately twice that in the horizontal dimension. Making an allowance for this, you correctly guessed that the phase angle was about 90°. You are keenly perceptive. Proceed to Item 506.

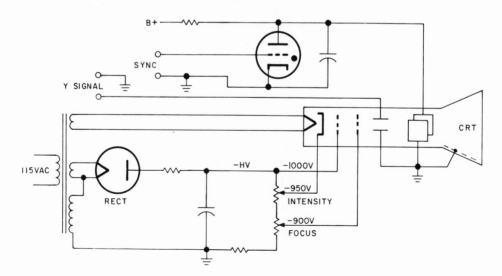

FIGURE 5-5 Basic oscilloscope circuit.

Figure 5-5 shows a brief but workable circuit diagram for an oscilloscope. Starting with the electron-gun section of the CRT, we have heater voltage from a transformer. A negative voltage of approximately 50 to 100 volts relative to the cathode is supplied to the intensity grid through the intensity control, and minus 50 to plus 50 volts is supplied to the focus electrode or second anode. A relatively high voltage of 1000 volts is applied to the Aquadag coating or final accelerator electrode. In this circuit, we have no final accelerator electrode. In this circuit, we have no deflection amplifiers, and the deflection signals are applied directly to the deflection plates.

The sawtooth voltage is developed by a gas tube or thyratron. When the plate-to-cathode voltage becomes sufficiently high to ionize the gas molecules within this tube, the gas ionizes, or "breaks down," and conducts a heavy current. This discharges the voltage accumulated on the capacitor very quickly. When the voltage across the capacitor decreases to a low value, the potential is insufficient to maintain the gas ionized, and the tube shuts off, or de-ionizes. The voltage across the capacitor builds up at a reasonably constant rate because of the charging current through the resistor. The cycle repeats itself when the plate-to-cathode voltage becomes high enough.

The sweep may be synchronized to an external Y signal by applying a small synchronizing voltage between the grid and cathode. This has the effect of decreasing the plate-to-cathode—ionization potential slightly, so that the tube fires just before it ordinarily would. This permits the tube to be synchronized to a repetitive signal.

Q506 What must be the time base of the sweep generator in order to see two complete sine-wave cycles[1] as shown here?

ITEM 506a   One-half the period for one sine wave.

ITEM 506b   Twice the period of one sine wave.

ITEM 506c   The period of one sine wave.

[1] Hint: Remember that the relationship between frequency and time here is inverse.

ITEM 506a

You answered that the time base of the sweep generator, in order to see two complete sine waves, is **one-half the time period for one sine wave.**

Well, if the time base is exactly one-half of one sine wave, you are going to see just one-half of one sine wave, or a positive bump. You will be missing the rest of the pattern. The period of the time base of the linear sweep voltage and the complete period of the two sine waves must agree. Figure this one out, and try a different answer back on Item 506.

ITEM 506b

You answered that the time base of the sweep generator, in order to see two complete sine waves, must be **twice the period of one sine wave.**

Very good. You realized that the periods of the linear sweep voltage and the complete sine waves must be identical in order to see two sine waves. You have to take time enough to see two sine waves, and the only way you can do that is to take the same amount of time as taken by two sine waves. Nice going; go on.

The same sort of reasoning applies to Lissajous figures. If you want to compare the frequency ratio of two signals, you have to adjust the controls so that you can count the number of times the signals touch each edge of the scope or come close to each deflection plate. Continue with Item 507.

ITEM 506c

You answered that the time base of the sweep generator, in order to see two complete sine waves displayed, must be **the period of one sine wave.**

Well, now that you have stopped to think about it, this one doesn't quite make sense, does it? How in the world are you ever going to see two complete sine waves if the time base is just the period for one? Wouldn't the time base show you just one and chop off the second one? Now that you have your thinking jogged, try another answer on Item 506.

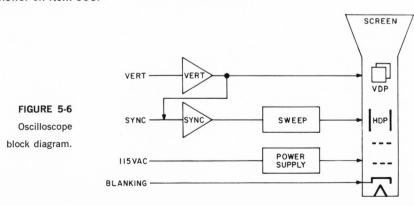

FIGURE 5-6
Oscilloscope
block diagram.

Now that you have some idea of the circuitry associated with making a cathode-ray tube work, let's take a look at the other components in a typical test oscilloscope. Locate the blocks in Fig. 5-6. The cathode-ray tube has an associated power supply. Also recognizable by now as an old friend is the horizontal sweep generator. In addition, there is a vertical amplifier to amplify low-level signals to a sufficient level (approximately 50 to 200 volts) to deflect the electron beam in the vertical direction. Note that a signal may be tapped off to supply a synchronizing signal to the sweep generator in the horizontal section. The vertical amplifier typically has an attenuator to reduce large signals to keep them on the screen, instead of allowing them to expand beyond it.

The horizontal amplifier typically is much like the vertical amplifier. However, it may accept synchronized sweep signals from the sweep generator, or an external signal may be applied to the horizontal amplifier. Thus the horizontal signal may portray the vertical signals against a linear sawtooth from the sweep generator, or it may portray them against a sine wave externally applied for the generation of Lissajous patterns.

Note that an external blanking signal may be applied to the intensity grid. When a linear sawtooth is applied to the horizontal deflection plates, the retrace normally is blanked so that it is invisible. The blanking signal very conveniently is taken from the discharge pulse of the thyratron's shorting the charging capacitor. This provides a short pulse coincident with the return of the sweep from the right side of the screen.

Q507 Which axis corresponds to the pen-writing channel of the oscillograph?

ITEM 507a The X axis with its linear sweep.

ITEM 507b The Y axis with its unknown dependent signal.

ITEM 507c The Z axis with its trace blanking.

ITEM 507a

You answered that the X **axis with its linear sweep** is similar to the pen-writing channel on an oscillograph.

Nope, this one won't work. The X axis corresponds to the paper's motion uniformly under the writing pen. The X axis simply provides a component in that it makes the beam move linearly from left to right, simulating the motion of the paper. Try another answer on Item 507.

ITEM 507b

You answered that the Y **axis of an oscilloscope with its presentation of test signals** is similar to the pen-writing channel on an oscillograph. Correct and right on the button! The linear sweep makes the spot move linearly from left to right, as in reading, to simulate the motion of paper under the writing pen. The unknown signal makes the beam move in the scope's Y axis; its variations then add to the linear motion to produce a pattern exactly like that seen on an oscillograph. Go to Item 508.

ITEM 507c

You answered that the Z **axis of a scope with its trace blanking** is similar to the writing-pen channel of an oscillograph.

Nope, not on this one. The Z axis typically is used for retrace blanking or modulating the electron beam to produce time markers. Moreover, the Z axis does not deflect the spot laterally or vertically. The writing pen on an oscillograph definitely has a deflection laterally across the paper. Try a different answer on Item 507.

Several different types of sweep circuits may be utilized to generate a linearly rising sawtooth waveform to sweep the electron beam back and forth across the oscilloscope at a time base. As we showed previously, the commonest circuit is an RC circuit with some method to discharge the capacitor when it has reached a certain voltage. The circuit shown before utilized a thyratron (Fig. 5-5). We could also use a multivibrator to discharge the capacitor or a less well-known circuit involving a single pentode, the phantastron circuit. However, these will not be discussed here; all depend upon producing a linearly rising voltage waveform by charging the capacitor at a constant current: The time derivative of the current is equal to zero.

A second type of sweep circuit utilizes a linearly changing current through a coil and resistor, an LR circuit. The voltage is equal to the inductance times the time rate of change of current. To produce a constant voltage across the inductance, or coil, the second time derivative must be zero so that the rate of change of the current with respect to time is a constant but not zero.

Let's consider another type of commonly used sweep-generating circuit. Refer to Fig. 5-7 which shows the basic circuit for the Miller integrator circuit. Let's start by assuming that the gate tube (first tube) operates as a switch and that it is normally conducting. Consequently the integrator (second tube) will also be in a conducting state with its plate voltage at some moderately high value. Let's apply a negative gate such that the gate period will equal the total time period of the output sawtooth. This negative gate cuts off the gate tube. As the name implies, this tube acts as an open switch for the duration of the gate pulse. This permits the plate voltage of the gate tube to rise to B+ which couples a positive rectangular pulse to the integrator tube.

ITEM 508A

This positive pulse tends to produce more plate current in the integrator tube, but the feedback capacitor (coupled from the plate to grid) produces a negative drop across the resistor R_g. Thus the feedback voltage bucks, or opposes, the plus gate from the gate tube. A stalemate ensues until the feedback capacitor has time to charge slightly, permitting the plate to go slightly negative. The grid voltage thus is seen to be the vector sum of the gate pulse and the time derivative of the feedback plate voltage. Because of the gain of the tube, a very linearly decreasing waveform results for the duration of the pulse. If the gate pulse stops before the plate current saturates, an extremely linear waveform is produced. This circuit is used quite often to generate sweeps for test oscilloscopes or radar sets.

Q508 In the discussion above for the Miller integrator, we considered the gate pulse negative. Will this same circuit work with a positive gate pulse, one that drives the gate tube into saturation so that it still acts as a switch but in the opposite direction?

ITEM 508a No, the circuit will not work with a plus gate because of the saturation of the integrator stage.

ITEM 508b Yes, the output tube will yet act as an amplifier-integrator.

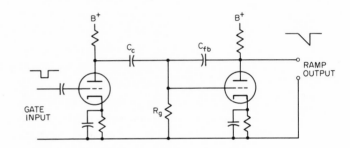

FIGURE 5-7 Miller integrator sweep circuit.

You answered: **No, the circuit will saturate, and the Miller integrator will not operate with a plus gate.**

Both tubes had cathode bias such that they could be expected to operate with a bias somewhere in their linear class-A region. The key point is whether the plate voltage of the output tube, the Miller integrator, will have to decrease or increase linearly from its resting plate voltage. With cathode bias, this is the case; the output tube can change in either direction linearly. The gate tube likewise has a cathode bias and could produce a positive or negative switching gate for the Miller integrator. Thus the circuit will operate quite well with the positive gate as well as with a negative gate. True, operation will remain somewhat easier with a negative gate because then the circuit operates a little bit simpler since the gate is coupled merely through $R_1 C_c$. But try the other answer on Item 508.

You answered: **Yes, the circuit will operate okay with a plus gate.**

Both tubes have cathode bias such that they operate in their linear class-A region. The critical point is whether the gate-tube output can produce a positive or a negative gate; whether the plate voltage of the gate tube can rise or whether it can decrease to a low saturation value. Similarly, the Miller integrator output tube can have its plate voltage changed in either direction since it's biased in the class-A region with cathode bias. Thus the Miller integrator tube could operate with a plus or minus gate, although operation is possibly somewhat easier with a negative gate. Go to Item 509. You were correct.

The noteworthy characteristics about vertical amplifiers in an oscilloscope are their frequency response and gain. These two characteristics are closely related to dollar value. An amplifier with a wide-frequency response and a high gain costs considerably more than amplifier with lower figures. A typical frequency response is one flat from 5 cps to 500 kc; the amplifier gain is flat within this region and 30 percent off (3 db down) at those two frequency points. A common high-quality frequency response runs from direct current to 5 Mc; that is, the gain at 5 Mc is 70 percent of that at 3 or 4 Mc.

To extend the frequency response of an oscilloscope to direct current or vhf limits when these are beyond the capacity of the existing vertical amplifier, some oscilloscopes permit the connection directly to the deflection plates of the external signal. When this results, the deflection sensitivity is in the order of 20 to 50 volts/cm. The gain figure, or range of amplification, for a typical amplifier may range from its most sensitive range of 1 mv/cm to unity.

A calibrated oscillator may be included with an accurate signal attenuator to check the gain and voltage of the signal displayed on the oscilloscope face. The calibrated oscillator puts out a square wave with a peak-to-peak amplitude that is known very accurately. This oscillator signal may then be attenuated by an accurate voltage divider to provide a known peak-to-peak signal amplitude. Thus the oscilloscope deflection may be calibrated so that, in addition to looking at a signal's waveform, you may read peak-to-peak voltage accurately to within 5 percent.

Dc coupling is used to extend the low-frequency response of an amplifier to direct current; dc amplifiers are used throughout to amplify a signal before applying it to the vertical deflection plates. Without direct coupling, the low-frequency response of the oscilloscope is set by the RC coupling network with the lowest or shortest time constant. This commonly is the input coupling RC network, where typical input values are 1-megohm impedance and a 0.1-μf capacitor. This produces an RC time constant with a low-frequency cutoff of 16 cps.

ITEM 509A

INPUT CHANNEL VARIATIONS

The high-frequency response of the amplifier is limited by the shunt capacity in the circuit and its effective plate resistance. Shunt capacities, such as the tube's plate-to-cathode impedance, the various wiring capacities, and any shunt capacitors to ground, effectively increase the total shunt capacity and lower the maximum frequency of the amplifier. For an amplifier to have an extremely high cutoff frequency, the effective load resistance and the effective shunt capacity must indeed be quite low.

Differential amplifier inputs may be utilized to balance out or cancel some undesired signal such as hum. These are dual-input amplifiers where the signal is fed in push-pull to the amplifier input. Any signal to both inputs in phase will be rejected to a high degree; typically such a common-mode signal may be rejected even though it is 30 to 100 times (30 to 40 db) stronger in amplitude than the desired signal fed in push-pull or differentially to the amplifier input. This feature permits the rejection of common-mode noise and hum for very-low-level differential signals.

Another feature of the oscilloscope is that quite often the vertical amplifier will have a dual-trace capability. An electronic switch is used so that two signals may be displayed simultaneously. The electronic switch is nothing more than a fast-acting double-pole double-throw (DPDT) switch. One signal is displayed with the positive half of a square wave. This puts this first signal on the upward trace of an oscilloscope. The second signal is presented simultaneously with the negative half of a large square wave, and this second signal is accordingly displayed on the lower part of the oscilloscope face. Separation between the two signals can be varied, as well as the frequency at which the electronic switch operates.

Q509 The most common ratings for vertical amplifiers (special features aside) are:

ITEM 509a The frequency response and gain.

ITEM 509b The rise time and calibration oscillator.

ITEM 509c The amplifier's rise time and frequency response.

ITEM 509a

You answered that the two most common ratings for a vertical amplifier, special features aside, are the amplifier's **frequency response and gain characteristics.**

The frequency response of the amplifier is indeed one of two most common characteristics; you are very much interested in the low-frequency cutoff, preferably down to the direct current, as well as extending the high-frequency response as high as possible. The second characteristic, of course, is the sensitivity, or the range of gain characteristics, of the deflection amplifier. You were right on the ball when you picked this answer. Proceed, maestro; go to Item 510.

ITEM 509b

You answered that the most common ratings for vertical amplifiers, aside from special features, are the amplifier's **rise time and a calibrated oscillator.**

Rise time is defined as the time it takes a pulse to go from 10 to 90 percent of its final value. Calibrated oscillators are extremely handy gadgets to have, but there are other ways to calibrate the voltage response of an oscilloscope. (For instance, you might just put in a known battery voltage and watch how far the spot deflects.)

In this case, I am afraid the presence of a calibrated oscillator is a special feature. Do you remember that we said we were trying to ignore special features? Rise time when calibrated is one of the two important features of an amplifier. But you haven't even gotten close to the other one. Reread the material on Item 509, and try again.

ITEM 509c

You answered that the most common ratings of vertical amplifiers, special features aside, are **the amplifier's rise time and frequency response.**

Frequency response and rise time are interrelated characteristics. Rise time is the time it takes a pulse to rise from the 10 percent level to 90 percent of its final value. Frequency response is directly related to this since a greater high-frequency response also means a shorter reaction time to pulses. Since these are two inter-related characteristics, you missed one important feature of amplifiers. Back to Item 509; keep one of these two features in mind, but find another to match it.

For maximum utility, the linear sweep that moves the spot from left to right repetitively across the scope face must have rather extreme linearity (uniform motion with respect to time), and the time base, or repetition frequency, must be known with a fair degree of accuracy. Often what is done is to utilize an RC generating circuit with a constant charging current to produce a linear increase in voltage across the capacitor. This ensures sweep linearity. Producing an accurate time base is a different story, however. Highly calibrated current sources and highly accurate RC networks are needed to ensure that the time base reflects accurately what the dial says for that particular sweep speed. Sweep speeds or time bases range from 10 sec/cm to 10 μsec/cm, with decade or intradecade intervals between them.

To determine frequencies more accurately than the 5 to 10 percent typical of a calibrated-sweep time base, one may use an external frequency from a standard frequency generator or a Lissajous pattern if the frequencies are close harmonically. Usually one Lissajous signal is an unknown sine wave and the second, or standard, sine wave comes from a variable-frequency generator. Another way to provide a frequency reference is to provide marker bursts, or pips, from crystal reference oscillators. The unknown signal frequency is estimated from knowing the frequencies of its two closest markers, just as in reading a ruler or scale.

An interesting additional feature about some oscilloscopes is that the sweep base may be magnified. This feature is particularly important with narrow pulses. When the time base is set so that one pulse is visible on the scope, there may be a considerable off time before the next pulse appears. The sweep magnifier magnifies or expands any desired portion of the synchronized sweep. Typically the sweep may be expanded by any integral factor up to 10 or 50.

Q510 For the waveform shown, what is the signal frequency with the sweep speed set at 2μsec/cm?

ITEM 510a   3.0 Mc.

ITEM 510b   1.5 Mc.

ITEM 510c   0.167 Mc.

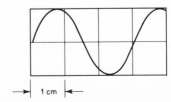

1 cm

ITEM 510a

You answered: **The signal frequency was 3.0 Mc.**

Each line segment on the graph represents 1 cm, and the waveform completed one complete cycle (that is, it starts again) in exactly 3 cm. Do you remember that frequency is the inverse, or reciprocal, of period? You simply take the reciprocal of the period in seconds, and you will have the right answer. Turn back to Item 510 and find it.

ITEM 510b

You answered: **The signal frequency was 1.5 Mc.**

Each line segment on the graph represents 1 cm. The waveform went through one complete cycle in three marks, or 3 cm. Do you know how to convert the time for one complete cycle (the period) to frequency? Frequency is simply the reciprocal of the period in seconds. Now that you know how to work this problem, try a different answer on Item 510.

ITEM 510c

You answered: **The signal frequency was 0.167 Mc.**

On the graph, each line segment is 1 cm. The waveform started to repeat itself in exactly 3 cm, so that the period was 6 μsec. Remembering that frequency is the reciprocal of period, you picked the correct answer in this case. Nice going. Proceed to Item 511.

Previously we covered the basic operation of oscilloscopes, how an oscilloscope traces some dependent variable as a function of time, and how to make rough phase measurements using Lissajous figures. Now we will discuss how to set up a scope to view waveforms.

A problem that confronts all beginners in using an oscilloscope is the following. You have connected an input signal to the vertical input terminals of your oscilloscope, and you see a series of fine vertical lines that are indistinct. You have a deflection in both X and Y dimensions, but the lack of a definite pattern means that your repeating, or cyclical, signal applied to the vertical deflection plates is not synchronized or stopped. Here signal frequency is much faster than sweep frequency.

How do you "stop" a vertically applied signal so that you may see it? Well, on a scope such as the Tektronix 541A, set the mode switch to automatic, and ignore the trigger level and slope controls. Set the source switch to a moderate setting. This should immediately result in seeing the pattern on the scope stop because the trigger generator in the automatic mode is capable of synchronizing the sweep to any signal from 50 cps up to 2 Mc. On other scopes, set the "sync amp" to moderate; turn the "freq vernier" until the pattern stops.

To compress or expand the sweep to see one entire cycle of the waveform, vary the sweep in coarse steps by turning the time/centimeter switch on the T541A. On other scopes, turn the "coarse freq" control. As you vary this switch, you will see more and more of a waveform until eventually you see an entire cycle of the vertical signal. Advancing the switch more will permit you to view several cycles and then many cycles on one sweep. To vary in small increments the amount of the signal seen, turn the variable time/centimeter knob, or fine frequency, which is a fine sweep adjustment control.

Q511 What control(s) is the most important in synchronizing a vertically applied signal so that just one full cycle may be seen on the scope? Assume that you have the triggering mode set to automatic on a scope such as the T541A.

ITEM 511a Vertical sensitivity, trigger level.

ITEM 511b Trigger level, time/centimeter.

ITEM 511c Source switch, time/centimeter.

ITEM 511A

With the mode switch in the automatic mode, the stability and triggering level controls do not have to be adjusted to see a waveform on the scope face. You do have to adjust the triggering source switch to internal and apply an input signal. Plus or minus slope is relatively unimportant. No other control adjustments are required to stop the waveform on the scope face. However, you may wish to vary the time/centimeter control so that you see a fraction of a cycle, one cycle, or many cycles of your vertically applied signal on a single sweep. You may also wish to adjust the vertical sensitivity, but 511c was the best answer.

ITEM 512

SAMPLING OSCILLOSCOPES

When repetitive waveforms above 1 Gc (1000 Mc) must be measured, a special type of oscilloscope called a "sampling scope" is used. If we took a sample at a slightly later time in the pulse on successive sweeps shown below by the circles, we would be able to plot the circled-dot samples at a much slower rate than that at which we were taking samples. If we moved the sweep in the many-step staircase pattern shown below, we should be able to reconstruct the pulse from the sample amplitudes, as shown in the third figure. This is exactly what a sampling oscilloscope does.

There are some special-purpose oscilloscopes that will plot singularly occurring pulses when the frequency is in the gigacycle range. A typical use is measuring nuclear events.

That is enough of this chapter on basic functions of oscilloscopes. Turn now to the Quiz 5, Item 513.

1–SIGNAL SAMPLES(0)   2-SWEEP   3-DISPLAY

FIGURE 5-8 Sampling oscilloscope signals.

ITEM 513   Check your written answers on the next page.

QUIZ 5 **1** What are the essential features of the CRT? *(D)*

2 How can a CRT be used like an oscillograph? *(I)*

3 What are the three axes, or dimensions, of the oscilloscope presentation? *(G)*

4 How would you obtain the following pattern (with which scope)?
  a Sampling scope
  b Dual-trace vertical amplifier
  c Horizontal sweep magnifier
  d Differential-input vertical amplifier
  e Any of these *(B)*

5 What is the horizontal-vertical frequency ratio for this Lissajous pattern:
  a 3:1
  b 2:1
  c 1:1
  d 1:2
  e 1:3 *(E)*

6 Which of the following are components of the electron-gun section of a cathode-ray tube: **a.** heater, **b.** cathode, **c.** intensity grid, **d.** focusing grid, **e.** accelerator (Aquadag coating) electrode, **f.** screen or scope face, **g.** all these. *(K)*

7 Why isn't the vertically applied signal seen on the scope face when the linear horizontal sweep is returning to its starting point?
  a The spot is moving too fast.
  b The electron beam is cut off.
  c The vertical signal is clamped to zero.
  d The retrace may be seen as a thin line.
  e All these. *(H)*

8 What kind of signal may be applied to the horizontal deflection plates?

a A linearly rising repetitive sawtooth.

b A singly occurring sawtooth sweep.

c An externally generated sine wave.

d An externally generated sawtooth sweep.

e Any of these. *(F)*

9 What are two basic characteristics of sweep generators? *(A)*

10 An oscillograph could have its time axis (paper flow) modified to present an *XY* plot of two variables, as is done with an oscilloscope for Lissajous patterns. (True/False) *(C)*

11 What is the rise time of this waveform (1 cm $=$ 1 μsec)?

a 0.1 μsec.

b 0.2 μsec.

c 0.5 μsec.

d 1.0 μsec.

e 3.0 μsec. *(J)*

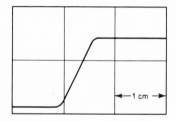

12 Rise time for a pulse and bandwidth of an *RC* amplifier are inversely related, so that the product $T_R \times$ BW equals a constant. What is this typical constant?

a. 0.4, **b.** 0.71, **c.** 1.0, **d.** 2.2, **e.** 4.4 *(M)*

13 What pattern results when two sine waves of equal height of the same phase are applied to an oscilloscope with the same vertical and horizontal deflection sensitivities?

a. ◯ **b.** ╱ **c.** *O* **d.** | **e.** — *(L)*

14 What happens if the voltage above has a phase angle of 90°?

a. ◯ **b.** ╱ **c.** *O* **d.** | **e.** — *(N)*

ITEM 514

ANSWERS TO QUIZ 5

A A linearly changing voltage that abruptly resets and then repeats.

B **b**

C True.

D An electron gun, deflection system, and phosphorescent screen within an evacuated glass envelope.

E **a**

F **e**

G The horizontal dimension *X*, vertical dimension *Y*, and the electron-beam-intensity dimension *Z*.

H Possibly all except **c.**

I Move the electron beam uniformly in one direction while making it follow the variations of a signal to "write" in a second direction at right angles to the first.

J **c**

K **a** through **d.**

L **b**

M **d**

N **a**

FIGURE 6-1   Photograph of the HP 130C oscilloscope.

OSCILLOSCOPES 17 QUESTIONS

ITEM 601

THE HP 130C OSCILLOSCOPE

Refer to Fig. 6-1 on the facing page, which shows a picture of the HP 130C oscilloscope. Study this panel layout and the controls. The panel controls are color-coded and functionally arranged. An internal-graticule CRT is supplied.

The HP 130C oscilloscope is a general-purpose instrument with identical vertical and horizontal amplifiers, a 500-kc bandwidth, and a 0.2 mv/cm maximum sensitivity. The phase characteristics of the vertical and horizontal amplifiers permit the measurement of relative phase shift between the signals with 1° accuracy up to 100 kc. Both amplifiers are dc coupled and provide sensitivity in 1:2:5:10 steps from 0.2 mv/cm to 20 volts/cm.

The sweep generator provides linear horizontal sweep voltages from 1 to 5 sec/cm in 1:2:5 steps. Sweep-magnifier positions allow trace expansion up to 50 times. A vernier control provides for continuous adjustment between calibrated sweep time increments and lowers the slowest sweep rate to at least 12 sec/cm. A single sweep switch allows observations of singular events.

The front panel control provides a selection of triggering modes. Automatic triggering starts the trace as the trigger source passes through zero, and in this position a base line is displayed whether or not a trigger signal is connected. In other modes, the sweep may be set to start at any point on the trace or the sweep may be set to run freely.

A beam-finder switch returns the trace to the screen when it might otherwise be out of view. The Model 130C operates either on 115 or 230 volts, 50 to 1000 cps, and with a power of approximately 90 watts.

Q601 On the 130C oscilloscope, the sweep is:

ITEM 601a   Started automatically by the trigger source.

ITEM 601b   Independent of any trigger source.

ITEM 601c   Free-running, but synchronized with the trigger.

ITEM 601a

You answered that the oscilloscope sweep is **started automatically by the trigger source.**

The sweep generator in this oscilloscope is gated on and off by the trigger generator. The trigger generator in turn can be set to free-run, produce a single gate, or to be synchronized with either an internal signal from the vertical amplifier or from an external signal. Thus your answer was indeed correct; there is quite a variety of trigger sources in this oscilloscope. Turn to Item 602.

ITEM 601b

You answered that the sweep is **independent of any trigger source.**

When the sweep switch is set to free-run, the sweep on the oscilloscope is independent of the trigger source, as the name implies. The sweep is running freely and has no relation to any trigger source. However, this is not the usual operation of the oscilloscope. Turn back to Item 601, and discover for yourself the other trigger modes.

ITEM 601c

You answered that the sweep is **free-running, but it can be synchronized with the trigger source.**

A free-running sweep circuit typically utilizes a multivibrator or thyratron to permit the sweeps to be generated and then synchronized to some trigger source. In this particular case, however, the sweep generator does not run freely and has to be gated on and off in response to a trigger. Although your answer is a possible answer and it is close for some characteristics, a more appropriate answer is yet to be found on Item 601.

Refer to and study the block diagram (Fig. 6-15) at the end of the chapter.

The vertical and horizontal amplifiers are almost identical, with the minor exception of their actual gains. The vertical amplifier accepts signals at its external input terminals, amplifies the signal, and drives the vertical deflection plates of the cathode-ray tube (CRT). The horizontal amplifier will accept a signal from the internal sweep generator. The deflection sensitivity is approximately 20 volts/cm in the vertical channel and approximately 30 volts/cm in the horizontal channel at the CRT terminals.

The sweep generator receives a synchronizing signal from one of three sources: the vertical amplifier, the line voltage, or from an external source. The synchronizing signal is converted into a starting trigger which opens the gate, starts the sweep, and turns on the CRT beam. The sweep is coupled to the horizontal deflection plates. The sweep then turns itself off through the holdoff circuits to prevent the start of another sweep until all circuits have recovered from the current sweep.

There are four low-voltage supplies that supply regulated operating voltages for the oscilloscope. The high-voltage power supplies receive their power from the low-voltage supply through a high-voltage power oscillator and regulating circuits. The electron gun or CRT controls are included in the high-voltage supply.

Q602 Looking at the block diagram, how many of the power supplies[1] in the oscilloscope are regulated?

ITEM 602a All the low-voltage and high-voltage supplies.

ITEM 602b All the low-voltage supplies, +250, ±100, and +12.5 volts dc.

ITEM 602c The three dc voltage supplies, +250, ±100 volts.

[1] Hint: Here's one small part of the answer: The high-voltage supply with rectifier No. 2, V305, is regulated against changes in the input supply voltage of +250 volts to the high-voltage oscillator.

ITEM 602a

You answered that **all the low-voltage and high-voltage supplies** in the oscilloscope are regulated. All four low-voltage supplies are indeed regulated, with three of the supplies being more closely regulated than the $+12.5$ volts supply. The high-voltage regulator circuit technically regulates a negative high voltage applied to the cathode-ray-tube cathode, and thus both high-voltage supplies are regulated with respect to the load variations, although only the cathode supply is regulated with respect to power-input variations. This was the correct answer. Turn to Item 603.

ITEM 602b

You answered: **All the low-voltage ($+250$, ±100, and $+12.5$ volts) supplies are regulated.**

Well, you can read a block diagram correctly, at least in part. All the low-voltage supplies are indeed regulated; some of them more highly regulated than others. In addition, however, you ought to go back to Item 602, and also take a look at the high-voltage section of the block diagram.

ITEM 602c

You answered: **Only the $+250$- and ±100-volt low-voltage supplies are regulated.**

You had better take another look at the block diagram. The $+12.5$-volt supply is indeed regulated, although its regulation is merely that of one stage instead of a two-stage amplifier-regulator design as in the other low-voltage supplies. While you're at it, take a look at the high-voltage supplies. Back to Item 602!

On the HP 130C block diagram at the end of this chapter, locate the vertical-amplifier section. Note that there is a two-section attenuator, part of which directly attenuates the signal input or Y signals and the second part of which works in connection with the emitters of the first differential amplifier to change gain. Following the differential amplifier is an output amplifier with a differential output that goes to the VDP of the CRT.

The high-frequency 3-db limit of the amplifiers is 500 kc or better. The maximum circuit impedance at which accurate measurements can be made is inversely proportional to the input capacitance of the measuring instrument and the signal frequency. For high-impedance circuit measurements at high frequency, a compensated voltage-divider probe is used, so that the frequency response is flat to the maximum usable frequency.

The low-frequency limit of the amplifiers is direct current, with the amplifier coupling switch in direct current.[1] With the amplifier coupling set on alternating current, the low-frequency limit varies from 10 cps at the higher voltage ranges to 25 cps at the most sensitive settings. The low-frequency cutoff on ac coupling is similar in effect to the better-known high-frequency cutoff. At the low-cutoff frequency, the amplifier response is down thirty percent with an accompanying 45° phase shift typically. Lower frequencies may yet be amplified but at an unknown gain and phase shift unless the scope amplifiers are calibrated. This may be desirable in some cases; 5 percent amplitude-measurement accuracy is typical.

The vertical and horizontal amplifiers may be operated single-endedly or differentially (balanced to ground). A feature of differential operation is common-mode rejection, in that a signal which is applied in phase to both input grids is rejected by a large margin in comparison to a signal applied out of phase to the input grids. This common-mode rejection varies from 30 to 40 db, depending upon the sensitivity range; a signal 30 to 100 times larger than a differential signal can be rejected.

Q603 Referring to the block diagram, how many controls affect the vertical sensitivity of the oscilloscope? Note— the input coupling switch and dc balance control should be excluded. Controls are identified by an unattached circle near the control's symbol and its label or title. (A line through the circle indicates a screwdriver control adjustment instead of a front panel control.)

ITEM 603a Five.   ITEM 603b Four.

ITEM 603c Three.   ITEM 603d Two.

[1] The dc position is used when you want to measure voltage levels of a waveform with reference to something other than the waveform average.

ITEM 603a

You answered that there are **five** controls on the vertical-amplifier section of the block diagram that affect the vertical sensitivity.

The two controls most obviously affecting the vertical sensitivity are the range switch and the vernier control for vertical sensitivity. In addition, the gain control, the vertical calibrate, the dc balance, and the amplifier switches also feed into this section. See if you can figure out just which ones of these affect the vertical sensitivity, and you will have no trouble picking the correct answer back on Item 603.

ITEM 603b

You answered that there are **four** controls in the vertical-amplifier section of the block diagram that affect the vertical sensitivity.

The vertical sensitivity switch sets the range of the voltage amplification in the vertical channel in four steps while the vernier vertical sensitivity control allows small adjustments, such as for calibration purposes. Possibly you looked at the vertical position switch or the vertical calibrate signals or the balance control which do feed into the vertical-amplifier section, but they do not affect the vertical sensitivity by itself. Study the block diagram a little more carefully, and turn to Item 603.

ITEM 603c

You answered that the number of controls that affect the vertical sensitivity in the amplifier block diagram is **three.**

You neglected to include such controls as the vertical position, the dc balance, and the input and amplifier coupling switches, but you neglected them quite correctly. There are indeed just three controls that affect the vertical sensitivity: the range switch, the vernier control, and the gain switch, a screwdriver adjustment.

Go to Item 604.

ITEM 603d

You answered that there are **two** controls on the block diagram which affect the vertical sensitivity.

Quite possibly you noticed the vertical sensitivity switch which sets the overall sensitivity range from 0.002 to 20 volts/cm and the sensitivity vernier which provides for adjustments in the vertical sensitivity, particularly calibration adjustments. Take a closer look at the vertical-amplifier section of the block diagram, however, and see if you can find at least one more control that you may have missed. Turn to Item 603.

Refer to the circuit diagram for the vertical amplifier (Fig. 6-2) and to the overall block diagram (Fig. 6-15) at the end of the chapter.

Basically, the amplifier circuit consists of an input attenuator, a feedback amplifier, and a differential output amplifier. The input attenuator provides steps of 10 and 100 gains (20 and 40 db), with a maximum sensitivity of 200 μv/cm. The remaining and intermediate gain steps are provided by the emitter or interstage attenuator. The input stage provides high-input impedance. Degenerative feedback from the emitter terminals of Q_3 and Q_4 to the cathodes of the input tube V_1 makes the differential feedback amplifier relatively independent of stage characteristics. In single-ended operation, one of the differential input terminals is grounded. The differential output amplifier provides the necessary voltage swing to drive the vertical deflection plates of the CRT. The vertical sensitivity of the CRT screen is approximately 20 volts/cm, and approximately 200 volts is required to drive the spot from the bottom line to the top line.

The position control in the output-cathode circuitry requires a constant-current source V_3 to stabilize the ac gain of the output stage when the position control is varied. The position control feeds back a difference current to the transistor emitters of Q_3 and Q_4 resulting in a dc difference in the respective collector currents and a corresponding voltage at the grids of the output amplifier. V_2 amplifies this difference and applies it to the CRT deflection plates for position control. The dc balance controls equalize this positioning voltage to prevent a change in sensitivity setting resulting from causing a shift in trace position. Changing a dc balance control will shift the signal pattern up and down on the CRT face without affecting the signal amplitude.

Q604 On the diagram, figure out how the beam-finder switch works.

ITEM 604a It increases the current through the constant-current source to swamp out the deflection signals.

ITEM 604b It mechanically switches the signals off the deflection plates.

ITEM 604c It reduces the current from the constant-current source to practically zero.

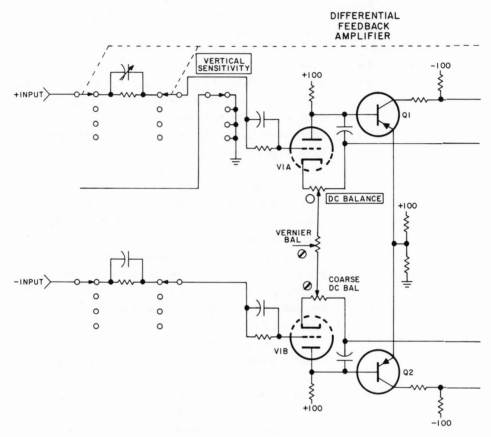

FIGURE 6-2 Simplified HP 130C vertical-amplifier circuitry.

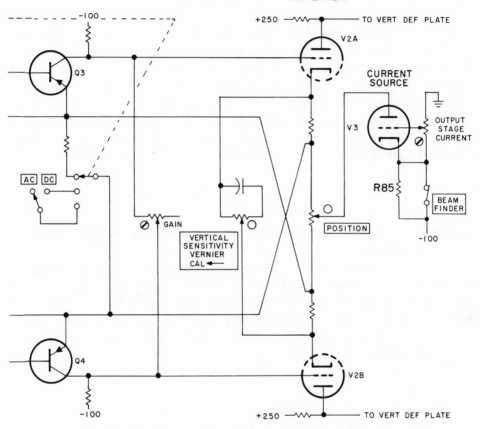

You answered: **The beam-finder switch works by increasing the current through the constant-current generator to swamp out any deflection signals.**

Well, you are getting hot but not hot enough. Look at the circuit diagram for the vertical-amplifier section of the oscilloscope. Find the beam-finder switch at the lower right-hand corner, and note that when the switch is in the open or depressed position (the switch is shown in its normal, or closed, position), a resistor R_{85} is unshorted and thus puts a high resistance in series with the constant-current source to -100 volts. Instead of providing a lot of current to swamp out the signals, the beam-finder switch appears to provide action in the opposite direction. Trace the circuitry down a little bit further, and see what effect this has on the current of the output differential cathode followers. Then select a different answer on Item 604.

You answered: **The beam-finder switch works by mechanically switching signals off the deflection plates.**

One way, obviously, to find the beam when it is deflected off the face of the CRT would be to mechanically insert a switch and simply switch the signals off. However, how would you tell the direction in which the beam had been deflected off the face? You would have no indication of the direction, but upon further scanning of the circuit diagram, you can figure out that there is a different action to the beam-finder switch. Find it on Item 604.

You answered: **The action of the beam-finder switch reduces the current from the constant-current source to practically zero.**

On the circuit diagram (Fig. 6-2) for the vertical amplifier, locate the beam-finder switch on the right side of the drawing. When the switch moves from its normally closed position to the depressed, or operated, position, the resistor R_{85} is unshorted and presents a 10,000-ohm resistance in series between the -100-volt source and the constant-current tube. This upsets the constant-current aspect to the extent that the output differential cathode followers are practically cut off. Since the tubes are balanced in push-pull with practically no current going through them, the beam is returned to practically the center position even though it had very large deflection voltages before. The remaining small deflection indicates the direction of the previously off-screen beam. This is indeed the action of the beam-finder switch. You were right on the money with this one. Turn to Item 605.

Refer to the circuit diagram (Fig. 6-3) for the horizontal amplifier. The circuit is basically the same as that of the vertical amplifier. The feedback resistors are slightly smaller to increase the gain; the higher gain is needed because the horizontal deflection plates are somewhat less sensitive than the vertical plates. This is because the horizontal deflection plates are slightly closer to the face of the cathode-ray tube and the electron beam is moving faster at this point. There are other differences in the horizontal amplifier compared with the vertical amplifier to allow a flexibility of internal and external sweep positions. The horizontal-position—control circuitry also is slightly different. The output-position—control circuitry is similar to that in the vertical amplifier. In the internal sweep position, however, an additional position control is added at the input of the amplifier to permit viewing any part of the trace in the $\times 1$ to $\times 50$ (magnified) internal sweep positions. Normally, just the center part of the sweep, even though magnified, is presented on the CRT. With this additional position-control potentiometer, sufficient range is added to the horizontal position control to permit viewing either end of the sweep on even the fastest magnified sweep positions.

On internal sweep, the horizontal amplifier has a sensitivity of 0.1 volt/cm in the $\times 1$ position. The voltage dividers present a 100:1 ratio, requiring a sweep voltage from a sweep generator of 10 volts/cm, or 100 volts peak-to-peak, to sweep the electron beam fully across the graticule. The remaining internal sweep positions increase the gain of the horizontal amplifier expanding the sweep about the center of the screen. Thus these positions present a magnified view that is equivalent to a higher-speed sweep trace.

Q605 With the sensitivity switch set on the $\times 2$ internal sweep position, what is the peak-to-peak voltage from the sweep generator to provide full 10 cm of horizontal deflection?

ITEM 605a   50 volts.

ITEM 605b   100 volts.

ITEM 605c   200 volts.

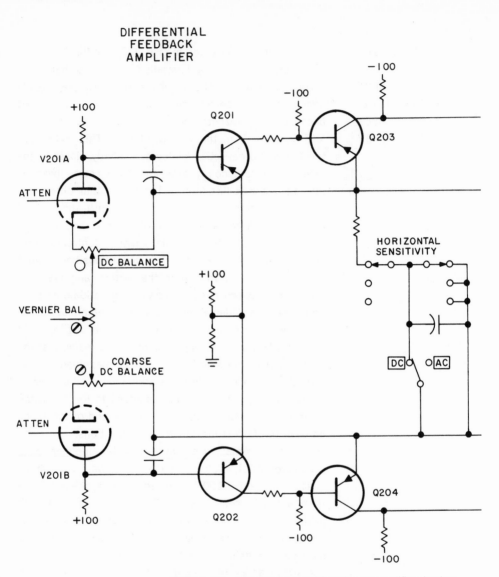

DIFFERENTIAL
FEEDBACK
AMPLIFIER

FIGURE 6-3 Simplified HP 130C horizontal-amplifier circuitry.

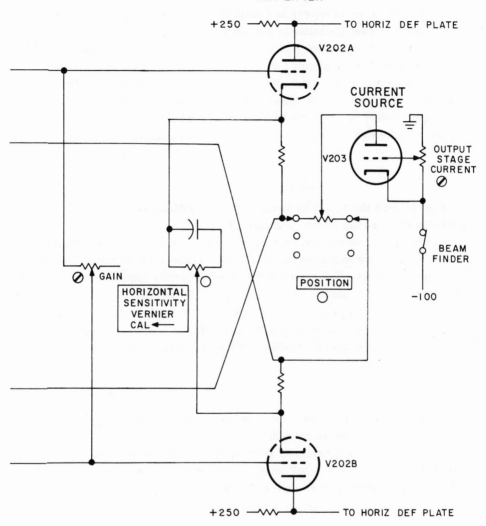

DIFFERENTIAL
AMPLIFIER

+250 —WW— TO HORIZ DEF PLATE

V202A

CURRENT
SOURCE

V203

OUTPUT
STAGE
CURRENT

GAIN

HORIZONTAL
SENSITIVITY
VERNIER
CAL ←

POSITION

BEAM
FINDER

−100

V202B

+250 —WW— TO HORIZ DEF PLATE

ITEM 605a

You answered: **With the sensitivity switch on the ×2 internal sweep position, it takes 50 volts from the sweep generator to provide a full 10-cm horizontal deflection.**

You followed the reasoning of the paragraph consistently. The gain is doubled in the ×2 position such that only half as much voltage from the sweep generator is required as when it is in the ×1 position. Also, you clearly discriminated between the voltage required in the internal sweep position to drive the horizontal amplifier and the horizontal deflection sensitivity which is approximately 30 volts/cm at the deflection plate. You're right on the ball with this one. Continue with Item 606.

ITEM 605b

You answered: **With the sensitivity switch on the ×2 internal sweep position, 100 volts is needed to provide a full 10-cm horizontal deflection.**

Possibly you remembered that it always takes the same voltage, approximately 100 volts, to make the spot sweep a full 10 cm of horizontal deflection. Well, that is fine except that we were talking about the sweep-generator output voltage. Actually the horizontal deflection sensitivity is of the order of 30 volts/cm so that it would take approximately 300 volts to make the spot deflect from the left edge of the matrix to the right edge of the matrix, or graticule, on the screen. What the sweep generator has to supply to the horizontal amplifier is different. Figure it out back on Item 605.

ITEM 605c

You answered: **With the sensitivity switch on the ×2 internal sweep position, 200 volts will provide a full 10-cm horizontal deflection.**

It appears that you have your calculations reversed on this one. As the gain increases from the ×1 to the ×2 position, less input voltage is needed, not more. Check your calculations again on Item 605, and pick the right answer.

ITEM 606

TRIGGER GENERATOR

Refer to the block diagram (Fig. 6-15), and note that there are two major sections to the sweep circuitry, the trigger generator and the sweep generator. At this point we are going to discuss only the trigger generator. Refer to the circuit diagram (Fig. 6-4).

The output of the trigger generator is a negative-going synchronized pulse across diode CR111. The trigger-generator circuit itself is a Schmitt trigger[1] with narrow switching limits or low hysteresis for good sensitivity. To produce the required negative-going trigger across the output diode, a negative-going step must be present at the output of the trigger, V102B-1. Therefore the trigger signal at the grid of V102A must cross the negative-going switching limit of V102 at the time the trigger pulse is generated. This will occur during the negative-going portion of the input signal for a signal fed to the grid of V101A or during the positive-going portion for a signal fed to the grid of V101B. Either polarity may be selected by means of the trigger source-slope switch S101.

The trigger source-slope switch S101 selects the source and slope of the trigger signal. The trigger source may be external, internal, or line. When the switch is in the internal position, the trigger signal comes from the vertical amplifier. When on external, an external trigger must be connected to the terminal binding post. In line, the sine-wave line voltage serves as the trigger, the frequency varying from 50 to 1000 cps. The triggering waveform may be a sine wave, square wave, or pulse or complex waveform, and it may be repetitive or one-shot. The point on the waveform at which the trigger is generated is selected by the level control.

---

[1] A "Schmitt trigger" is a flip-flop circuit that can be only in one of two exclusive states at a time. That is, V102A can be ON, heavily conducting, while V102B is OFF, nonconducting, or vice versa. In the absence of a signal, V102B normally is OFF because of its grid-bias arrangement to —100 volts.

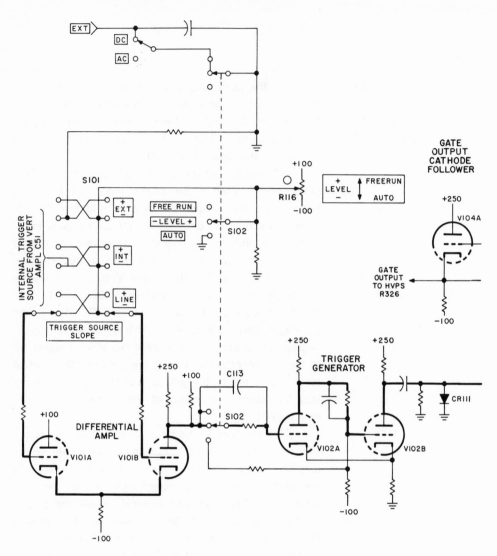

FIGURE 6-4 Simplified HP 130C trigger-generator circuitry.

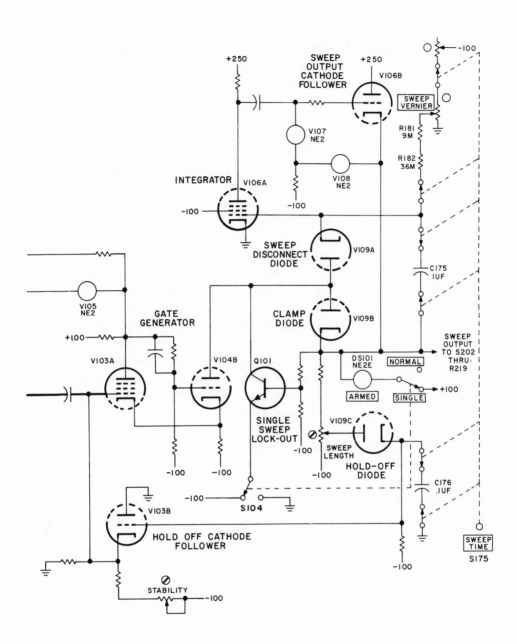

ITEM 606A

The setting of the level control R116 adjusts the bias to the differential amplifier V101, determining the voltage level on the trigger-signal waveform at which V101B will actuate the trigger generator. The level control is ganged with switch S102 to establish certain conditions at the two extremes of rotation. With level fully counter-clockwise, S102 is in auto position. The control is then grounded, causing the trigger to be generated as the trigger signal passes through zero in either direction. S102A inserts a capacitor to block any direct current from the external trigger source to ensure that the signal will pass through zero. Another section of switch S102 modifies the voltage level of the trigger generator for automatic operation so that V102 is a free-running multivibrator. The resulting 40 to 50 cps repetition rate is determined by the grid RC time constant of V102. The auto mode establishes a base line on the screen so that in the absence of a trigger signal there is a reference line. In the free-run position, a new sweep starts at the end of the holdoff period without the need of a trigger. The free-running rate depends on the setting of the sweep-time switch S175.

Q606 When the trigger signal is absent and S102 is in the level position, the input section V102A of the trigger generator is:

ITEM 606a   Biased for class-A operation.[1]

ITEM 606b   Cut off.

ITEM 606c   Conducting.

[1] Class-A operation essentially is linear amplification; a small signal is amplified by the same ratio as a large signal.

ITEM 606a

You answered: **When the trigger signal is absent, the input section of V102A of the trigger generator is biased class A.**

    This is a multivibrator, and a multivibrator with part of it biased class A is a rare bird. It does happen occasionally but certainly not in this circuit. Check out the biasing for the trigger generator, and remember it is basically a flip-flop. The two triodes are alternately cut-off or saturated, conducting as hard as possible. This is certainly far from class-A operation where a signal goes in and linear amplification takes place to produce a linear output signal. Check over the biasing for both triodes in the trigger generator in the circuit diagram, and then pick a different answer on Item 606.

ITEM 606b

You answered: **When a trigger signal is absent, the input section of the trigger generator V102A is normally cut off.**

    Refer to the sweep-circuit diagram (Fig. 6-4) for the trigger generator. Note that the grid for the left-hand section may be either connected to the plate and B+ of the previous differential amplifier or left floating through a coupling capacitor. The grid for the right-hand section is coupled to the plate of the left-hand section V102A, but the bias resistor also returns to -100 volts. The inference is that it's much easier for the right half of the tube to be cut off than the left half of the tube. Thus, with no trigger signal present, your answer isn't correct. Analyze the circuit a little bit further, and you will have no trouble picking the correct answer on Item 606.

ITEM 606c

You answered: **When a trigger signal is absent, the input section V102A of the trigger generator is normally conducting.**

    Let's look at the circuit diagram (Fig. 6-4). The left-hand section of the tube is either connected through the plate of the previous differential amplifier to B+ or is left floating when capacitor C113 is in the circuit. The grid of the right-hand triode V102B is connected through the plate of the left-hand triode V102A to B+, while a biasing resistor also connects this grid to -100 volts. Thus, it is easier for the right-hand tube to be off from a biasing point of view than the left-hand section. This is indeed the case when there is no signal; the right-hand tube V102B is cut off, and the left-hand tube V102A is conducting.

    This was the correct answer. Proceed now to Item 607.

ITEM 607

**SWEEP
GENERATOR**

Refer to the circuit diagram (Fig. 6-5). Also refer to the block diagram (Fig. 6-15), and note that the gate generator has several outputs and inputs. The negative-going trigger comes from the trigger generator, and the gate generator supplies a negative-going gate to the integrator for the gating of the sweep. The gate generator also supplies a plus gate to the CRT grid to intensify the trace during the sweep time. Also note the circuitry associated with stopping and starting the sweep to establish the desired initial conditions.

The gate generator V103A and V104B is a Schmitt trigger circuit similar to the trigger generator except that it has wide switching limits. Prior to the start of the sweep, the sweep output of the grid of the Miller integrator V106A is held at ground level by disconnect diode V109A and clamp diode V109B; therefore the sweep-time capacitor C175 is discharged. The incoming negative-going gate turns off both diodes, leaving the grid of the integrator tube V106A free to go negative. As the grid starts to go negative, however, the high gain of the tube drives the sweep-output side of the sweep capacitor C175 positive much faster than the grid goes negative. The result is that the grid voltage of the Miller integrator remains almost fixed, and a constant current flows from the −100-volt supply to charge C175 at a linear rate. The positive-going side of the sweep capacitor represents the output-sweep waveform.

The charging resistors R181 and up have a 5:2:1 ratio corresponding to the first three positions of the attenuator switch. As long as the grid voltage to integrator V106A is substantially constant, the current through capacitor C175 will vary in the inverse ratio to the charging resistance and the sweep time will vary directly with the series resistances. While capacitor C175 is being used as the sweep capacitor, C176 determines the holdoff time after a sweep is finished. Further step positions of the switch move to adjacent capacitors so that one sweep capacitor serves as the holdoff capacitor for the next sweep position.

ITEM 607A   The sweep voltage is fed back through the holdoff cathode follower V103B to the gate generator. When the output voltage exceeds a certain preset level, determined or set by the sweep-length adjustment R146, the holdoff diode conducts, turning on the holdoff cathode follower which applies a positive pulse to the grid of the gate generator V103A. This positive pulse is the opposite of the negative initial trigger which started the cycle. Thus the gate generator flips off, and the circuit regenerates. The sweep disconnect diode allows the sweep capacitor C175 to discharge, resetting the integrator. The holdoff diode V109C turns off, leaving control of the holdoff cathode follower to the holdoff capacitor C176. The time constant of capacitor C176 and resistor R148 keeps the gate from turning on again for a short time until all circuits have recovered from the previous sweep. As the sweep rate increases, this holdoff capacitor becomes smaller, making the recovery time shorter for faster sweep times.

The single-sweep lockout transistor Q101 is in the circuit only when switch S104 is set to single. It holds the sweep disconnect diode V109A cut off after the sweep so that the integrator cannot recover, thus disabling the sweep until armed by flipping switch S104 back to normal.

Q607 Looking at the circuit diagram for the sweep generator, when does the holdoff diode V109C turn off in the sweep cycle?

ITEM 607a   When the cathode voltage from C176 decreases below the anode voltage.

ITEM 607b   When the anode voltage of V109C goes negative with respect to the cathode.

ITEM 607c   When the gate comes on again and the plate voltage of V104B has decreased.

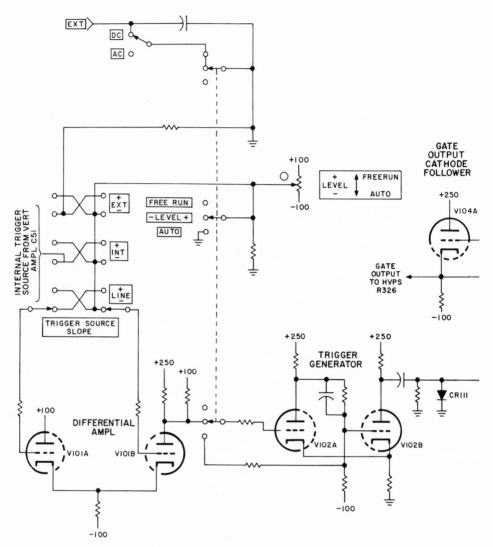

FIGURE 6-5 Simplified HP 130C sweep-generator circuitry.

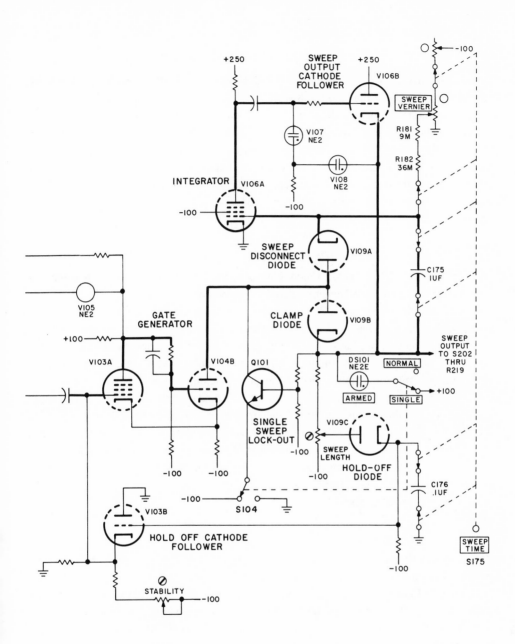

SWEEP GENERATOR 607A

ITEM 607a

You answered that the holdoff diode V109C turns off when **the cathode voltage from C176 decreases below the anode voltage.**

The gate is turned off at the end of the sweep cycle and the holdoff diode conducts when the positive-going waveform exceeds the bias on the holdoff diode. When the gate turns off, the positive-going output waveform is removed abruptly, and the diode is cut off immediately. It is cut off, however, by having the anode voltage reduced below the cathode voltage. This is the opposite polarity to that given in the answer you selected. Take a closer look at the circuitry, and figure out the correct answer on Item 607.

ITEM 607b

You answered that the holdoff diode V109C turns off in the sweep cycle **when the anode of V109C goes negative with respect to the cathode.**

The holdoff diode V109C conducts briefly when the positive-going output sweep waveform is applied to the anode of this diode, which causes the diode to conduct and charges capacitor C176. This same conduction, however, turns the gate off, which stops the just previously positive-going output waveform. The cessation of the output waveform causes the anode of the holdoff diode V109C to go negative with respect to the cathode, turning off the holdoff diode. The cathode is held momentarily at its previous value by the action of the holdoff capacitor C176. Thus the diode turns off, as any good little diode should, whenever its plate voltage is less than the cathode voltage. Your answer was very much correct. Nice going. The delay time provided by holdoff capacitor C176 provides time for recovery or resetting of the integrator circuits. The capacitors cannot instantaneously reset to their initial conditions. Proceed to Item 608.

ITEM 607c

You answered that the holdoff diode V109C turns off in the sweep cycle **when the gate comes on again and as the plate of V104B goes negative again.**

Let's figure normal operation for this circuit. We know that a negative trigger starts the gate; this would cut off V103A and turn on V104B, the other half of the gate generator. When the second half V103A is turned on, its plate voltage would go quite negative. This in turn would cut off both diodes V109A and B, causing the start of the positive-going output waveform. All this time diode V109C has been held cut off until the output waveform reaches a sufficiently high voltage so that it can conduct. This is a different part of the cycle than we asked for in the question; the diode in the discussion here is off in the sweep part of the cycle. The question asked about the turnoff of the holdoff diode in the sweep cycle. Follow this reasoning a little bit farther along, and see if you can discover what is associated with the turnoff of the holdoff diode V109C. Return to Item 607.

ITEM 608

POWER SUPPLY

Refer to the block diagram (Fig. 6-15) and to the circuit diagram (Fig. 6-6) for the power supply. There are three regulated supplies supplying output voltages of +250, +100, and −100 volts. Each of these three regulated supplies has its own separate control amplifier and reference to hold the output voltage constant. The +250 voltage is obtained from a 150-volt supply added to the top end of the +100-volt supply. The 12.5-volt supply furnishes heater voltage for the input stages for the vertical and horizontal amplifiers. The regulation for the heater power supply need not be as great as with the B supplies, and the regulation is much simpler and less intensive.

The high-voltage supply is generated by a high-frequency oscillator at a frequency of about 70 kc. The output voltage of the oscillator tube V301 is stepped up by transformer T301 to approximately 3000 volts and is rectified by two rectifiers V304 and V305. On the circuit diagram (Fig. 6-6), note that the rectifier circuit for V304 supplies −2850 volts to the cathode of the CRT and that the circuitry associated with rectifier V305 supplies the grid voltage for the CRT. Note that the positive intensifying gate from the sweep generator is also applied to this second supply. This positive trigger supplies a ground, or reference point, for the supply. The reference, or ground end, of the other supply, associated with rectifier V304, is through the intensity control. The intensity control thus affects the output voltage from rectifier V304.

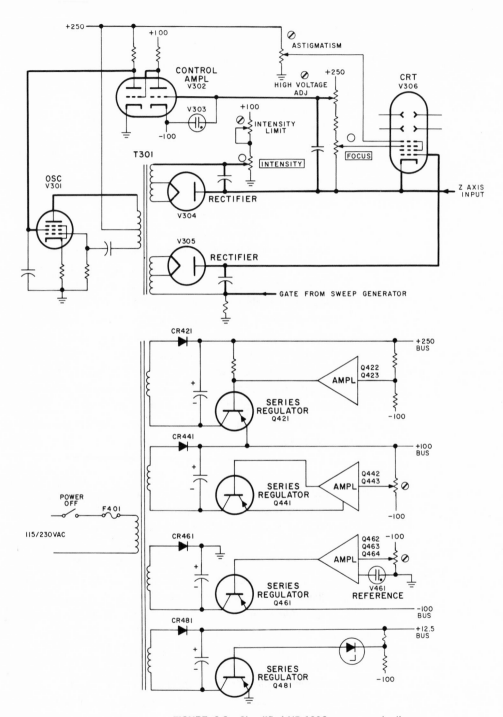

FIGURE 6-6 Simplified HP 130C power-supply diagram.

ITEM 608A   The high voltage is regulated via a series resistor string from the cathode of the CRT to the +250-volt supply. This resistor string includes the focus control and the high-voltage adjustment potentiometer R312. The control amplifier V302 picks off a predetermined percentage of the −2850 volts, amplifies it in a dc fashion, and applies it to the power oscillator tube. Assume that the minus high voltage has increased in voltage output, or gone more negative, let us say to −3000 volts. This results in a more negative voltage being applied to the control amplifier, which is amplified, and appears as a negative-going output voltage at the plate of the control amplifier V302. This reduced plate voltage reduces the screen voltage of the oscillator tube V301, thus reducing its output power.

The reduced sine-wave output of the oscillator produces less voltage output for rectifier V304, and the −3000 volts excursion of the supply is brought back to its nominal −2850 volts. Note that the control amplifier is sensitive to minus high-voltage changes only in the rectifier circuitry associated with V304, and not with high-voltage changes associated with rectifier V305. When you assume a constant current or constant load for the grid circuitry of the cathode-ray tube, however, the output voltage at the CRT grid also is regulated.

Q608 How does the intensity control[1] operate?

ITEM 608a Through the action of the high-voltage regulator circuit, it affects the grid voltage of the CRT.

ITEM 608b It directly varies the grid-to-cathode voltage of the CRT.

ITEM 608c It changes the CRT cathode voltage by adding a small dc voltage in series with the minus high-voltage supply going to the CRT cathode.

---

[1] This one is involved; there's more to this than meets the eye at first glance. Study the high-voltage regulator circuit and its discussion above. Which high voltage where is kept constant? If this one is loaded down, what happens to the other high voltage?

ITEM 608a

You answered that the intensity control works **through the action of the high-voltage regulator circuit to affect the grid voltage of the cathode-ray tube.**

The intensity control taps off some of the +100 volts and adds it in series with the output of the minus high voltage from rectifier V304. The regulator keeps the cathode bus voltage at a −2850 volts regardless of how much voltage the intensity control has added in series with it. However, the control amplifier has compensatingly changed the output of the minus high voltage from rectifier V305, which is applied to the grid of CRT. Thus your answer is indeed correct. The answer is quite sneaky and is considerably more involved than it appears at first. Congratulations for having figured this one out! Proceed to Item 609.

ITEM 608b

You answered: **The intensity control directly varies the grid-to-cathode voltage of the CRT.**

Take a good look at the circuit diagram (Fig. 6-6) for the high-voltage supply. The intensity control is located quite a way from the grid and cathode of the CRT, isn't it? The intensity control adds a small voltage in series with the high-voltage output of rectifier V304. Since the −2850-volt supply is regulated, this supply line will stay at a constant −2850. The output of the intensity control thus is puzzling, isn't it? It is not at all obvious and certainly is not as direct as was your answer. Return to Item 608 and puzzle out the correct answer.

ITEM 608c

You answered that the intensity control works **by adding a small dc voltage in series with the minus high-voltage supply going to the CRT cathode.**

The intensity control does tap off a certain amount of the +100 volts and does add it in a series with −2850-volt supply. The action of the regulator circuit, however, is to ensure that the −2850 volts does indeed stay just that, −2850 volts. What is happening, then, is that the intensity control adds in a small voltage so that the transformer output voltage supplied to the rectifier V304 is changing to compensate for the dc voltage added in by the intensity control. Therefore, the cathode voltage, in spite of the intensity-control action, remains a constant −2850 volts. Your first impression in this case is not good enough. Turn back to Item 608 and puzzle out this tricky circuit a little bit further.

ITEM 609

**TEKTRONIX 541A
OSCILLOSCOPE**

Refer to Fig. 6-7, which shows a picture of the 541A oscilloscope. Study the picture, and become familiar with the general layout of the panel and the controls. The Tektronix Type 541A oscilloscope is a general-purpose laboratory instrument. Plug-in preamplifiers are used in the vertical deflection system so that the instrument may be used with wideband, dual-trace, low-level, differential, high-frequency-response, high-rise-time, or transistor-checking preamps. The vertical-deflection system characteristics depend upon the plug-in unit in use. A delay line is used to delay the vertical signal 0.2 μsec so that the leading edge of pulses may be seen.

A variety of triggering modes are available for the horizontal sweep system: automatic, ac low-frequency reject, ac, dc, and high-frequency sync. The sweep may be triggered internally, externally, or set to run freely. The sweep rate may be varied in accurately calibrated steps from 0.1 μsec to 5 sec/cm. A five times (5$\times$) magnification of the center 2-cm portion of the oscilloscope display may be used. External horizontal deflection signals may be applied from direct current to 240 kc.

A built-in square-wave amplitude calibrator at a frequency of approximately 1 kc is used to calibrate both sweep systems. The power supplies are electronically regulated. Line-voltage requirements for operation are 115 volts or 230 volts, 50 to 60 cps, at approximately 500 watts.

Q609 What is the most outstanding feature of the vertical deflection system of the T 541A oscilloscope?

ITEM 609a The wideband preamplifier with a frequency response of direct current to 24 Mc.

ITEM 609b The availability of the many different plug-in units with special characteristics.

ITEM 609c The delay in the vertical-amplifier section to permit the sweep to start sufficiently early that the leading edge of pulses may be viewed.

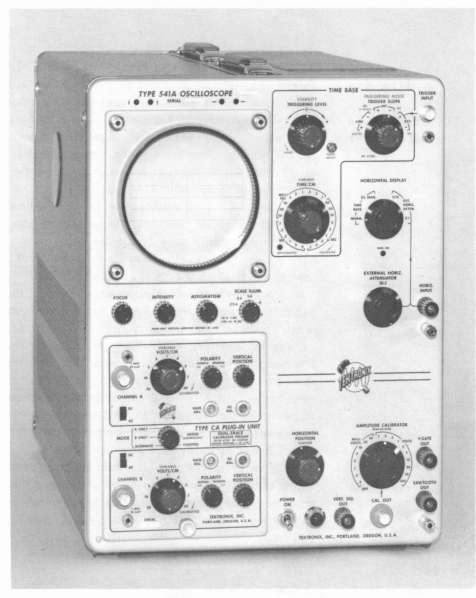

FIGURE 6-7 Photograph of the Tektronix 541A oscilloscope.

ITEM 609a

You answered that the most outstanding characteristic of the vertical deflection system is **the wideband preamplifier with a frequency response of direct current to 24 Mc.**

The type K plug-in amplifier for use in the vertical deflection system does indeed have a wide bandpass characteristic. However, the most outstanding feature of the vertical deflection system is that a wide variety of preamplifiers are available to cover many different user situations. Turn to Item 609.

ITEM 609b

You answered: **The most outstanding characteristic of the vertical deflection system is that many different plug-in preamplifier units for a variety of different applications are available.**

This is indeed the most outstanding characteristic. This is what makes this oscilloscope so versatile. Some of the different plug-in preamplifiers available are the following: a wideband dc-coupled preamp, a high-gain wideband dc-coupled preamp, a dual-trace dc-coupled preamp, a high-gain dc-coupled differential preamp, a low-level ac-coupled differential preamp, a wideband dc-coupled differential preamp, a fast-rise-time dc-coupled preamp, a fast-rise-time high-gain dc-coupled preamp, a pulse-sampling preamp, and a differential comparator. They may also have a strain gage, check transistor rise time, or measure semiconductor diode recovery.

Turn to Item 610.

ITEM 609c

You answered that the most outstanding feature of the vertical deflection system is **a delay line to delay the vertical signals so that the sweep may be started in time to view the leading edge of pulses.**

One interesting feature of the vertical deflection system is indeed this delay line. However, in not all cases would you be interested in a fast rise time and in viewing pulses. Sometimes you might be interested in very low-level low-frequency signals or in a differential application. The most outstanding feature of the vertical system of the T 541A oscilloscope is the availability of many types of preamplifiers for many different applications. Turn to Item 609.

Refer to the block diagram, Fig. 6-16, for the 541A oscilloscope. The vertical deflection system uses a dc-coupled push-pull main vertical amplifier to drive the delay line in the vertical deflection plates of the CRT. The main units are the input amplifier V1014 and V1024, the cathode-follower driver V1033 and V1043, and the distributed six-stage output amplifier.

Just above the CRT face on the front of the panel of the oscilloscope are located the beam-position indicators B1083 and B1087. These indicators show the relative position of the trace with respect to the center of the graticule. When the beam is centered vertically, the potential across the neon lights is insufficient to light them. If the beam is positioned above or below the screen, however, the appropriate indicator amplifier will draw sufficient current to light one of the neon lamps to indicate the direction in which the electron beam has been deflected off the scope.

The time-base trigger in the horizontal deflection system develops a pulse to start the time-base generator. A triggering mode switch allows the operator to select the type of triggered operation he desires. Auxiliary controls are used in setting the triggering point on waveforms. To display signals above 5 Mc, the time-base trigger is bypassed and a synchronizing signal is applied directly to the sweep-gating multivibrator in the time-base generator, with no choice of triggering slope in this mode.

The trigger circuit produces a negative pulse input which is differentiated to trigger the time-base generator appropriately. The time-base generator consists of three major circuits: a sweep-gating multivibrator, a Miller run-up circuit, and a holdoff circuit.

The horizontal amplifier converts the single-ended sawtooth output of the time-base generator into a push-pull signal for driving the horizontal plates of the CRT. The gain of the amplifier may be varied by a factor of 5 to provide a $5\times$ magnification. Controls are also provided here for horizontal positioning and adjusting horizontal linearity.

The low-voltage power supplies are driven by a

single power transformer. The power supply will maintain regulated output voltages over line-voltage changes from 105 to 125 volts or 210 to 250 volts. Bridge rectifiers are employed for five separate full-wave power supplies, with regulated output voltages of -150, $+100$, $+225$, $+350$, and $+500$ volts. A single 60-kc Hartley oscillator furnishes power for three power supplies providing accelerating voltages for the CRT.

Q610 When the spot or trace on the scope face disappears upon applying a Y, or vertical, signal, you should:

ITEM 610a   Look at the beam-position indicators.

ITEM 610b   Push the beam-finder switch.

ITEM 610c   Increase the intensity setting.

ITEM 610a

You answered: **When the spot or trace disappears upon applying a vertical signal, I should look at the beam-position indicators.**

This is precisely what you should do. When the spot disappears, look to see which of the four neon bulbs is lighted to tell you which way the spot has been deflected off the scope. Then move one of the positioning controls appropriately to bring the spot and trace back into view. Sometimes, of course, you might want to turn up the intensity at the same time because the spot is deflected so fast by a large signal that it becomes almost invisible. But most of the time the trouble is simply that the spot is just off the CRT face. Go to Item 611.

ITEM 610b

You answered: **When the spot or trace on the scope disappears upon applying a vertical signal, I would push the beam-finder switch.**

Turn back to the picture of the front panel of the 541A oscilloscope. Look it over carefully and see if you find a beam-finder switch there. There isn't one, is there? But you're certainly on the right track. While you're looking at the same picture, see what else you can find that has to do with the beam position; there is something there. Reread the material on Item 610 and try again.

ITEM 610c

You answered: **When the spot or trace on the scope disappears upon applying a vertical deflection signal, I would turn up the intensity control.**

This is a good check to make in general, but if you had had a signal present until you applied the vertical deflection signal, don't you think that something else might be at fault? What if the vertical signal had shoved the spot clear off the face of the scope? Turn back to Item 610 and select a different answer.

ITEM 611

541A VERTICAL DEFLECTION SYSTEM

Refer to Fig. 6-8, the simplified vertical-amplifier circuitry. Also, look at the system block diagram (Fig. 6-16) at the end of the chapter.

The signal input from the plug-in unit is coupled to the input amplifier stage. The gain is varied by cathode degeneration. The input amplifier feeds its output signal to the cathode followers in the distributed amplifier to isolate the distributed amplifiers from the input amplifier and provide a low-impedance drive.

The output stage is the six-section distributed amplifier. Note the tapped inductors in the transmission line between each grid and between each plate for isolation purposes. The reason for using a distributed transmission line is that the capacitances of each tube are isolated this way and do not add to the total amplifier capacitance. However, the transmission line does permit the adding of the gain of each stage. Thus the transconductance of six tubes is obtained at the expense of the capacitance of just one.

The vertical signal is delayed 0.2 μsec between the input to the grid line and the vertical deflection plates to ensure that the front, or leading, edge of fast vertical signals can be observed. This permits the same vertical signal to trigger the sweep and yet still be seen just after the sweep has started. This is one way to have your cake and eat it too.

ITEM 611A

Unless compensated, dc components in a complex waveform may shift in passing through the amplifier since the very-low-frequency gain is less than the midfrequency gain. Such compensation is provided via a low-frequency—boost network in the plate line and via the use of a long time constant in one plate line to provide a small amount of positive feedback. Variable resistor R1091, the dc shift control, provides the proper compensation.

When internal triggering of the time-base generator is used, a sample of the vertical signal is used to develop the triggering pulse. This is obtained from the trigger pickoff circuit and also is available at the front panel binding post, vertical signal output.

The vertical-amplifier output signal goes through the balanced delay line to the vertical deflection plates. The function of this delay line is to retard the arrival of the signal waveform to the deflection plates until the CRT has been unblanked and the horizontal sweep started. The delay line is terminated in its characteristic impedance to avoid reflections; this dissipates both the signal energy in the line and dc energy.

The use of a distributed amplifier provides high gain and wide bandwidth but at the same time introduces problems. The first problem is that at some high cutoff frequency, the gain may approach infinity, which shows up as ringing or oscillation. Secondly, to avoid reflections and further instability, a delay line must be used and terminated in its characteristic impedance.

Q611 Why is a distributed amplifier used in the vertical deflection system?

ITEM 611a   To provide high gain at all frequencies.

ITEM 611b   To provide a low driving impedance for the delay line.

ITEM 611c   To provide a highly stable pulse delay.

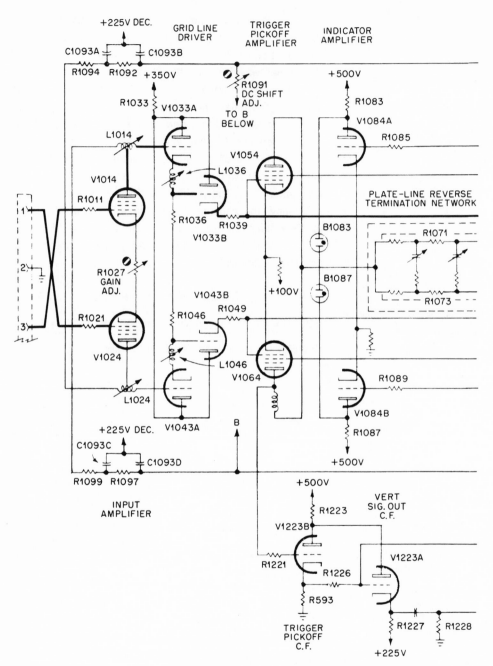

FIGURE 6-8 Simplified T 541A vertical-amplifier circuitry.

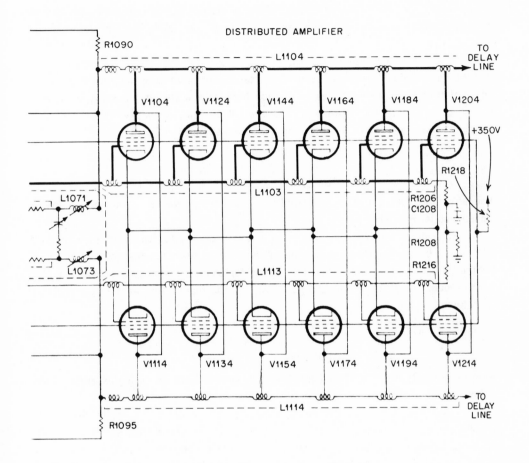

DISTRIBUTED AMPLIFIER

R1090

L1104

TO DELAY LINE

V1104 V1124 V1144 V1164 V1184 V1204

+350V

R1218

L1103

R1206
C1208

L1071

L1073

R1208

R1216

L1113

V1114 V1134 V1154 V1174 V1194 V1214

L1114

TO DELAY LINE

R1095

→ TO TIME-BASE TRIG.

VERT
SIG. OUT

ITEM 611a

Your answer was that the reason for using a distributed amplifier in the vertical deflection system is **to provide high gain at all frequencies,** including high frequencies.

That is entirely correct; providing high gain with a wide bandwidth is very much of a problem whether you are talking about video or radio frequency. The distributed amplifier has the unusual characteristic of permitting the adding or paralleling of tube transconductances to provide high gain while, at the same time, providing for the shunt capacitance of only one tube. This is done via the distributed coupling delay line, which isolates the tube capacitances. Go to Item 612.

ITEM 611b

You answered that a distributed amplifier is used **to provide a low driving-source impedance for the delay line.**

The delay line does need a relatively low driving-source impedance, namely 600 ohms, but the delay line could be driven by a cathode follower instead of a distributed amplifier. So this is not the reason for using a distributed amplifier in this oscilloscope. What are its advantages? Reread the material on Item 611 and figure out why.

ITEM 611c

You answered that a distributed amplifier is used because of its **highly stable pulse delay.**

Certainly, the delay provided by the distributed delay line in the distributed amplifier is a highly stable one. The delay line provides even more than this, however. If only a highly stable delay were desired, it would be enough merely to have a distributed line, not a distributed amplifier. No, the reason for using a distributed amplifier is something other than the highly stable delay characteristic. See if you can find the something else on Item 611.

ITEM 612

THE
TRIGGER
SYSTEM

Refer to Fig. 6-9, the simplified trigger circuitry, and to the block diagram at the end of the chapter as necessary.

The time-base trigger develops a pulse to start the time-base generator below 5 Mc. The trigger slope switch allows the operator to select either the positive or negative slope of the vertical signal to trigger the sweep. Above 5 Mc the time-base trigger is bypassed and the synchronizing signal is applied directly to the sweep-gating multivibrator in the time-base generator.

Triggering signals may be developed from several sources, the most common being the internal vertical-amplifier circuitry of the oscilloscope. With this source, either triggered or synchronized operation is available. The same holds true for an external trigger source. The trigger also may be picked from the power line.

The trigger input amplifier is a polarity-inverting cathode-coupled amplifier and provides a negative-going signal to drive the following stage as well as enabling the operator to choose the triggering signal level.

ITEM 612A

The trigger multivibrator is a dc-coupled multivibrator. In the normal, or quiescent, state ready to receive a signal, tube section V45A is conducting. The grid of the second section V45B is held below cutoff so that plate voltage of V45B is high and no output is developed. As the grid of V45A is driven negative, its plate voltage starts to rise. This is coupled to the B section, and V45B accordingly starts to conduct. The multivibrator flips over rapidly regardless of how slowly the input grid voltage to V45A falls. When the input signal reverses, the action with V45A reverses itself.

With the triggering mode switch in the auto position, the trigger multivibrator is changed from a bistable to a free-running multivibrator. The dc coupling is replaced by ac coupling to provide this. The multivibrator runs freely in the absence of a triggering signal; an input signal now will synchronize the multivibrator's frequency.

The trigger multivibrator produces a square wave which is fed to the time-base generator. In the time-

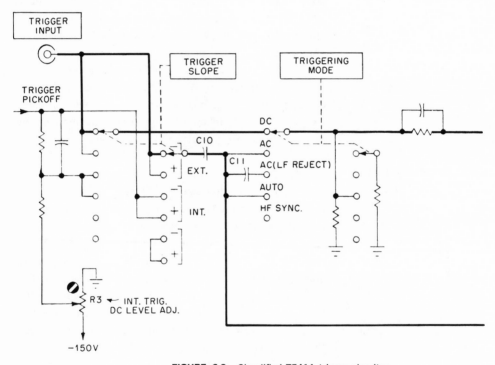

FIGURE 6-9 Simplified T541A trigger circuitry.

base generator this square wave is differentiated to produce a sharp negative-going pulse to trigger the generator at the proper time in the signal cycle.

Q612 Study the circuit diagram from trigger input to output. In the high-frequency sync position, the triggering multivibrator is:

ITEM 612a A synchronized free-running multivibrator.

ITEM 612b Not used because the trigger signal bypasses it to go directly to the time-base generator.

ITEM 612c Triggered only by the high-frequency signal components.

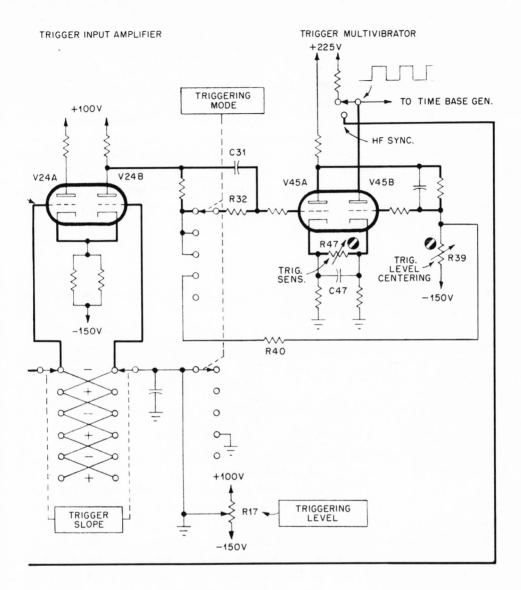

TRIGGER INPUT AMPLIFIER

TRIGGER MULTIVIBRATOR

ITEM 612a

You answered: **In the high-frequency sync position the trigger multivibrator is a synchronized free-running multivibrator.**

Refer to the circuit diagram for the trigger circuitry. Find the trigger switch, the trigger mode selector switch, and note that it has several sections. In the high-frequency sync position, note that the input signal bypasses the trigger multivibrator to go to an output section of the switch and then to the time-base generator. The trigger multivibrator is disconnected in this position. In addition the trigger multivibrator is free-running only in the next position back, the one called auto. Try a different answer on Item 612.

ITEM 612b

You answered that in the high-frequency sync position, **the trigger multivibrator is bypassed.**

Referring to the circuit diagram, you were completely correct on this. In this position the trigger input signal bypasses the trigger multivibrator and goes directly to the time-base generator where it synchronizes the gating multivibrator. You were very much on the ball with this answer, and proceed now to Item 613.

ITEM 612c

You answered that in the high-frequency sync position, the trigger multivibrator is **triggered only by the high-frequency signal components.**

Refer to the simplified trigger-circuitry diagram. Note that in the high-frequency sync position, the trigger input signal takes a wire and path completely around the trigger circuitry to the output circuitry of the trigger multivibrator to go to the time-base generator. You have the situation partially correct and partially incorrect. In the high-frequency sync position, the sweep is triggered only by the high-frequency signal components, but that is a different story than stating that the trigger multivibrator does the triggering. It doesn't. The trigger multivibrator is completely out of the circuit in this switch position.

Turn to Item 612.

Refer to Fig. 6-10, which shows the time-base generator's simplified circuit. Refer to the detailed block diagram (Fig. 6-16) at the end of the chapter as necessary. The negative-going square wave from the trigger generator is coupled to the time-base generator, where it is differentiated to produce a sharp negative-going triggering impulse. The three main circuits are the sweep-gating multivibrator, the Miller run-up circuit, and the holdoff circuit.

The sweep-gating multivibrator operates in a bistable mode. Normally V135A is conducting and its plate voltage is low, which cuts off the second half of the tube V135B. When an impulse comes along, the situation reverses. The normally off state of the Miller circuit is determined by the dc network between plate and grid. This network is the neon glow tube B167, the run-up cathode follower V173, and the on-off diodes V152. The network sets the plate voltage of the Miller tube such that the tube will operate above the knee of the characteristic curve and thus operate linearly.

If the stability and triggering level controls are adjusted for triggering operation, the sweep-gating multivibrator is forced into its other state where V145 is the conducting tube. When this happens, the on-off diodes V152 are cut off. The grid of the Miller tube and the cathode of the cathode follower are then free to change. The grid voltage of the Miller tube starts to drop since it is connected to the −150-volt bus through timing resistor R160. Consequently the plate of the Miller tube starts to rise, carrying along the grid and cathode of cathode follower V173. This raises the voltage of the top of the timing capacitor C160 which in turn, in a bootstrap fashion, pulls up the grid of the Miller tube and keeps it from dropping. The increase in voltage on the timing capacitor C160 is offset by the negative voltage from the timing resistor. Thus the grid voltage is kept constant to within a fraction of a volt for the duration of the sweep. The linear rise in voltage of the cathode follower is used as the sweep time base. The timing capacitor C160 and timing resistor R160 are selected by the time/centimeter switch. This RC time constant determines the sweep length and repetition rate.

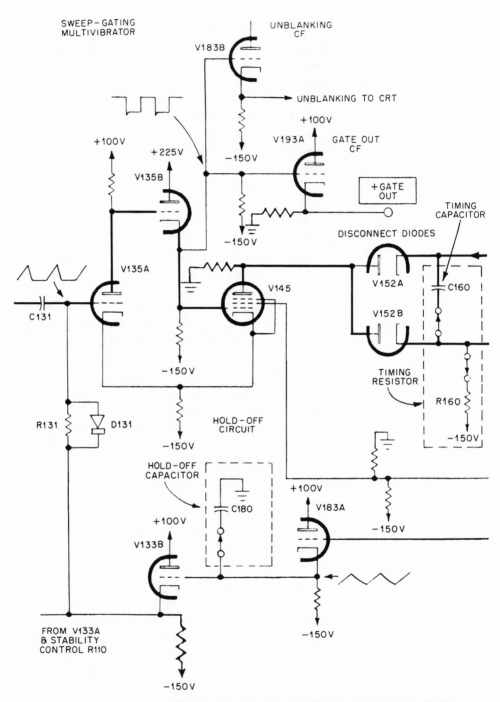

FIGURE 6-10 Simplified T 541A time-base-generator circuitry.

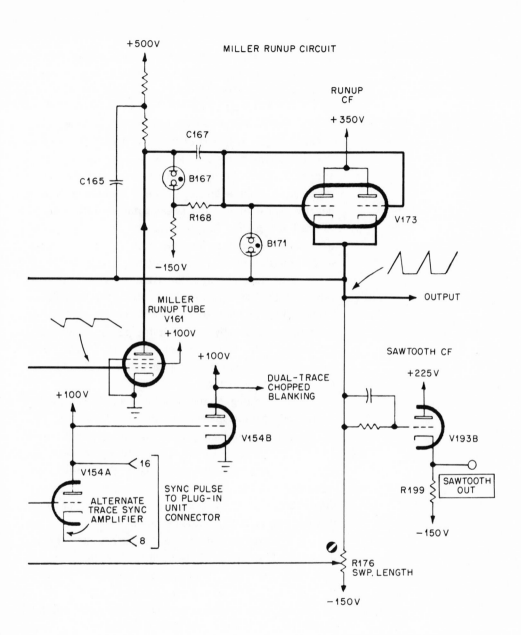

MILLER RUNUP CIRCUIT

+500V

RUNUP
CF

+350V

C167

C165

B167

R168

V173

−150V

B171

MILLER
RUNUP TUBE
V161

+100V

OUTPUT

+100V

SAWTOOTH CF

+225V

DUAL-TRACE
CHOPPED
BLANKING

+100V

V154B

V193B

16

V154A

SAWTOOTH
OUT

ALTERNATE
TRACE SYNC
AMPLIFIER

SYNC PULSE
TO PLUG-IN
UNIT
CONNECTOR

R199

−150V

8

R176
SWP. LENGTH

−150V

ITEM 613A   The sweep rate is the speed at which the electron spot moves across the face of the CRT. The length of the sweep, or the distance that the spot moves across the face of the scope, however, is determined by the setting of the sweep length control R176. As the output sweep voltage rises, part of this is coupled back through the sweep-length resistor R176 through triode V183A and its associated triode V133B to the input grid of the sweep-gating multivibrator V135A. Remember that a negative spike flipped the sweep-gating multivibrator on to start the gate. This positive voltage resulting from the positive sweep waveform fed back through the sweep-length resistor turns the sweep-gating multivibrator off.

The holdoff capacitor C180 charges up quite rapidly to the peak sweep voltage, so that it will hold the sweep-gating multivibrator off until capacitor C180 has discharged sufficiently to permit the gating multivibrator to reverse. This causes the clamp or disconnect diodes to discharge the sweep-timing capacitor C160 and reset the Miller run-up circuit.

The setting of the stability control R110 determines the operational mode of the time-base generator. For triggered operation the stability control is adjusted so that the grid of V135A of the sweep-gating multivibrator is just high enough to keep the multivibrator from free-running. Adjusted thus, a sweep can be produced only when an incoming negative trigger pulse drives the grid of V135A below cutoff.

Moving the arm of the stability control toward ground, but not so far as to reach the preset switch, will raise the grid level of V135A and prevent the gating multivibrator from being triggered, which would turn off the sweep. Moving the arm towards the −150-volt side drops the grid voltage of V135A to where the discharge or the holdoff capacitor C180 can switch the multivibrator. Adjusted in this manner, the sweep-gating multivibrator will free-run and produce a recurrent sweep.

Q613 Which is not a function of the disconnect diodes V152A and B:

ITEM 613a   Stop the sweep when the diodes are just conducting.

ITEM 613b   Determine the holdoff time by their dynamic resistance.

ITEM 613c   Start the sweep when just cut off.

ITEM 613a

You answered that it is not the function of the disconnect diodes V152A and B **to stop the sweep when the diodes are conducting.**

The sweep starts its retrace when the two diodes are heavily conducting, as when the control tube V146 is cut off. The heavy conduction of the two diodes swamps, or shorts, the retrace timing capacitor C160. Thus, when the diodes are conducting or just conducting, the sweep is just stopped. The time that the diodes are conducting is the reset period, and the sweep-timing capacitor is being reset to zero in its low-voltage state. Thus, one function of these two diodes is very much to stop and start the sweep. Try a different answer on Item 613.

ITEM 613b

You answered that it is not the function of the disconnect diodes V152A and B to **determine the holdoff time by means of their dynamic resistance.**

When the diodes are heavily conducting, their dynamic resistance is a shunt circuit for the timing capacitor C160. During the sweep resetting time, this RC time constant determines the sweep retrace time. But this is different from the holdoff time, since the sweep desirably is held cut off longer than the retrace time to ensure a stable resetting of the timing capacitor. Thus, you were quite right. One process that is not a function of the disconnect diodes is to determine the holdoff time, although the disconnect diodes do determine the sweep retrace time. Nice going; that showed clear thinking on your part. Go to Item 614.

ITEM 613c

You answered that it is not the function of the disconnect diodes V152A and B to **start the sweep when they are just cut off.**

In the reset condition, the pentode control tube V146 is cut off, and thus the anodes of the two disconnect diodes are at ground potential. Since their cathodes go to minus supplies, the diodes are conducting heavily. This heavy conduction swamps, or shorts, the timing capacitor C160. Thus, when the diodes are cut off, the timing capacitor C160 is permitted to charge to produce the sweep. This is exactly how the sweep is started—when the diodes are just cut off. Try a different answer on Item 613.

ITEM 614

DUAL-TRACE OPERATION

Dual traces may be produced on the CRT face. Refer to Fig. 6-11. If a square wave is fed into the vertical deflection system along with the vertical signal, the electron spot will be alternately raised and lowered so that two separate sweeps are viewed on the scope's face. Synchronizing pulses for dual-trace preamplifiers are supplied by the dual-trace tube V154A. When the multivibrator tube V145 cuts off, a differentiated pulse from its screen is coupled to the grid of V154A, producing a negative trigger at its plate. This trigger then switches the multivibrator in the dual-trace unit, producing sweeps that are alternately high and low.

The square wave, in addition to being put on the scope in synchronism with alternate sweeps, may be put on independently of the sweep signal. The sweep may be chopped into many small pieces so that the spot is deflected alternately high and low along with the usual vertical input signal. In this condition the dual-trace multivibrator is connected for free-running operation and produces chopped sweeps. A negative pulse comes from the multivibrator to the grid of V154B, producing a positive pulse at the plate which is coupled to the cathode of the CRT to blank the beam.

Q614 The switching multivibrator for dual-trace operation provides a square-wave vertical deflection signal that is:

ITEM 614a   Independent of the time-base generator.

ITEM 614b   Either synchronized with, or independent of, the time-base generator.

ITEM 614c   Synchronized with the time-base generator.

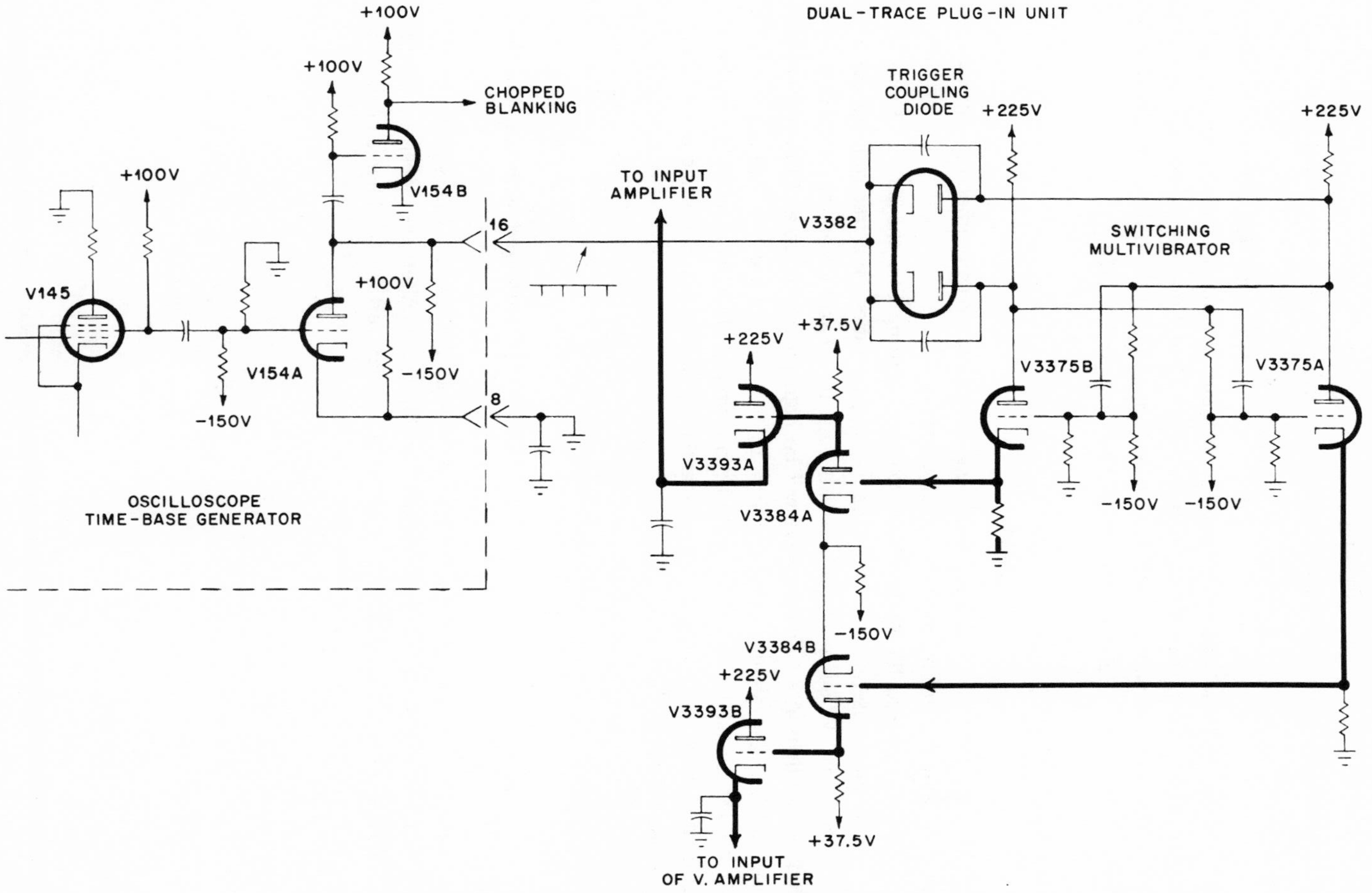

FIGURE 6-11 Simplified T 541A dual-trace circuitry.

ITEM 614a

You answered that the dual-trace switching multivibrator is **independent of the time-base generator.**

The dual-trace multivibrator can indeed be connected for independent operation; such is the case when it is free-running and produces chopped sweeps. The chopping frequency is completely independent of the time-base generator and produces a square wave which alternately deflects the spot up and down to produce two traces on the scope. But you have an option. Turn to Item 614.

ITEM 614b

You answered that the dual-trace switching multivibrator can **either be synchronized with, or be independent of, the time-base generator.**

This is indeed the case. Nice going on figuring this one out. Although the circuit diagram does not show the free-running condition, the free-running certainly was discussed. When synchronized with the time-base generator or sweeps, the switching multivibrator's square wave will be high for one trace and low for the next sweep, so that the signals corresponding to the sweeps are alternatingly high and low. Or the switching dual-trace circuit can simply chop the signals to sweep the spot up and down at a fast rate independently of the sweep. The same effect results: two traces. Turn to Item 615.

ITEM 614c

You answered that the switching multivibrator is **synchronized with the time-base generator.**

In the synchronized mode, that is indeed the case. The switching multivibrator then is a bistable multivibrator, or flip-flop. Alternate sweeps produce a square-wave output that is added in with the regular vertical-amplifier signal. However, there is an option. Go to Item 614.

ITEM 615

HORIZONTAL AMPLIFIER

Refer to Fig. 6-12 and the block diagram (Fig. 6-16) at the end of the chapter. The input to the horizontal amplifier may come from an external signal, which is applied to the horizontal input connector, or may come as a sawtooth sweep waveform from the time-base generator.

In the input amplifier circuitry, a variable resistor R348 adjusts the length of the time base and the sweep by varying the signal attenuation. In the unmagnified sweep position, an additional attenuator is in series with the signal to cut its magnitude by a factor of 5 normally. This network is out in the 5× position. For positioning, the signal at the left-hand deflection plate is fed back to the input of the driver cathode followers via an adjustable resistor R348. By changing the dc voltage at this point, the user can adjust the positioning of the magnified sweep to look at any part of the unmagnified sweep.

Part of the signal appearing at the plate of the output amplifiers is used to drive the output cathode followers. Their purpose is to drive the capacity of the horizontal deflection plates and associated wiring. To assure a sufficient flow of current at a fast time when the cathode followers are cut off (and source impedance consequently high), a pentode V398 is used to supply current. This is necessary only when the left-hand deflection plate is negative-going and is not necessary during the retrace time. The grid signal to V398 is the right-hand deflection plate signal differentiated, so that faster signals result in more grid drive than slower ones. The bootstrap capacitors C364 and C384 are used to help supply the necessary charging current for fast-time bases.

Q615 The pentode V398 functions as the load for the left-hand cathode follower V364B and increases the high-frequency response by:

ITEM 615a Providing a low source resistance on negative signals.

ITEM 615b Supplying a constant current on positive signals.

ITEM 615c Supplying negative feedback from the right-hand deflection plate.

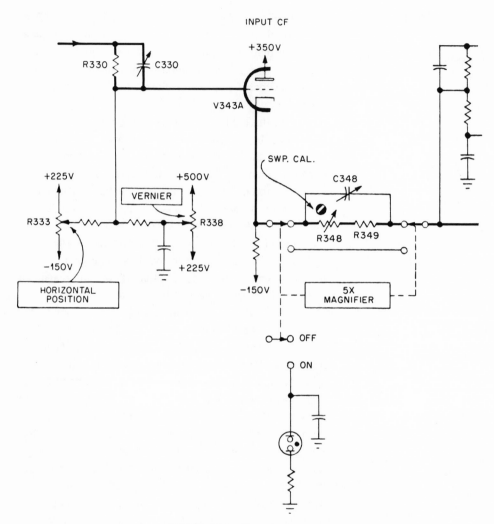

FIGURE 6-12 Simplified T541A horizontal-amplifier circuitry.

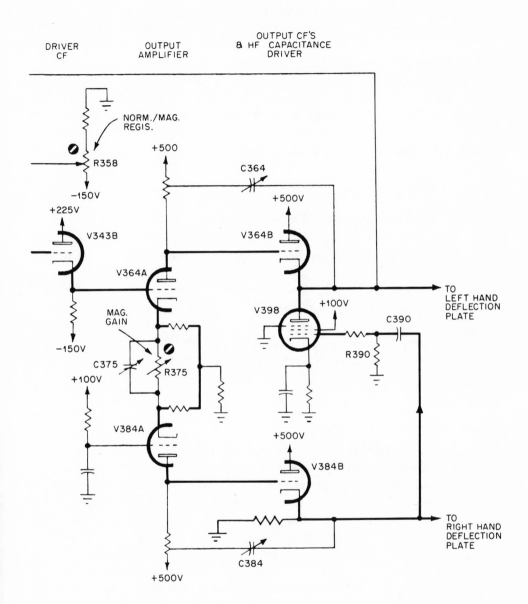

DRIVER
CF

OUTPUT
AMPLIFIER

OUTPUT CF'S
& HF CAPACITANCE
DRIVER

NORM./MAG.
REGIS.

R358

−150V

+225V

V343B

−150V

C375

+100V

MAG.
GAIN

R375

V364A

V384A

+500

C364

+500V

V364B

V398

+100V

C390

R390

+500V

V384B

TO
LEFT HAND
DEFLECTION
PLATE

TO
RIGHT HAND
DEFLECTION
PLATE

C384

+500V

You answered: **The pentode V398, functioning as the cathode-follower load, increases the high-frequency response by providing a low driving-source impedance on negative signals.**

With negative signals, falling as they do after positive signals, the cathode-follower output voltage is dropping; the triode is going toward the cutoff region. When cut off, its resistance is high, and it cannot drive the load voltage. In this case the pentode load steps in to supply the missing power. Its drive comes from the other deflection-plate signal and is phase-inverted, as well as differentiated, to supply the needed current. This showed clear thinking on your part. Nice going, Dr. Holmes. Turn to Item 616.

You answered that the pentode-load resistance for the left-hand cathode follower increases the high-frequency response by **supplying a constant current on positive signals.**

The pentode does indeed have a constant-current characteristic which is used on positive signals when the triode V364 cathode follower is conducting. But there is more to the story than that. The source resistance of the cathode followers is quite low when the triode is conducting, but when it is cut off, where is the current going to come from? Think about this for a minute, and select a different answer on Item 615.

You answered: **The pentode V398 increases the high-frequency response by supplying negative feedback from the right-hand deflection plate.**

The grid drive for this pentode V398 does come from the right-hand drive to the deflection plate. However, the signal is differentiated so that more drive is applied to the pentode grid at the high frequencies than at the lower frequencies. This doesn't quite sound like the usual application of negative feedback to linearize an output, does it? No, I'm afraid not in this case. The signal appears to be negative feedback, but it really is in phase. There is negative feedback around the loop, however, from the left-hand cathode-follower output back to the input of the driver triode V343B. But there is another possibility that you have overlooked. See if you can find it on Item 615.

ITEM 616

THE LOW-VOLTAGE SUPPLY

Refer to Fig. 6-13 and the block diagram as necessary. The reference voltage for the −150-volt supply is furnished by the gas-diode voltage-reference tube V609. This tube has a constant voltage drop of −87 volts. This reference voltage is sent into one half of the difference amplifier V624A, and the grid voltage for the other half of the amplifier comes from the −150-volt supply bus via the −150-volt adjust control R616.

When line voltage or load fluctuations try to change the output voltage, an error signal exists between the two grids of the difference amplifier; this error signal is amplified and applied to the grids of the series resistance tubes, changing their resistance such that the output voltage is compensated to remain at a constant −150 volts.

The +100-volt supply is regulated by comparing the potential obtained from the voltage divider R650-R651 between the +100-volt bus and the −150-volt supply. The dc amplifier passes any error signal on to the series regulator tube to maintain a constant +100 volts on the bus.

The voltage for the +225-volt supply has 125 volts added on to the +100-volt bus. This difference voltage of +125 volts comes from a separate transformer winding and rectifier. The supply is regulated by sensing the voltage at a point near ground obtained from voltage divider R680-R681 which compares the +225-volt bus and the regulated −150-volt bus. The error voltage here is amplified by the difference amplifier and coupled to the cathode follower to compensate for any changes. This supply also furnishes an unregulated output of about +325 volts for the oscillator in the CRT high-voltage supply.

Q616 Which is true for the power supply?

ITEM 616a The low-voltage power supplies have individual adjustments for their output voltages.

ITEM 616b The −150-volt supply serves as the voltage reference for the other supplies.

ITEM 616c All the low-voltage outputs are regulated.

ITEM 616a

Low-voltage power supplies have individual adjustments for their output voltages.

Refer to circuit diagram Fig. 6-13. Do you see any voltage-adjustment potentiometers feeding the dc amplifiers in any of the regulated supplies except for the −150-volt supply? Take a very close look; how many of them do you see? Now you will have no trouble picking the answer back on Item 616.

ITEM 616b

The −150-volt supply serves as the voltage reference for the other low-voltage supplies.

On Fig. 6-13 locate in turn the dc amplifiers for each of the regulated supplies. In each case you will find a voltage divider where the lower end is returned to the −150-volt supply. Thus indeed, the −150-volt supply is the voltage reference for the other regulated supplies, although a gas diode V609 serves as its reference. Thus, adjusting the −150-volt supply with resistor R616 sets all the other voltages correctly through the precision voltage dividers. Go to Item 616A below.

ITEM 616c

All the low-voltage supplies are regulated.

On Fig. 6-13 at the right-hand side of the page are all the output voltages. Scan down the list, and see if you see any marked "unregulated." There is one, the +325-volt supply, which furnishes power for the r-f oscillator in the high-voltage supply. Go back to Item 616, reread, and try another answer.

ITEM 616A The rectified and filtered voltage is added to the +100-volt supply to furnish power for the +350-volt supply. The reference point is near ground potential, obtained from voltage divider R710-R711 connected between the regulated +350-volt bus and the reference −150-volt supply.

The rectified voltage for the 500-volt supply is added to the regulated side of the 350-volt supply to furnish power to the +500-volt regulator. The reference for the dc amplifier V754 compares the +500 volts from the divider connected between the +500-volt bus and −150-volt supply, divider R740-741.

The time-delay relay K600 delays the application of dc power to the amplifier tube for about 25 sec. This is to allow the tube heaters to come up to operating temperature before operating potentials are applied.

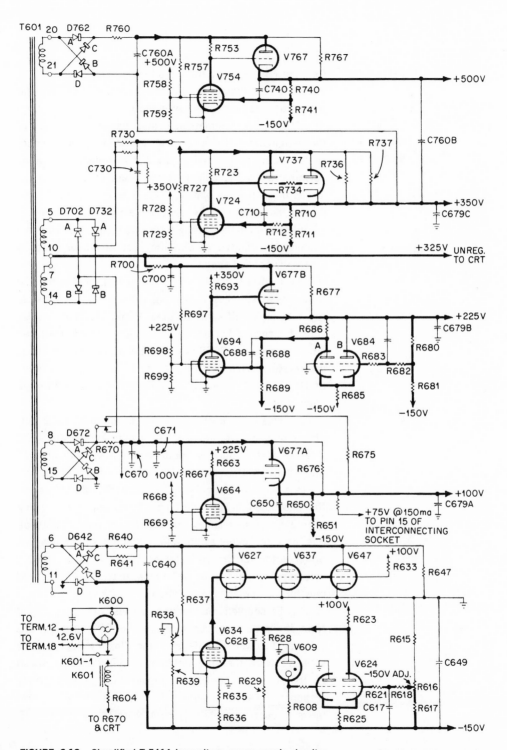

FIGURE 6-13 Simplified T 541A low-voltage power-supply circuitry.

ITEM 617

THE HIGH-VOLTAGE SUPPLY AND CRT CONTROLS

Refer to Fig. 6-14 for the simplified CRT circuitry.

The cathode-ray tube has the usual intensity and focus controls associated with the electron-gun circuitry. In addition, an astigmatism control varies the voltage at the astigmatism anode to focus the spot in both dimensions continuously, and a geometry adjustment varies asymmetrically the field that the beam encounters as it leaves the deflection plates. This is to control the linearity at the extremes of spot deflection. An intensity modulation signal also may be inserted in series with the cathode to brighten or dim the spot in response to an externally applied signal.

A 60-kc r-f oscillator furnishes power for the three power supplies furnishing voltages to the cathode-ray tube. A half-wave rectifier V862 provides −1350 volts for the CRT cathode. A half-wave voltage-tripler circuit provides +8650 volts for the Aquadag post anode accelerator. This provides the total accelerating voltage of 10 kv. Both supplies are tied to the +100-volt regulated supply.

Finally a floating half-wave rectifier V822 furnishes bias voltage, about −1450 volts for the CRT grid. Floating this supply is required to provide dc-coupled unblanking pulses to the CRT grid. The −1350-volt cathode supply is regulated by comparing its voltage to the decoupled +100-volt bus. If variations in loading should occur to change the voltage on the −1350-volt bus, an error signal exists and is amplified to change the power output of the oscillator accordingly. The +8650-volt supply and the negative-bias supply are regulated only for the line-voltage variations.

Dc-coupled unblanking pulses are transmitted from the time-base generator to the CRT grid via the cathode follower V183B and the floating high-voltage supply. Note that the unblanking pulse is ac coupled at the intensity control to provide for high-frequency response. The dc component of the unblanking pulse feeds through the intensity control itself.

Q617 Which is true of the high-voltage supplies for the CRT:

ITEM 617a All high-voltage supplies are regulated with respect to load changes.

ITEM 617b There is one high-voltage tripler and one high-voltage half-wave rectifier.

ITEM 617c The +100-volt supply is the reference for the high-voltage supply.

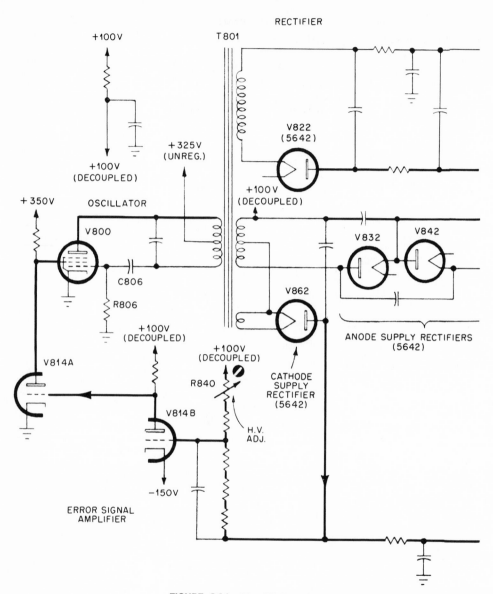

FIGURE 6-14 Simplified T 541A high-voltage and CRT circuitry.

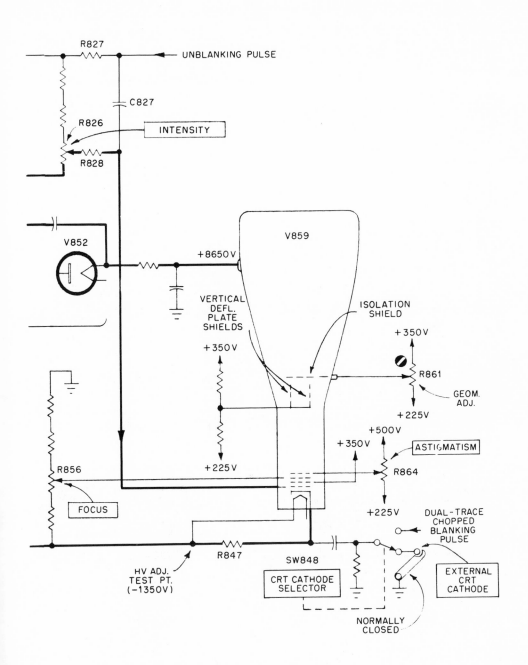

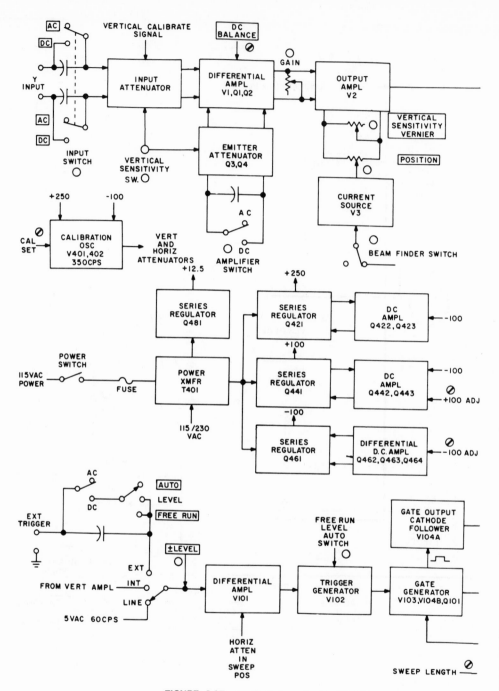

FIGURE 6-15 Block diagram for the HP 130C oscilloscope.

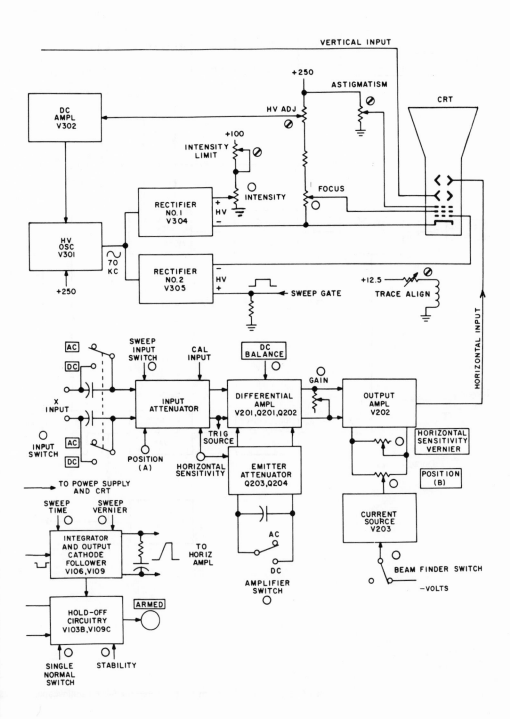

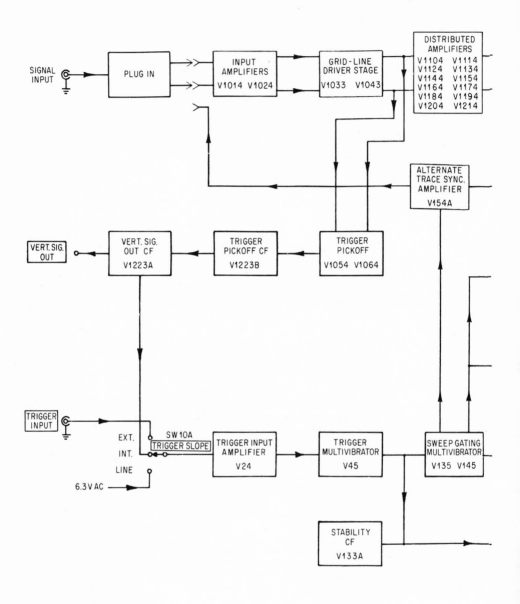

FIGURE 6-16 Block diagram for the Tektronix 541A oscilloscope.

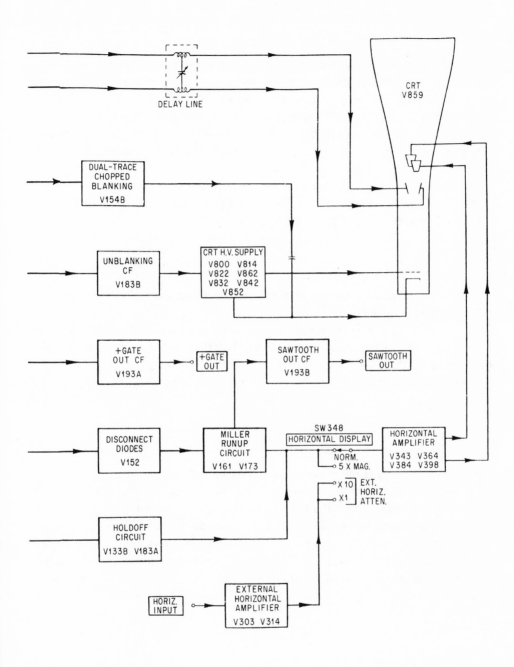

DELAY LINE

CRT
V859

DUAL-TRACE
CHOPPED
BLANKING
V154B

UNBLANKING
CF
V183B

CRT H.V. SUPPLY
V800   V814
V822   V862
V832   V842
V852

+GATE
OUT CF
V193A

+GATE
OUT

SAWTOOTH
OUT CF
V193B

SAWTOOTH
OUT

DISCONNECT
DIODES
V152

MILLER
RUNUP
CIRCUIT
V161   V173

SW348
HORIZONTAL DISPLAY
NORM.
5 X MAG.

HORIZONTAL
AMPLIFIER
V343 V364
V384 V398

X 10   EXT.
        HORIZ.
X1   ATTEN.

HOLDOFF
CIRCUIT
V133B V183A

HORIZ.
INPUT

EXTERNAL
HORIZONTAL
AMPLIFIER
V303 V314

ITEM 617a

All the high-voltage supplies are regulated with respect to load variations.

The regulation of the high-voltage supplies comes from varying the r-f input power to all three high-voltage supplies. The cathode minus high-voltage supply is the reference and is the regulated supply. Locate on the diagram the input to the control amplifier V814B. Note that the cathode supply is coupled to one end of the voltage-divider reference source. Thus the cathode high-voltage supply is regulated for input power, for line-voltage changes, as well as for load changes. The other supplies, however, are regulated only for input power variations, and not for load changes, since there is no way for a change in their output voltage to be coupled into the control amplifier. Try another answer on Item 617.

ITEM 617b

The high-voltage supplies consist of one high-voltage half-wave tripler and one high-voltage half-wave rectifier.

Look at Fig. 6-14 and count how many diodes you have. There are three diodes associated with the one high-voltage tripler, but there are two other high-voltage diodes, one for the cathode supply and one for the grid supply. Thus there are two half-wave rectifiers in addition to the high-voltage tripler. Pick another answer back on Item 617.

ITEM 617c

The +100-volt supply is the reference for the minus high-voltage supply.

Actually you ought to be able to figure this one out without referring to the circuit diagram (Fig. 6-14). The logic is that the voltage reference always compares one polarity voltage with another one. Earlier you discovered that the minus high-voltage supply for the cathode of the CRT was regulated. This would obviously have to offset a plus voltage, not a negative voltage. Thus this answer is quite correct, whether or not you referred to the circuit diagram. Nice going. You have now finished another chapter, and it is time for another quiz. Turn to Quiz 6, Item 618.

ITEM 618

QUIZ 6

As before, write down your answers on a separate sheet of paper. Then check your answers by the corresponding letter on the next page.

1 What are the major functional divisions, or areas, of the two oscilloscopes studied? *(C)*

2 What feature(s) of the vertical circuitry facilitate(s) measuring voltage in waveform signals? *(A)*

3 The high-voltage supplies for both scopes (have/do not have) the high voltage regulated, and the high-voltage–rectifier input power comes from (the ac line directly/an r-f oscillator). *(D)*

4 Which plug-in preamp for the T 541A scope would you use for directly comparing the output of an amplifier with its input? *(B)*

5 What feature of these two scopes is useful in determining a signal's frequency? *(G)*

6 Both scopes in their sweep generation use (a transistorized linear ramp generator, a synchronized thyratron relaxation oscillator, a gate multivibrator plus Miller integrator). *(K)*

7 What provisions are made in the two scopes for finding an off-the-face electron beam? *(F)*

8 For what purpose(s) might you use the intensity modulation terminals of a scope to apply a signal directly to the CRT grid? *(H)*

9 Why might you want to use the vertical amplifier dc-coupled instead of ac-coupled? *(E)*

10 Suppose the input impedance (1 megohm shunted by 45 pf) of the vertical amplifier loads the circuit being measured too heavily. What would you do about this? *(I)*

11 What is the purpose of a delay line in the vertical-amplifier channel? *(J)*

12 What is typical measurement accuracy for a calibrated scope in the x or y channel? *(L)*

ITEM 619

A The calibrated vertical-gain feature, with a wide range of 1:2:5 step changes, and calibration oscillator.

B A dual-trace preamplifier so that the input would be displayed on one trace and the output on the other.

C Vertical and horizontal amplifiers, trigger and time-base generators, power supplies, and CRT.

D The input to the regulated high-voltage supplies comes from a 60-kc oscillator.

E The dc level of any point on the signal waveform can be measured with respect to ground or some other reference not on the waveform.

F In one, a beam-finder switch reduces the deflection voltage to very low values to center the beam, and in the other, an off-beam position is indicated by neons.

G The calibrated time-base generator with a wide coverage in 1:2:5 steps.

H Unblanking when using an external sweep or trigger, and for providing time-marker pulses on the sweep.

I Use a compensated 10:1 or 50:1 voltage-divider probe with its much higher impedance.

J It delays the signal applied to the VDP while the undelayed signal picked off earlier in the chain starts the sweep. This permits viewing fast-rise-time pulses.

K Gating multivibrator plus Miller integrator.

L Typically 5 percent for a calibrated scope—this can be somewhat better with care and much worse without calibration.

Take a break; then tackle "lucky seven."

CHAPTER SEVEN

APPLICATIONS OF SCOPES

ITEM 701

**PHASE
MEASUREMENT**

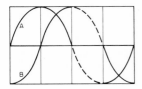

Phase measurement on sine waves can be made within 1° easily and often times to the nearest ½° with the following measurement scheme. Two scope channels are used which have identical gain and bandwidth response characteristics. The *A* channel of the dual-trace amplifier is triggered by the input signal. The scope controls are adjusted until the *A*-channel signal occupies the entire base width of 10 cm. The amplitude is adjusted to the maximum height of 10 cm on the vertical scale. Then the *B*-channel signal is adjusted so that its height is the same as the *A* signal's.

A precision potentiometer is used to provide a delayed trigger. This produces a pulse which blanks out part of each sine wave on the oscilloscope. This blanking occurs at a very precise instant on the time base and is used to find the time at which each sine wave in turn goes through a particular point, such as zero.

First, the delayed trigger is adjusted with the precision potentiometer (Helipot) until the *A*-trace blanking hits zero voltage on the *X* axis. The Helipot dial is read to three figures. Then the *B* trace is blanked just as it crosses the *X* axis. The Helipot dial is read again. Since the Helipot dial covers 1000 increments and represents the entire 10 cm to move the blanking completely across the scope face, each Helipot increment represents one-thousandth of one revolution, or 0.36° per digit. The two time readings are merely subtracted and multiplied by this factor to give the phase difference directly.

Q701 The dial readings (0 to 1000) in this phase-measurement procedure indicate:

ITEM 701a Parts per thousand of the time for one cycle.

ITEM 701b Phase in degrees to the second zero crossing.

ITEM 701c Voltage corresponding to the sine of the phase angle.

ITEM 701a

You answered: **The dial readings directly indicate the relative distance in parts per thousand (ppt) of the waveform displayed, which is adjusted to be one full cycle.** The dial readings are converted to degrees by the multiplying factor of 360/1000, or 0.36.   Right.

Turn to Item 702.

ITEM 701b

You answered that the dial readings indicated **phase in degrees to the second zero crossing.**

The dial readings indicate 0 to 1000 linear increments.   A sine wave by definition is nonlinear, and the dial numbers represent 1000 linear increments across one cycle of a recurrent waveform but only when the scope is adjusted such that one full cycle occupies the complete X dimension on the scope face.

Return to Item 701.

ITEM 701c

You answered: **The dial readings indicate a voltage corresponding to the sine of the phase angle.**

No, for a sine wave, the voltage applied to the vertical axis, or Y dimension, corresponds to the sine of the signal phase angle.   Here the dial reading indicates blanking delay along the X axis.   With the time base adjusted so that one complete sine wave takes up the entire X axis, the 1000 linear dial increments can be interpreted as something else.

Turn to Item 701.

A delayed sweep is quite useful in case you wish to trigger the sweep at the start of a pulse and then view the trailing edge of the pulse to check on the variation of the pulse width, called "jitter." See the illustration below. Or you might wish to see the variation in time between pulses. You could extend this to view a long string of pulses if the sweep is triggered from the master pulse generator. A delayed sweep is required to permit you to magnify a small section of the desired waveform since the short sweep operates at such a fast rate.

Let's assume that you wish to view the trailing edge of this pulse and that the trigger started on the leading edge. If you triggered on the trailing edge of the pulse, you would not see any jitter in the overall pulse width. Delay the sweep until 90 percent of the pulse has passed. Then start the sweep at a fast rate compared to the delay time, and continue the sweep on past the end of the pulse. The ratio of the delay to sweep time might be 5:1, and the magnification ratio would be 5:1 to view in detail the trailing edge of the pulse.

To ensure that variations in the time delay do not contribute to variations in the sweep delay, a highly stable time delay is desired. Typically, circuitry similar to a sweep generator is utilized. A circuit to produce such a delayed sweep is shown here. The delay generator produces a gating output pulse at a stable time delay after the input trigger.

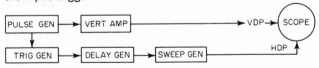

Q702 A delay generator is used to delay the start of a sweep so that later features in a cyclical waveform may be viewed in great detail. The most important characteristic about this time delay is:

ITEM 702a Variations in its time delay.

ITEM 702b Wide range of triggering levels.

ITEM 702c Variations in output pulse amplitude.

ITEM 702d Its output impedance.

The most important characteristic about a time-delay generator used to delay sweeps is that the time delay be highly stable, that is, have very little variation in the time-delay period (answer **a**). This means that regulated power supplies, accurate components, and a stable ramp generator such as a Miller run-up circuit are used.

ITEM 703

SAMPLING
SCOPE
HP 185B

Next we are going to give you briefly the theory of operation of the HP 185B oscilloscope and present some information on how it is used to make rise-time measurements on very fast pulses.

The Model HP 185B oscilloscope provides a visual display for very-high-speed pulses with repetition rates up to 1 Gc (1000 Mc). The HP 185B obtains its high-speed characteristics by using a sampling technique. The entire signal is scanned, and each succeeding sample of the signal is taken at a slightly later point on successive pulses. Each time such a sample is taken, the spot on the scope is moved along one step. Thus a complete picture of a repetitive high-speed pulse is synthesized by a buildup of image-retaining dots on the oscilloscope face. As below, a graph is plotted point by point of the samples taken.

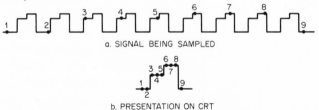

a. SIGNAL BEING SAMPLED

b. PRESENTATION ON CRT

Figure 7-1 shows a picture of the Model HP 185B sampling oscilloscope. This scope provides 10 basic time scales ranging from 10 μsec/cm to 10 nsec/cm, depending upon the setting of the time scale switch. Any part of this basic time scale can be expanded by adjusting the time scale magnifier switch. Built-in time and amplitude markers provide a ready means of checking calibration of both scope axes. Intensity of the trace is independent of pulse duty cycle. For supplemental output, the HP 185B provides output signals for XY

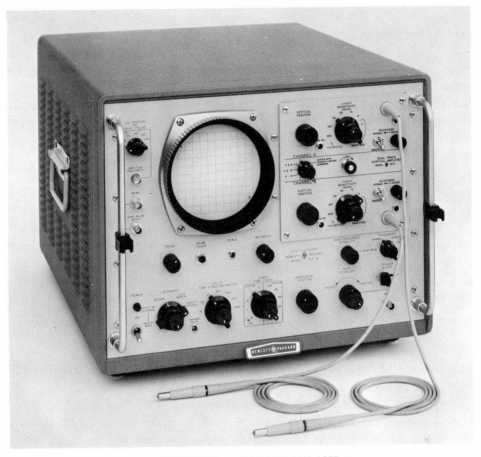

FIGURE 7-1   Photograph of HP 185B scope.

recorders and provides means for controlling the display manually or externally.

The vertical system includes a plug-in vertical amplifier, such as the Model HP 187B. It is this amplifier which determines vertical characteristics such as bandpass and sensitivity. This plug-in unit is not a part of the basic HP 185B scope.

Q703 In the HP 185B sampling oscilloscope, samples[1] are taken at a frequency that is:

ITEM 703a   An exact submultiple of the signal frequency.

ITEM 703**b**   Not related to the signal frequency.

ITEM 703**c**   Very slightly different from an exact submultiple of the signal frequency.

[1] Refer to the above sampling diagram.

ITEM 703a

Samples are taken at **an exact submultiple of the signal frequency.**

If you do this, the samples are always taken at the same relative spot on a repeating pulse. Accordingly you would see a constant amplitude signal for the entire trace duration on the scope face. This answer is close to the desired answer but not close enough. You have to have a slight variation in the sampling frequency in its relationship to the signal frequency. Triggering the sweep is done at a constant ratio, however.

ITEM 703b

Samples are taken at a frequency **not related to the signal frequency.**

This would be all right if you had a pulse that appeared just once on the scope. But when the pulse repeats and you sample at random intervals, you would get a random-appearing signal or noise on the scope face. So you do need some relationship between the signal frequency being sampled and the frequency at which such samples are taken.

ITEM 703c

Samples are taken at a frequency only **slightly different from an exact submultiple of the signal frequency.**

This is true. If you took samples at an exact submultiple of the signal frequency, you would have a constant phase relationship and you would be sampling the same point on the pulse with each successive sample. You would see only a straight line on the scope. Your sampling frequency has to slip slowly, similar to the way mechanical motion is stopped with a stroboscope. With a strobe, when the flash frequency bears an exact relationship to the rotating frequency, the machinery appears to stop. This also happens in the sampling oscilloscope. When the strobe frequency is slightly different from the rotating machinery's frequency, the machinery appears to rotate very slowly. That is exactly what we want to happen with the sampling oscilloscope.

ITEM 704

SIGNAL SAMPLING

The action of the sampling oscilloscope is similar to that of a strobe light slightly out of synchronization with the turning device, which results in an apparent slow motion. This is the same effect as results from taking moving pictures of a rapidly spinning wheel when the camera shutter speed is nearly the same as the time for one rotation of the wheel, causing the wheel to appear to be turning very slowly or even backward.

The sampling of the signal with this oscilloscope is done the same way. The plug-in amplifier in this case represents the camera shutter and lens. The sampling circuit is open for very short periods of time and the input voltage at that time carefully measured. This occurs repetitively with each succeeding sample taken on a later pulse and at a slightly later time with respect to the start of the pulse.

There is a certain minimum and maximum time between which the sampling oscilloscope can take each observation. In the HP 185B, the minimum time is 0.3 nsec, and the maximum time 100 μsec. This time for taking samples is called the "viewing window" and opens 120 nsec after a trigger is received. Accordingly, signals with a period greater than 100 μsec require special triggering techniques to view the leading edge of the pulse.

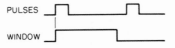

Q704 Why are special procedures necessary to view the leading edge of a pulse when the period between pulses is greater than 100 μsec?

ITEM 704a The window opened after the pulse started.

ITEM 704b The window closed before the start of the next pulse.

ITEM 704c The trigger for the window can't be delayed until the next sweep is to start.

ITEM 704a

Special procedures must be used to view the leading edge of a pulse where the inter-pulse period is greater than 100 μsec because **the window opened after the pulse started.**

That is quite correct. The window takes 120 nsec to open, and when the interpulse period is greater than 100 μsec, the window cannot be started on the first pulse in time to view the leading edge of the first or second pulses.

Turn to Item 705.

ITEM 704b

Special viewing procedures must be used because **the window closed before the start of the next pulse.**

This is true and is part of the overall reason why special procedures must be utilized. If the interpulse period is shorter than 100 μsec, the sweep can be triggered on one pulse and the end of the window extended to include the leading edge of the next pulse. The reason the window can't be opened to see the leading edge of the triggering pulse is that it takes 120 nsec to get the window open.

Turn to Item 705.

ITEM 704c

Special procedures must be utilized because **the trigger for the window can't be delayed until the next sweep is to start.**

One special procedure would be to delay the signal itself with a delay line so that the delayed signal could be presented on the sampling scope face after the trigger had started the sweep. Or a delay-trigger generator could be used to delay the trigger so that the next pulse could be seen, even though the interpulse period was longer than 100 μsec. This special delay-trigger generator and delay line are not part of the HP 185B scope and consequently would merit the terms of special procedures.

Turn to Item 705.

ITEM 705

SAMPLING GATE

Let's take a look at how the sampling works in practice. The sampling oscilloscope is a combination of a regular oscilloscope and a plug-in vertical amplifier, combination HP 185B and HP 187B. This scope senses the amplitude of a particular 0.5 nsec section of an input signal and applies this signal to the vertical amplifier on the scope. The sensing, or sampling, occurs as determined by the HP 185B and occurs slightly later on each recurrence of the input signal. Each time a sample is taken, the scope beam moves a short distance horizontally corresponding to the added time delay of the later sample.

This scope has a feedback device which detects any difference or error between the input voltage being sampled and the previously stored output voltage. Refer to the illustration below. This difference is then nullified by changing the stored output voltage via the amplifier and stretcher circuit. When the sampling gate closes, the probe capacitance starts to charge in the direction of the input voltage. Any error between the input voltage and the stored output voltage appears as a voltage change across this probe capacitance. This voltage change is amplified, stretched, and used to correct the output voltage to make it equal the input voltage at the time of the sample. The sampling gate opens before the probe capacitor has had time to charge fully. Positive feedback in the amplifier is used to compensate for this. The overall loop gain is unity, and via feedback, the probe capacitor is fully charged to the level of the input after only one sample.

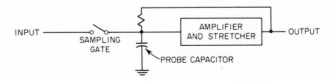

Q705 The sampling probe capacitor charges fully:

ITEM 705a When the sampling gate is closed.

ITEM 705b Just after the gate has opened after a sample.

ITEM 705c Just before the next sample is taken.

ITEM 705a

The capacitor in the sampling probe charges to the full input voltage **during the time that the gate is closed.**

No, it doesn't charge fully at that time; the capacitor charges to approximately 15 percent of the input voltage when the gate is closed.

ITEM 705b

Soon after the gate has opened, the amplifier and stretcher combination operate by positive feedback and unity gain to bring the probe capacitance charge up to the full input voltage.

Turn to Item 706.

ITEM 705c

The sampling probe capacitor charges fully **just before the next sample is taken.**

The amplifier and stretcher do not require the whole intersampling period to bring the probe capacitor up to the full voltage of the input. This is because the stretching period varies considerably on the different time scales. The circuitry is designed such that the probe capacitor is brought up to the input voltage soon after the gate is opened rather than waiting until close to the next sample.

Let's discuss briefly the methods available to trigger the sampling oscilloscope. The HP 185B must be synchronized with a signal that is time-related to the signal in the vertical amplifiers. This scope must be externally synchronized because the sampled signal never actually enters the oscilloscope vertical circuits and thus is not available internally for synchronization. The signal is sampled with the probes and doesn't get any further into the scope circuitry.

Triggers with a repetition rate between 50 cps and 1 Gc can be utilized in the HP 185B scope. An internal holdoff circuit limits the maximum sampling rate to about 100 kc in spite of the frequency of the signal being sampled. A stability control provides limited control over this holdoff circuitry to adjust for maximum stability when the trigger rate exceeds 100 kc. For signal frequencies above 100 Mc, a countdown circuit reduces the frequency of the trigger signal to approximately 10 Mc. A separate high-frequency stability control is provided for this countdown circuitry.

When limited time-scale speed is not a problem nor is jitter, the simplest method of synchronizing this scope is to trigger on one pulse and to view one or more later pulses on the screen. For this to be possible, the signal frequency must be at least 10 kc so that at least one later pulse will occur in the 100-μsec window. This is illustrated in the three lines below. The first represents a repetitive pulse signal, the second shows the trigger from the first pulse, and the third line represents the delayed window which samples the second pulse in the train.

PULSE SIGNAL
SWEEP TRIGGER
DELAYED WINDOW

Under these circumstances the trigger signal is taken from the circuit being tested and applied to the trigger input. The signal being sampled is applied to the vertical input as usual.

Q706 The usual trigger source for a signal with a repetition frequency above 10 kc is:

ITEM 706a Internally from the vertical amplifier.

ITEM 706b From an external trigger generator.

ITEM 706c Supplied externally to the trigger input.

ITEM 706a

The usual trigger source for a signal above 10 kc is obtained **internally from the vertical amplifier.**

This is not possible because the signal being sampled never gets further than the sampling device, typically the scope probe. Consequently, the vertical signal is not available within the scope circuitry.

ITEM 706b

The usual trigger source for a signal above 10 kc is **from an external trigger generator.**

Although an external trigger generator can be used to provide additional delay or for special timing purposes, it isn't needed in the usual case. The circuit under test provides video signals for the vertical amplifier as well as a trigger directly to the oscilloscope trigger input. The sampling window has sufficient delay and aperture so that it can display the second pulse in a series as well as later pulses for signals which have pulse periods that range from 100 μsec down to 1 nsec.

ITEM 706c

The external signal goes directly to the scope trigger input.

This is indeed the case. The scope must be triggered by the circuit under consideration since the vertical-amplifier signal does not correspond to the signal frequency; it is chopped up or sampled. An external trigger generator is not necessary because the window has both sufficient width and delay to display the second pulse in a series as long as the pulse repetition rate is above 10 kc.

Turn to Item 707.

ITEM 707

SCOPE SETUP

Getting a trace, or sweep line, on this sampling oscilloscope is about the same as the sequence of operations for the ordinary oscilloscopes with which you are more familiar. For instance, you would set up your various mode switches and then turn up the intensity control. If the spot or trace were visible, then you would position it appropriately with the horizontal and vertical position controls. If you do not see a trace or spot when you turn the intensity control up to maximum, press the beam-finder switch, reduce the intensity as necessary, and readjust the position controls. Then adjust the focus control for a sharp trace.

Q707   Refer to Fig. 7-1. Using your previous knowledge of how to adjust the controls of an oscilloscope, which of the following is the correct sequence of operations to obtain a sharp trace on this sampling oscilloscope when the sweep is free-running:

ITEM 707a   Set the scanning to internal and the mode switch fully clockwise. Increase the intensity control until a trace is visible, and adjust the focus control to make the trace as sharp as possible. Position the trace, if visible, with the positioning controls, or use the beam-finder switch if the trace is not visible until you can reposition the trace.

ITEM 707b   Set scanning to internal and the mode switch fully clockwise. Increase the intensity control until a trace is visible. Use the positioning and beam-finder switch as necessary to put the trace where you want it; make the trace as sharp as possible with the focus control.

ITEM 707c   Turn up the intensity control until you see a trace, use the position and beam-finder controls to position the trace as desired, and focus the trace sharply. Then set the scan control to internal and the mode control fully clockwise.

The sequence of operation of controls was:

ITEM 707a

Set the scanning on internal and the mode control fully clockwise; increase the intensity to get a visible trace, and focus it. Position the trace until visible, or use the beam-finder switch to find it and reposition the trace.

The only thing wrong with this answer is that you have to have a trace on the scope before you can focus it sharply.

ITEM 707b

Set the scanning on internal and the mode control fully clockwise; increase the intensity until the trace is visible. Position the trace as desired, using the beam-finder switch if necessary. Focus the trace as sharply as possible.

Yes, this was the correct sequence of operations. Turn now to Item 708.

ITEM 707c

Turn up the intensity control until the trace is visible; position the trace as desired, using the beam-finder switch if necessary. Focus the trace sharply, and turn the scanning control to internal and mode control fully clockwise.

This is fine in general, except that you should have set the scanning and mode controls first. Unless these controls are set, you will not have a free-running trace to see at all.

ITEM 708

SCOPE SETUP
(continued)

After you have a trace on the oscilloscope, you would like to get the sweep triggered or synchronized with the vertical signal being applied. So, connect the trigger signal to the trigger input. Turn the trigger slope positive if you want the sweep to be triggered by a positive pulse slope, or vice versa. The vertical-amplifier probe would be attached to the circuit under test at the point where you wanted to pick up a signal to be analyzed.

Q708 Refer to Fig. 7-1. Assume that you have set the vertical sensitivity to the desired signal amplitude on the scope. See if you can puzzle out what would be the sequence of adjusting the other controls and switches in order to see an unmagnified trace of the signal being sampled:

ITEM 708a Set the time scale magnifier to X1, adjust the triggering controls, and set the mode control counterclockwise as far as possible. Adjust the vertical sensitivity for the desired signal amplitude, and then turn to the appropriate time scale desired. Set the density switch as far clockwise as possible while keeping the flicker to a minimum. Touch up the stability control as necessary.

ITEM 708b Set the time scale desired. Turn the density control as far clockwise as possible, and adjust the stability control for a stable sweep. Set the triggering at the desired setting with the mode control as far counterclockwise as possible. Then adjust the vertical sensitivity control for the desired signal height.

ITEM 708c Set the trigger sensitivity and vertical sensitivity as desired. Select the appropriate time scale; turn the mode control fully counterclockwise and the density control as far clockwise as possible. Adjust the stability control for a stable sweep.

The sequence of operation of controls was:

ITEM 708a

Set the time scale magnifier to X1, adjust the triggering sensitivity, and set the mode control as far counterclockwise as possible. Adjust the vertical sensitivity for signal amplitude desired, and then set the time scale appropriately as desired. Turn the density control as far clockwise as possible, while keeping flicker to a minimum. Adjust the stability control as necessary for a stable sweep.

This was the correct answer and is indeed the sequence in which you would set up the controls. Turn to Item 709.

ITEM 708b

Select the desired time scale; turn the density control as far clockwise as possible while maintaining minimum flicker. Adjust the stability control for a stable sweep. Set the trigger sensitivity as desired, and turn the mode control as fully counterclockwise as possible, yet keeping a stable sweep. Adjust the vertical sensitivity as desired.

There are two things wrong with this approach. First, you should set up your controls with the time scale set on X1 rather than on your final time scale. This is because the adjustments are easier to make before you start magnifying the trace, as well as your troubles. Secondly, the density control is adjusted last for a minimum flicker, and the stability control should be just a touch-up operation.

ITEM 708c

Set the trigger sensitivity and vertical sensitivity as desired. Select the time scale desired, turn the mode control as far counterclockwise as possible, still keeping stable triggering. Set the density control as far clockwise as possible, yet with minimum flicker. Then touch up the stability control.

Basically you should set up the trace on as slow a time scale as possible because it is easier to do this before you switch to faster sweeps where the settings are more ticklish. Also, the vertical sensitivity setting might not be adjustable until you have a pulse displayed so that you know how high you want to see the pulse. You may get a wrong idea about the vertical signal amplitude until the pulses are stopped.

Reread Item 708.

Many times you will have to delay the trigger signal by hook or crook, so that you can see the leading edge of a pulse applied to the vertical amplifier of the sampling oscilloscope. As "hook or crook" implies, you may delay the vertical signal itself sufficiently so that the trigger circuitry and sweep start before the signal is applied to the vertical deflection plates. Alternatively, you may delay the sync signal more than the delay maximum (100 μsec) available in the HP 185B. Using this second method, the sync generator in the scope triggers the sweep circuitry and then sometime later triggers the circuit under test. Thus, even if the pulses are spaced farther than 100 μsec apart, the sweep has started sufficiently early so that the second pulse put out by the circuit under test will be visible when applied to the vertical deflection plate on the oscilloscope. There are other variations of these two basic methods.

Figure 7-2 illustrates both of these methods. The top part of the circuit shows a delay line used to delay the signal to the vertical amplifier by 120 nsec. The trigger circuitry starts with the leading edge of the pulse so that the sweep starts 120 nsec before the signal is applied to the vertical deflection plates. The vertical-amplifier signal is delayed by the delay line; the window is delayed by the triggering and sweep circuits. The lower circuit in Fig. 7-2 shows that the sync generator in the HP 185B first triggers the sweep circuit a variable time before a delayed pulse is sent to the circuit under test to trigger it. Delays of considerably more than 120 nsec may be utilized with this circuit, depending entirely upon the pulse delay in the sync generator.

Q709 What is the advantage of using the scope's sync generator in viewing fast pulses?

ITEM 709a Seeing the leading edge of the pulse.

ITEM 709b No delay line is required.

ITEM 709c Greater stability of the sync signal.

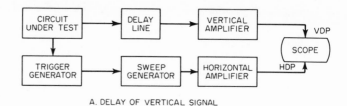

A. DELAY OF VERTICAL SIGNAL

FIGURE 7-2

Delay methods.

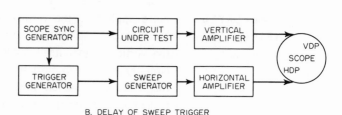

B. DELAY OF SWEEP TRIGGER

The advantage of the scope's sync generator is:

ITEM 709a

Seeing the leading edge of pulses.

Actually you can observe the leading edge of pulses with several different methods, depending on whether the circuit under test can be triggered or must be left free-running. All the methods are aimed at letting it be the leading edge. Therefore, this answer choice is important, but there is more to the question than this.

ITEM 709b

No delay line is needed when the scope's sync generator is used.

This is quite correct. The delay line is a piece of external equipment, whereas the HP 185B does have an internal sync generator. This method can be used, however, only when the circuit under test can be driven by the delayed trigger from the sync generator. Turn to Item 710.

ITEM 709c

The stability of the sync generator is greater than that of a delay line or external delay generator.

Actually there is no jitter whatsoever when a signal goes through a delay line since no active circuitry is involved but merely the passive transmission of pulses down a cable. A delay generator does have to be quite stable, but even the best of delay generators has some amount of jitter, or start-time variation from one pulse to the next one. The delay line doesn't have any of this. So reread Item 709.

ITEM 710

**TIMING RAMP
GENERATION**

Now we are going to delve briefly into the overall function of the HP 185B. Refer to the block diagram (Fig. 7-3). The major sections are the input circuits, the ramp gate generator, the time-base circuits, the calibrator, the vertical amplifier(s) and electronic switch, the horizontal amplifier, and the power supplies. The input circuits accept the trigger signal, and the trigger controls provide for stable triggering from various kinds of input signal.

The ramp gate generator produces the basic timing pulse for the time-base circuits, which are the ramp generator, the comparator and blocking oscillator, and the horizontal-scan generator. Although the ramp gate generator may be set to run freely, usually it is energized by the input trigger signal. The repetition rate for the basic timing pulse is 100 kc for time scales 200 nsec/cm and faster, but it decreases in proportion to the selected time scale for slower scales, becoming about 5 kc at 10 μsec/cm. When the trigger rate is less than the maximum timing-pulse rate, one timing pulse is generated to each trigger pulse. But when the repetition rate exceeds the maximum pulse rate, the trigger signal is subdivided, or counted down. However, the basic timing pulse, the ramp gate pulse, always maintains a strict time relationship to the input trigger frequency or to some submultiple of the input trigger frequency. Sampling of the vertical signal is done at a slightly later time on successive ramps.

The ramp gate pulse has four functions: It is used to start the ramp voltage in the time-base circuits, to complete its own cycle in a feedback network, to trigger the ramp gate extender circuitry, and to initiate the delayed sync pulse and calibrator signals. The ramp gate extender circuit increases the duration of the ramp gate pulse, producing an extended pulse which has a duration that is dependent upon the time between the input trigger t_2 and the moment just after sampling t_4. The ramp generator produces a linearly rising voltage with a slope that is dependent upon the time scale.

Q710 The frequency of the ramp pulse generator:

ITEM 710a Is independent of the signal frequency.

ITEM 710b Increases linearly with the signal frequency.

ITEM 710c Is related subharmonically to the signal frequency.

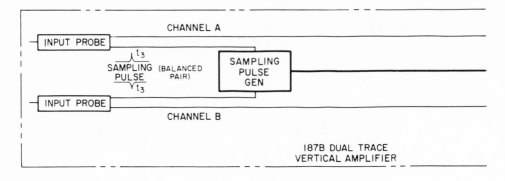

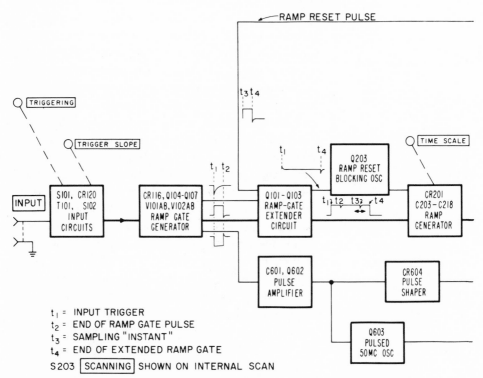

t_1 = INPUT TRIGGER
t_2 = END OF RAMP GATE PULSE
t_3 = SAMPLING "INSTANT"
t_4 = END OF EXTENDED RAMP GATE

S203 | SCANNING | SHOWN ON INTERNAL SCAN

FIGURE 7-3 Overall block diagram of HP 185B scope.

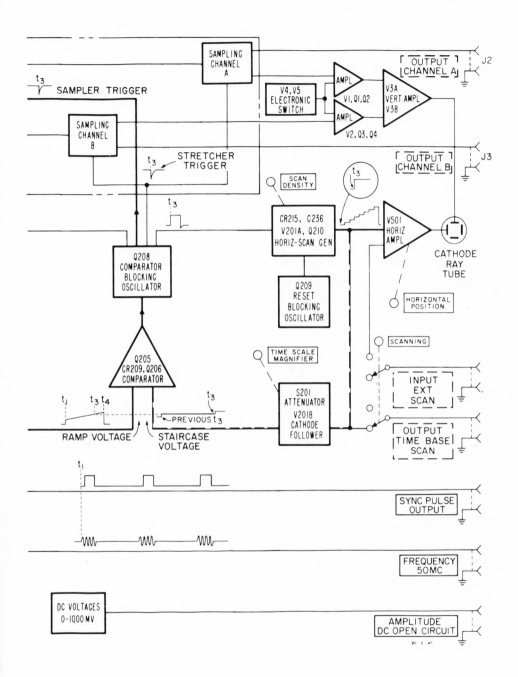

The frequency of the ramp pulse generator:

ITEM 710a

Is independent of the signal frequency.

No, there is a definite but variable relationship between the signal applied to the vertical deflection plates and the frequency from the ramp pulse generator.

ITEM 710b

Increases linearly with an increase in the signal frequency.

There is a strict time relationship between the signal trigger frequency and the ramp-pulse-generator frequency, but it isn't linear. For instance, the maximum frequency of the basic timing pulses is 100 kc for time scales 200 nsec/cm and faster. The ratio thus increases up to the maximum speed of 10 nsec/cm. This is not a linear relationship by any means.

ITEM 710c

Has a subharmonic relationship to the trigger frequency.

This is indeed the case. The trigger frequency is always related by some integral ratio, although it may be rather large, to the repetition frequency of the ramp pulse generator. The signal sampling time or phase is varied in keeping with the sweep voltage so that the sampling phase effectively varies, while the frequency ratio is held fixed between the signal frequency and the ramp-gate-generator frequency.

Turn to Item 711.

ITEM 711

**TIME-BASE
CIRCUITS**

Refer to Fig. 7-3. In the comparator circuit the ramp voltage is compared to the horizontal-scan voltage, a staircase voltage. When the ramp voltage reaches coincidence with the horizontal-scan voltage at time t_3, the comparator produces a pulse which triggers the comparator blocking oscillator. The comparator blocking oscillator has four outputs: The first two are the sample trigger and stretcher trigger which initiate the sampling action of the vertical signal, the third is used in the staircase generator, and the fourth initiates the end of the ramp voltage.

The output of the horizontal-scan generator goes to the horizontal amplifier and through the time scale magnifier switch to the comparator. There are four horizontal modes, determined by the setting of the scanning switch. In the internal mode, the scan voltage is derived in the staircase-voltage generator. In the manual mode, the scan voltage is derived by the positioning potentiometer, and moving this control moves the spot directly. In record, the scan voltage is derived from the charging voltage across a capacitor. In the reset or external mode, the scan voltage is derived from an external source applied through the external scan connector jack. This position is also used to reset the trace when in record.

Q711 In the internal mode, what determines the ramp voltage swing (from its lowest voltage to its highest voltage)?

ITEM 711a   The comparator circuit.

ITEM 711b   The voltage of one step in the staircase.

ITEM 711c   The accumulated staircase voltage.

ITEM 711d   The time scale control.

What determines the ramp voltage swing?

ITEM 711a

The comparator circuit.

This determines the time at which the ramp is stopped, but it does so only when the ramp voltage exceeds that of the staircase voltage. The comparator circuit does not determine the ramp voltage swing.

ITEM 711b

One step in the staircase.

This merely determines the rate at which the spot is swept across the face in the horizontal direction. To be compared with one step, the staircase voltage would have to be differentiated, and such a circuit is not shown on the overall diagram.

ITEM 711c

The accumulated staircase voltage.

The staircase voltage from the start of the sweep is what is compared with the ramp voltage each time the ramp starts. The fact that the staircase voltage has increased one step since the previous ramp is what permits the ramp to increase to a slightly higher voltage level before its termination this time. This assures that the sampling is done at a slightly later point for each step of the staircase.

Turn to Item 712.

ITEM 711d

The time scale control.

This determines the slope of the ramp and thus how fast the voltage rises each time to the coincidence point; there the ramp stops, and another step is added to the staircase. The time scale control thus determines how fast the samples are taken, or how slowly the samples are displayed. The slope of the ramp definitely does not determine the total voltage swing of the ramp itself.

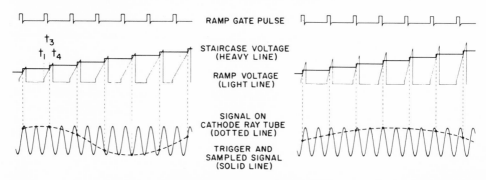

FIGURE 7-4   Time-base determination.

ITEM 712

TIME-BASE DETERMINATION

The actual speed of the beam horizontally across the scope face has no relation to the time base itself in seconds per centimeter. The time base is dependent entirely upon the time advance between successive samples as compared to the sweep deflection voltage. Two methods are used to vary the time advance. The first is to vary the slope of the ramp signal via the time scale control. The second is to vary the amplitude of the horizontal-scan voltage fed to the comparator versus that fed to the horizontal amplifier. This ratio is determined by the setting of the time scale magnifier control.

Figure 7-4 shows the effect of varying the slope of the ramp signal with the time scale control. With less slope (left figure), more time elapses between the ramp gate pulse t_1 and the time of voltage coincidence between the ramp and horizontal-sweep voltage t_3. Remember that the time of coincidence t_3 is the time at which the input signal is sampled. When the ramp slope is decreased, as in the left part of Fig. 7-4, the result is that a greater part of the input signal is covered between samples, thus giving more cycles per centimeter on the scope face.

Remember that the ramp signal begins when the input trigger occurs, plus a small inherent delay. Any time lapse between the input trigger and the comparator coincidence is a delay. The time scale is determined by the ramp slope and the amplitude ratio between the staircase signal to the comparator and to the horizontal amplifier. Differences in step amplitude of the staircase or nonlinear scan voltages have no effect on the time scale.

Q712 The time scale[1] is related:

ITEM 712a   Directly to the ramp slope.

ITEM 712b   Inversely to the ramp slope.

ITEM 712c   Inversely to the size of the staircase step in the comparator.

---

[1] Study Fig. 7-4 and its explanation carefully.

The time scale is related:

ITEM 712a

Directly to the ramp slope.

Increasing the ramp slope means that there is less time between taking successive samples which means that the signal has had less time to change.

ITEM 712b

Inversely related to the ramp slope.

Correct. Turn to Item 713.

ITEM 712c

Inversely to step size.

The step size by itself does not affect the time scale. The ratio of the overall staircase voltage fed to the coincidence comparator versus the same staircase voltage fed to the horizontal amplifier does determine the time scale. When the ramp and staircase voltages are the same, the coincidence circuit triggers. When the staircase step voltage is reduced, the horizontal-sweep gain is increased to keep sweep length constant on the scope face. At the same time, the ramp voltage has to go considerably less to equal this reduced staircase voltage. Correspondingly, successive signal samples would be taken closer together than before, at a faster time scale.

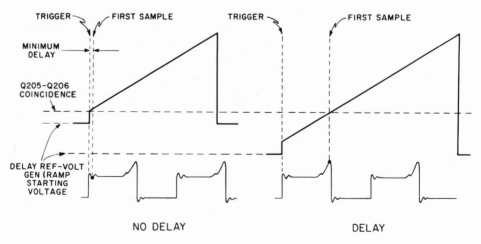

FIGURE 7-5 Effects of delay.

ITEM 713

TIME SCALE DETERMINATION

The delay control varies the fraction of the time interval, selected with the time scale control, which can be viewed at one time. The delay control effectively runs the viewing window along the time base from the trigger to whenever the ramp goes positive. The time scale controls the width of the window, and the delay determines the time at which the window opens.

Refer to Fig. 7-5. When the time scale multiplier is on the X1 position, the ramp starting voltage is varied with the delay control. A small amount of delay is built in the circuit to avoid any possible nonlinearity in the start of the ramp. The amount of delay which occurs before coincidence depends upon how far the ramp starting voltage was made negative, such as by the delay adjustments or the ramp slope.

When the time scale magnifier is at any position except X1, it inserts a resistive pad and attenuation between the horizontal amplifier and the comparator. As the attenuation is increased, the ratio between the staircase voltage applied to the comparator and that applied to the scope face is decreased, which decreases the time scale as seen on the scope. For example, in the X10 position only one-tenth of the signal is displayed on the scope, but this one-tenth of the previous voltage is magnified to full scope width. However, the ramp has to increase to only a tenth of its previous value before coincidence occurs and the sample of the signal is taken. Thus, the signal has had only one-tenth of its previous time to change.

Q713 The delay control determines:

ITEM 713a   The starting time of the ramp.

ITEM 713b   The initial jump at the start of the ramp.

ITEM 713c   The starting voltage of the ramp.

The delay control determines:

ITEM 713a

The starting time of the ramp.
The ramp starts with the extended gate pulse whenever a trigger is received, so the delay control does not affect the starting time of the ramp in this fashion.

ITEM 713b

The initial jump at the start of the ramp.
The little jump at the start of the ramp is essentially a constant voltage and is determined by the particular circuitry involved. The delay control does not affect the size of the jump voltage at the start of the ramp.

ITEM 713c

The starting voltage of the ramp.
The ramp control adds in a negative voltage as a handicap to the ramp before it starts. Remember that the comparator always triggers whenever the ramp voltage exceeds the current staircase voltage. If the ramp starts with a negative-voltage handicap, as is done by the delay control, the ramp has further to go before it reaches this coincidence point. Correct.
Turn to Item 714.

1 What two methods can be used to measure the phase relationship between two sine waves on an oscilloscope? *(J)*

QUIZ 7

2 State two reasons or uses for delaying the start of the sweep on a scope. *(C)*

3 What is the term for variations in pulse period? *(G)*

4 How does a sampling scope work? *(A)*

5 A sampling scope could be used to display a one-shot event. (True/False) *(H)*

6 Variations of the signal during the time the sampling switch is closed (are/are not) seen on the sampling scope. *(D)*

7 The sweep synchronization signal in a sampling scope may be taken from the vertical amplifier. (True/False) *(B)*

8 What delay methods can be used to see the start of a pulse? *(E)*

9 Discuss the frequency and phase relationship of the signal and ramp gate generator. *(I)*

10 How is the time advanced or controlled from one sample to the next on a sampling oscilloscope? *(F)*

A It takes samples of a repetitive voltage signal at slightly later times on successive pulses or cycles. These samples are the scope's vertical signal while the beam is stepped along horizontally on successive samples.

B False. Once sampled, there is no recurrent frequency component in the signal samples for triggering.

C To see the end of a pulse with greater stability and to magnify or expand pulse details occurring late in a pulse.

D The average value of the signal at sampling time is stored and held until the next sampling takes place. Thus signal variations during sampling are not seen.

E The signal can start the sweep and also be applied to a delay line; the delayed signal is then applied to the VDP after the sweep has started. If the period isn't too long and jitter too great, the sweep can be started on one pulse and the next pulse displayed on the scope. Finally, if the signal source can be driven by a trigger generator, the sweep can be started before the source is triggered.

F A linear ramp voltage rises until it just matches the staircase sweep voltage; at this time, the sampling of the recurrent signal occurs. The slope of the ramp and the ratio of ramp voltages fed to comparator and to sweep are controllable to advance the pulse sampling from pulse to pulse.

G Variations from pulse to pulse in pulse period are called "jitter."

H A sampling scope takes samples of recurrent events at slightly later times in successive pulses. One-shot events would not have subsequent pulses.

I The ratio of the signal frequency to that of the ramp gate generator is a large-integral constant, such as 1000:1 or 643:1. This also means the phase relationship is fixed.

J Lissajous patterns and precise controlled blanking of the scope at signal zero-crossings.

You're done. Hurray!

BASIC ELECTRONICS TEST

I Electricity

A Name the electric parts represented by the following symbols:

1

a. inductance, b. switch, c. spring, d. resistance

2

a. contact, b. diode, c. spark gap, d. capacitor

3

a. coil, b. transformer, c. spring, d. resistance

4

a. switch, b. battery, c. diode, d. capacitor

5

a. battery, b. ac source, c. tube, d. resistance

B How much current is flowing in the following circuits?

6

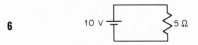

a. 50, b. 5, c. 2, d. 0.2

7

$$C = \frac{1}{1000\,\pi}\ \text{f}$$

10 V
100 CPS

a. 2, b. pi, c. 1, d. 0.2

C What is the value of the following combinations?

8

2 Ω   6 Ω

a. 1.5 ohms, b. 4 ohms, c. 6 ohms, d. 8 ohms

9

5 Ω

5 Ω

a. 2.5 ohms, b. 5 ohms, c. 10 ohms, d. 25 ohms

10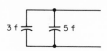

a. 0.6 farad, **b.** 4 farads, **c.** 8 farads, **d.** 15 farads

11

a. 0.50 farad, **b.** 1.34 farads, **c.** 3.0 farads, **d.** 6 farads

12

a. 0.40 henry, **b.** 2.50 henrys, **c.** 3.16 henrys, **d.** 7.00 henrys

13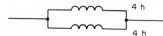

a. 2.0 henrys, **b.** 2.82 henrys, **c.** 8.0 henrys, **d.** 16.0 henrys

D How much power is dissipated in the resistor?

14

a. 25 watts, **b.** 5 watts, **c.** 2.2 watts, **d.** 1.0 watts

II Algebra

A Solve each of the following equations for x:

15 $I = E/x$
a. E/I, **b.** EI, **c.** I/E, **d.** E

16 $A = 2\pi fx$
a. $2\pi fA$, **b.** $2\pi f/A$, **c.** $2\pi/fA$, **d.** $A/2\pi f$

17 $C = \dfrac{1}{2\pi fx}$
a. $2\pi fC$, **b.** $2\pi f/C$, **c.** $C/2\pi f$, **d.** $\dfrac{1}{2\pi fC}$

18 $A = Bx + C$
a. A/B, **b.** $(A + C)/B$, **c.** $(A - C)/B$, **d.** $A/(B - C)$

III Trigonometry

A What is the angle θ in each of the following?

19 $\sin \theta = 1$
a. $0°$, **b.** $+45°$, **c.** $-90°$, **d.** $90°$

20 $\cos \theta = 1$
a. $0°$, **b.** $+45°$, **c.** $-90°$, **d.** $90°$

21 $\sin \theta = \cos \theta$
a. $0°$, **b.** $+45°$, **c.** $-90°$, **d.** $90°$

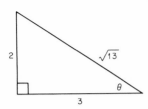

B

22 $\sin \theta =$
    a. $\sqrt{13}/2$, **b.** $3/\sqrt{13}$, **c.** $2/3$, **d.** $2/\sqrt{13}$

23 $\cos \theta =$
    a. $\sqrt{13}/2$, **b.** $3/\sqrt{13}$, **c.** $2/3$, **d.** $2/\sqrt{13}$

24 $\tan \theta =$
    a. $\sqrt{13}/2$, **b.** $3/\sqrt{13}$, **c.** $2/3$, **d.** $2/\sqrt{13}$

IV General

A What is the numerical value of pi?
  25   **a.** 2.73, **b.** 3.16, **c.** 2.98, **d.** 3.14

B What are the basic units of measure in the mks system?
  26 The unit of length is _____.
    a. centimeter, **b.** meter, **c.** kilometer, **d.** the earth's radius.
  27 The unit of time is _____.
    a. second, **b.** minute, **c.** hour, **d.** nanosecond.
  28 The unit of mass is _____.
    a. milligram, **b.** gram, **c.** kilogram, **d.** metric ton.

C What is meant by the following prefixes?
  29 Meg- . . . . . _____.   **a.** biilion, **b.** million,
                                       c. thousand, **d.** millionth
  30 Kilo- . . . . . _____.   **a.** thousandth, **b.** billion,
                                       c. millionth, **d.** thousand
  31 Milla- . . . . . _____.   **a.** billionth, **b.** millionth,
                                       c. thousand, **d.** thousandth
  32 Micro- . . . . . _____.   **a.** hundredth, **b.** thousandth,
                                         c. millionth, **d.** billionth

D Write the following numbers without the aid of the powers of 10.
  33 $5.34 \times 10^{-3} =$ _____.   **a.** 0.00534, **b.** 1/5.34,
                                               c. 0.000534, **d.** 0.0534
  34 $10^2 =$ _____.   **a.** 100, **b.** 102,
                                       c. 20, **d.** 10.2
  35 $9 \times 10^6 =$ _____.   **a.** 954, **b.** 540,
                                       c. 900,000, **d.** 9,000,000
  36 $2.54 \times 10^{-6} =$ _____.   **a.** 1.46, **b.** 0.000,002,54
                                       c. 0.000,000,254, **d.** 1/1.46

E General knowledge.

37 The most common voltage in houses and industry is _____.
   a. 440 volts, **b.** 24 volts, **c.** 220 volts, **d.** 115 volts

38 The most common line frequency in houses and industry is

   _____.

   a. direct current, **b.** 50 cps, **c.** 60 cps, **d.** 400 cps

39 Most commercial radio stations use _____
   modulation.

   a. continuous wave, **b.** phase, **c.** amplitude, **d.** digital

40 Most radio receivers are the _____ type.

   a. superheterodyne, **b.** superregenerative, **c.** regenerative, **d.** crystal
   detector

V Electronics

41 In a circuit with a battery E, a switch S, a capacitor C, and a
   resistor R connected in series around the loop, the current can
   be expressed as $i(t) = E/Re^{-Bt}$. What is B:
   a. C, **b.** C/R, **c.** RC, **d.** $1/RC$.

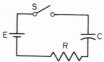

42 In a hot-wire vacuum diode with a normal negative plate voltage:
   a. A large current of electrons flows from cathode to plate
   b. Residual gas ions produce a moderate current flow from cathode
      to plate
   c. An equal number of electrons are emitted from the cathode and
      recombine with it
   d. None of these

43 What is the function of the grid in a vacuum triode:
   a. Repel cathode electrons in a controllable manner
   b. Attract electrons to divert them from the plate
   c. Generate secondary electrons to add to the plasma
   d. None of these

44 The majority carriers in p-type semiconductor material are:
   a. electrons, **b.** ions, **c.** holes, **d.** none of these

45 Current flow in this diode is:
   a. large
   b. slight
   c. zero
   d. none of these

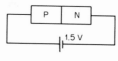

46 Voltage polarity flips the switch in the equivalent circuit for a diode. What percentage of the input voltage is dropped across this diode in the forward direction?

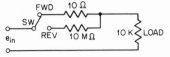

a. 0.1 percent

b. 1.0 percent

c. 90 percent

d. 99.9 percent

47 What percentage of the input voltage is dropped across the above diode in the reverse direction:

a. 99 percent, **b.** 99.9 percent, **c.** 99.99 percent, **d.** 90 percent

48 What is the effective dynamic plate resistance in ohms of the 6XYZ tube, given $E_p = 100$ volts, $I_p = 10$ ma, gain $= 40$, $G_m = 0.0012$ mho.

a. 3.3 kilohms, **b.** 4.8 kilohms, **c.** 33 kilohms, **d.** 48 kilohms

49 What is the tube analog of this circuit:

a. tetrode oscillator

b. grounded grid

c. grounded cathode

d. grounded plate

50 What is the major advantage of this transistor circuit:

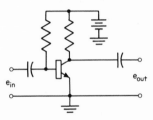

a. low output impedance

b. voltage gain

c. high input impedance

d. phase reversal

ANSWERS	**1**	d	**11**	b	**21**	b	**31**	d	**41**	d
TO BASIC ELECTRONICS	**2**	d	**12**	d	**22**	d	**32**	c	**42**	c
TEST	**3**	a	**13**	a	**23**	b	**33**	a	**43**	a
	4	b	**14**	b	**24**	c	**34**	a	**44**	c
	5	b	**15**	a	**25**	d	**35**	d	**45**	a
	6	c	**16**	d	**26**	b	**36**	b	**46**	a
	7	a	**17**	d	**27**	a	**37**	d	**47**	b
	8	d	**18**	c	**28**	c	**38**	c	**48**	c
	9	a	**19**	d	**29**	b	**39**	c	**49**	c
	10	c	**20**	a	**30**	d	**40**	a	**50**	d

INTERPRETATION OF SCORES

1 Count the number of answers you had correct above.

2 **Score range**   **Interpretation**

41-50   Adequate background to start this book.

31-40   Marginal background; review is suggested before starting this book.

30 & less   Inadequate background; you need to study basic ac-dc theory and electronics before starting this book.

INDEX TO ITEMS

NOTES

NOTES

NOTES

NOTES

NOTES

NOTES